D1276648

THE ESSENTIAL
Barbecue
COOKBOOK

THE ESSENTIAL BARBECUE COOKBOOK

THUNDER BAY
P·R·E·S·S
San Diego, California

Contents

VEGETABLES

SALSAS & DIPS

MARINADES

DESSERTS

Barbecue basics

Some barbecues can be as formal as a dinner party, others as relaxed as a picnic on the beach. Whatever the case, you will need to be prepared — choose the barbecue that suits you best, light the perfect fire and prepare the food to its maximum advantage.

Types of barbecues

Fuel-burning

Fixed barbecue Many gardens contain some sort of fixture for barbecuing; they are relatively simple constructions, usually made from bricks or cement or stucco and featuring two grates — the bottom for building the fire, the top for cooking the food. Grates (or grills) are not generally height-adjustable, so cooking can only be regulated by adjusting the fire, or moving the food away from or towards the fire. Being fixed these barbecues cannot, of course, be put out of high winds or moved to shelter in the event of rain. Despite this, fixed barbecues are easy to use and maintain, and quite often are large enough to cater for big gatherings.

Weber (kettle) barbecue One of the most popular styles of portable barbecue, the Weber features a tight-fitting lid and air vents at top and bottom which allow for greater versatility and accuracy in cooking. Webers can function either as a traditional barbecue, an oven or a smoker (see page 13 for preparation techniques). Weber barbecues only burn charcoal or briquettes (wood is not recommended) and are relatively small. The standard diameter is 24 inches, so if barbecuing for large groups more than one Weber is probably required.

Brazier This is the simplest style of fuel-burning barbecue, of which the small, cast-iron hibachi is probably best known. A brazier consists of a shallow firebox for burning fuel with a grill on top. Some grills

A Weber barbecue, although compact, can prepare a variety of foods

are height adjustable or can rotate. Braziers are best fitted with a heat-reflecting hood, so that food will cook at an even temperature.

Fuel

Although traditional, wood is not an ideal fuel for cooking. It can be difficult to light and burns with a flame. Charcoal or briquettes (made of compressed coal dust) are preferable. They will create a bed of glowing heat which is perfect for cooking. They do not smell, smoke or flare and are readily available in supermarkets or hardware stores. (Charcoal briquettes are sometimes known as barbecue briquettes and should not be confused with heating briquettes, which are not suitable for cooking.)

Firestarters or lighter fluid are essential for lighting charcoal or briquette fires. Firestarters are solid cubes of fuel and ignite instantly. Do not attempt to cook while either liquid or solid fuel is still burning, because they give off kerosene fumes. Generally, one or two firestarters will light about twenty pieces of charcoal or briquettes. Alternatively, use briquettes already permeated in fuel.

A 'normal' fire consists of about 50–60 briquettes or pieces of charcoal, and will last for several hours. All recipes in this book can be cooked over a normal fire.

Don't be put off by the pungent smell. It takes about 20 minutes to get coals glowing and even longer for briquettes. By then the firestarters have served their purpose and are quite odorless. When briquettes and charcoal are well lit, the flames will die down and a grey ash will appear all over the red-hot glowing coals. If preparing a Weber (kettle) barbecue, leave the lid off while the fire is developing.

Coals ready for cooking — the beads have developed a fine ash coating

Build the fire in the middle of the grate, so cooked food can be moved to the edge of the top grill and kept warm.

A good way to find out if the heat is right is to hold the palm of your hand about 4 inches above the glowing coals. If you pull it away within two seconds, you know the barbecue is ready for the food. Likewise, when cooking over a wood fire, make certain that the flames have died down completely to leave glowing coals, covered with ash, before starting to cook. The flavor is unique. Some leaves and twigs from certain trees, especially anything with a milky white sap, are not suitable to use on the barbecue so, if in doubt, leave it out. If you'd rather collect than buy wood, just be sure that what you're gathering isn't going to make your family cook-out front page news!

Smoke flavor can be achieved on even the humblest barbecue with the addition of water-soaked mesquite or hickory chips just prior to cooking. However, to smoke-cook food the indirect way, you will need to use some kind of covered barbecue. This method needs a drip pan (a baking dish will do) containing 4 cups of water to be positioned beneath food for smoking (see page 13 for details).

With indirect cooking on a gas barbecue, keep the burner lit under the wood chips and turn off the burner that's under the food. It's a slow-cooking method, but the smoke flavor will be much stronger than in direct smoke-cooked foods.

If cooking whole roasts, check for 'doneness' with a meat thermometer or, in the case of poultry, by inserting a metal skewer in the thigh and making sure that the juices that run out are clear. If the juices are pink, longer cooking time is needed.

If using a kettle barbecue, arrange the coals so that they are to the sides of the drip pan and place wood chips over coals. Place food to be smoked on a grill over the drip pan, but not touching the water. The steam helps to keep the food moist.

Temperature control

A fire's temperature can be lowered by damping down with a spray of water. (A trigger-style plastic spray-bottle is ideal.) Damping also produces steam which puts moisture back in the food.

The best and safest way to increase the heat of a fire is to add more fuel and wait for the fire to develop. Do not fan a fire to increase its heat; this will only produce a flame. Never pour flammable liquids on a fire.

Gas or electric barbecues

Although often more expensive, these barbecues are very simple to use. They do not require an open flame, only connection to their fuel source. In many cases, the gas or electricity heats a tray of reusable volcanic rock. Hickory chips can be placed over the rock-bed to produce a smoky flavor in the food, if desired. Sizes of models vary, the largest being the wagon style, which usually features a workbench, reflecting hood and, often, a bottom shelf for storage. While small portable gas models, which require only the connection of a propane gas cylinder, are greatly manoevrable, electric models are, of course, confined to areas where mains electricity is available. Most gas or electric barbecues have temperature controls; their accuracy is their primary advantage. Electric models can be fitted with rotisseries or spit turners for spit roasting.

A gas-filled barbecue featuring hood and work areas

Building your own barbecue

Basically, a brick barbecue consists of a metal griddle and/or grill rack suspended above a hearth that is bordered on three sides by brickwork. The design can be as simple or as grand as your outdoor setting can accommodate. Some elaborate barbecues incorporate a chimney but, unless you're a competent bricklayer, it's best to keep it all simple. Following are some hints that will help you build your own barbecue.

Decide on the size of grill rack you need; this will be governed by your partying ambitions. Cast iron is the best material. A flat, tiled area on one side of the barbecue to hold plates, drinks and general paraphernalia is also useful.

If the grill or griddle is to fit inside the barbecue, make sure you have fi in clearance from the grill or griddle to the brickwork. This allows for expansion in the metal. The height can be adjusted to what is most comfortable for you.

Correct placing of the barbecue is important. Think of the neighbors: smoke, and noise that you consider convivial, are often perceived as a nuisance by others. If at all possible, locate it in a protected place — one in close proximity to the kitchen.

Brick quantities

Once you've decided on the barbecue design, it's a good idea to make a plan before you start buying materials and to familiarise yourself with building techniques. Draw your barbecue to scale, say 1:5 or 1:10. Show a front view and a side view. You can then measure the area of brick-work and calculate how many bricks you'll need. Make sure you allow for the joints (usually fi in), and you should also allow at least 10 per cent extra for chips and breakages (just multiply the total number of bricks by 1.1 if you want to add 10 per cent). Note how the diagram on page 10 shows the hearth has a brick skin which is infilled with rubble and covered with a layer of concrete 3 in thick. Alternatively, if you have some old bricks, you could lay the whole thing in solid brickwork.

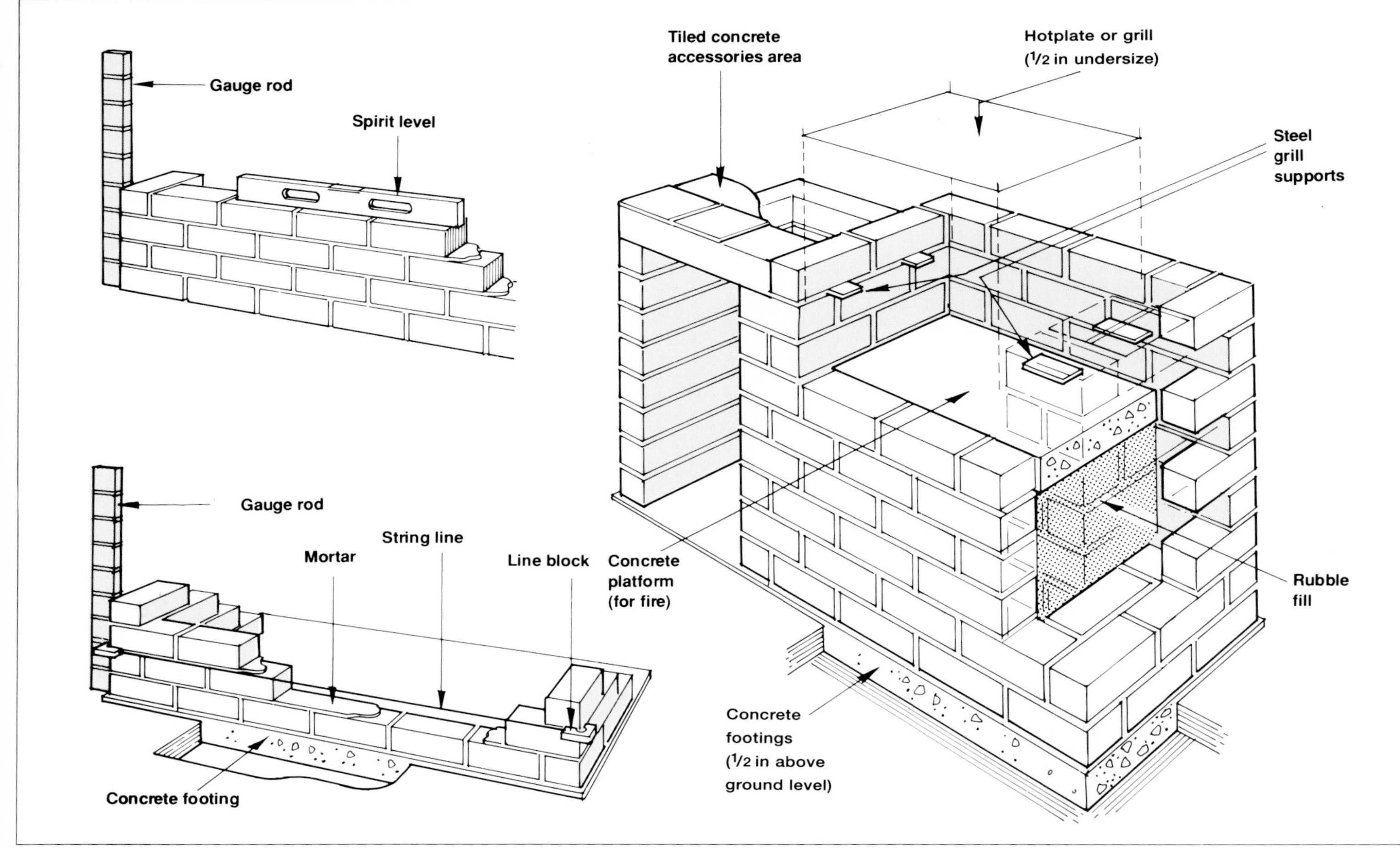

Barbecue construction, showing the back wall bricklaying

Mortar

The mortar in a barbecue should not be too strong or it will crack. A one part cement to one part lime to nine parts sand mix (with a bit of plasticizer in it to make laying easier) is ideal. Color the mortar with oxide to suit the bricks. The joints can be finished in a number of ways: made flush with the brick faces; raked out / in and left square; or ironed, which will leave the joint slightly concave.

Tools

Tape; pencil; lump hammer; a bolster for cutting the bricks; a shovel; a wheelbarrow; trowel; level; string line and blocks; a tool for ironing (making a rounded joint) or raking (making a square joint).

The footing

Ideally, the barbecue should be built on a level, 4 in thick, reinforced concrete slab. Make the width and length of the slab to suit brick sizes. It should project fi in above ground level so that the bricks are not touching the soil and getting wet all the time, which could lead to staining and mold.

Laying the bricks

The following instructions are only intended as a guide. Unless you are experienced in bricklaying, it is best to seek professional advice, even if you intend to build the barbecue yourself.

1 Prepare a gauge rod by drawing on a 2 x 1 in timber batten, to the full size, a series of bricks with fi in joints (see diagram). This rod will help you maintain even courses. Remember to start with a joint.

2 After wetting the bricks, measure out the mortar ingredients and mix them together with the shovel. If possible, select a waterproof surface on which to do your mixing; in a wheelbarrow is ideal. Mix ingredients thoroughly to a thick paste.

3 Starting on one of the back corners of the slab, lay a bed of mortar with the trowel. Lay the first corner brick in the mortar. Lightly tap it down with the handle of the trowel and cut away the excess mortar. Buttering the end of the next brick, repeat the procedure until the first course of one corner is laid and level. Start the next

course, bearing in mind that the brickwork overlaps on the corners (check the brickwork on your house if you're not sure). Use the gauge rod periodically to check the joint sizes (see diagram) and constantly use your spirit level to check for plumb and level.

4 When one back corner is done, build the one at the opposite end. Once both corners are complete, use two line blocks or pins and a nylon line to work to when filling the middle (but make sure you get the line on two opposite courses!).

5 The grill may be laid on top of the bricks. Alternatively, the grill may be suspended using four pieces of flat steel (e.g. 1 x fi in) or stainless steel rod (e.g. 4 x 4 in thick). These are built into the brick joints at an appropriate height. Make sure that 2 in of the steel rod projects out of the brick joints.

When laying the bricks, make sure you finish the joints before the mortar hardens. Brush off any excess mortar before it dries. If staining occurs, use a mix of one part hydrochloric acid to 10 parts water to clean the bricks. Then rinse with plenty of water.

6 If your barbecue design includes a tiled top, use glazed tiles as they are easier to clean. Make sure you have ⁄–fi in joints. When the glue has dried on the tiles, grout between them with a 3:1 sand and cement mix. Mortar usually needs two weeks to cure. Then you're ready to go ahead and call your friends round to give the barbecue a test run.

Equipment and accessories

If you know an avid barbecue chef, you'll never be stuck for ideas when it comes to birthday and Christmas gifts. Don't be intimidated by the list of utensils; you can make a good start with even the first half dozen.

❑ A stiff wire brush/scraper — for brushing and scraping away burnt-on food from the barbecue grill bars or griddle.

❑ Gas lighter — a must for gas barbecues without an automatic lighter.

❑ Long-handled tongs — for turning and moving food and coals while cooking (help to prevent singed hands and arms).

❑ Metal turner — good for lifting hamburgers, onion rings, fried eggs, fish pieces etc.

❑ Long, sharp knife — for carving large pieces of meat or poultry.

❑ Heatproof gloves — especially for handling skewers and cast iron skillets or saucepans.

❑ Water spray — to subdue flare-ups.

❑ A fire blanket — keep one on hand wherever you cook.

❑ Skewers — long, flat metal is preferred, but wood or bamboo works well if thoroughly soaked in water before use.

- ❑ Bristle basting brush or bulb baster — for coating with sauce or marinade.
- ❑ Wire fish frame — to hold fish together as it cooks and for easy turning.
- ❑ Rotisserie — for cooking large roasts of meat evenly.
- ❑ Meat thermometer — to test if large cuts of meat are done.
- ❑ Non-stick baking (silicone) paper and heavy duty foil — baking paper is an ideal cooking medium, perfect for roasting and baking. It's best not to cook directly in foil; sweet things are more prone to sticking or burning, while acid marinades can react with the aluminum.

Cooking techniques

Most of the recipes in this book call for the food to be cooked over a direct flame. Indirect cooking is only possible on Weber (kettle) style barbecues. (See page 13 for how to prepare a barbecue for indirect cooking.)

Retain moistness in the meat by searing quickly and turning once only

A barbecue griddle can be used to stir-fry vegetables

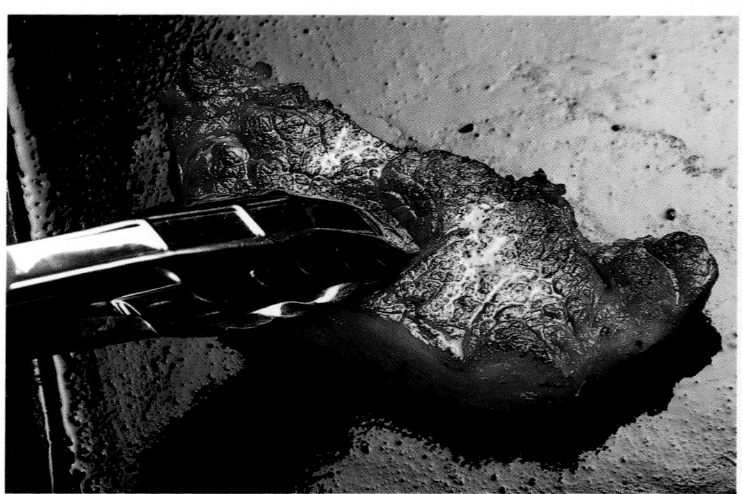
Test meat is cooked by pressing gently with tongs

Fish is ready when the flesh has turned opaque and flakes easily

Direct cooking

As with broiling or frying in the kitchen, the less turning or handling of the food the better. Once the fire is ready, lightly brush the grill or griddle with oil. Place the food over the hottest part of the fire and sear quickly on both sides; this retains moisture. Once seared, move the food to a cooler part of the grill or griddle to cook for a few more minutes. Barbecuing is a fast-cooking process, so even well-done food will not take very long. Techniques such as stir-frying are ideal for the barbecue griddle or you can use a cast iron skillet on the grill rack.

Test that meat is done by firmly pressing it with tongs or the flat edge of a knife. Meat that is ready to serve should 'give' slightly but not resist pressure too easily. At first, it may be difficult to judge when it is ready, but try to resist cutting or stabbing the meat; this not only reduces its succulence, but releases juice which may cause the fire to flare. Pork and chicken should not be served rare, so if in any doubt remove to a separate place and make a slight cut in the thickest part of the meat. If the juice does not run clear, return to the heat for more cooking. Test if fish is cooked by gently flaking back the flesh in the thickest part with a fork. Cooked flesh should be white and opaque, but still moist.

Smoking

Smoking chips or chunks come from hickory wood, mesquite, red gum or acacia trees and are available from barbecue specialists and some hardware or variety stores. Their smoke provides extra and unusual flavor to the food.

Smoking is best done on a covered barbecue (see below for technique) but can also be done on an open fire. Scatter some smoking wood throughout the coals. Once the wood is burning, damp down with a little water to create more smoke. Smoking wood is available in chips and chunks. Chips burn quickly so should be added towards the end of the cooking process. Chunks should last through the entire cooking process.

If glazing meat, such as ham, and smoking it, always glaze before adding wood. (Please note that some woods, such as pine, cedar or eucalyptus produce acrid smoke and are unsuitable for cooking. Use only wood sold specifically for smoking.)

Indirect cooking

Indirect cooking roasts or bakes food more slowly than direct cooking. It also allows for adding fragrant wood chips to the coals which introduces extra flavor to the food.

To prepare a Weber for indirect cooking:

1 Remove lid; open bottom vent.

2 Position bottom grate inside bowl and attach charcoal rails. Heap coals in rails; position firestarters inside coals.

3 Light fire and allow coals to develop to fine-ash stage. (Leave lid off while fire develops.) Place a drip tray or baking dish on bottom grate. Position grill rack; add food.

To prepare a Weber for smoking:

1 Prepare barbecue as above.

2 When coals reach fine-ash stage, add wood chips; fill drip tray or baking dish with 4 cups hot water. Cover with lid until fragrant smoke develops.

3 Remove lid; center food on the grill. Cover with lid.

Planning your menu

Now you have the barbecue, and the necessary equipment to get started, it's time to invite people round. Design your menu to take full advantage of the barbecue — vegetables, kebabs, breads, even desserts can be cooked or warmed easily.

Serve at least one salad with the cooked food. Salad dressings and special sauces can be made in advance and stored in a screw-top jar in the refrigerator. (See page 219 for salad dressing recipes.) Assemble salads up to one day in advance, but dress them just before serving.

Light the fire about an hour before using it. Check the fire occasionally — it can easily go out if unattended.

Assemble all necessary utensils and accessories, for example, tongs, forks, knives, plates and basting brushes, before cooking.

Have plenty of snacks and drinks available for your guests, but place them well away from the fire.

Have a hose or water bottle standing by in case of emergencies. (As a general safety rule, do not attempt to barbecue in strong winds.) A flashlight may be useful if barbecuing at night.

Always extinguish a fire once you have finished cooking on it. If possible, clean out the barbecue as soon as it has cooled down, brush or scrape grills and griddles, and discard ash and embers.

Place two or three firestarters in the coals; light fire, allow to develop

Place a drip tray underneath the grill when coals are ready

Spoon a generous quantity of smoking wood over the hot coals

Beef, lamb and pork

beef is always popular at a barbecue. Tender steaks, juicy roasts and burgers all play an important role. Choose good quality lean meat. The best beef cuts for barbecue roasting are whole pieces of rib eye, a thick slice of porterhouse, and boneless sirloin. If you will be marinating beef for the barbecue, economical cuts which will give good results include boneless top loins, top round, and flank. Rib steak, bone-in-blade, chuck and beef short ribs are also good choices.

Succulent and tender, lamb lends itself perfectly to barbecue cooking, either pink or well done. But be careful to avoid mutton, the older relative, which may prove tougher and takes much longer to cook. Lamb lends itself wonderfully to all kinds of marinades — from a yogurt-based tandoori mixture, to an oriental ginger-chili base.

Pork, too, is a good choice when barbecuing. It marries well with Asian-style ingredients like soy sauce, ginger and sesame oil to produce tender satays and finger lickin' ribs. Use leaner cuts and trim off the excess fat.

Nowadays there's no excuse for serving 'burnt offerings'. With a little practice, you will know when the meat is done with the touch of a finger or tongs. Choose steaks of an even thickness — about 1/ in is best — and remove excess fat. Score the edges of each steak with a sharp knife to prevent it curling on the barbecue. If refrigerated, allow the meat to return to room temperature before barbecuing — this ensures the meat cooks evenly.

Always preheat the grill or griddle (or skillet if you are using it on the grill) and brush lightly with oil before adding any food to prevent the food sticking. Sear meat steaks for one minute each side to firm the surface and retain the natural juices. Turn the meat once only and remember to always use tongs — never use a fork, because it may puncture the meat and release the juices, causing flare-ups and toughening the meat. Continue cooking the seared steaks on a cooler part of the barbecue until cooked to your liking.

For rare meat, cook only another minute or two each side. To test if the meat is done, press the steak with your finger or tongs. A rare steak should be soft and yielding to the touch. The inside of the steak should still be red with a thin edge of cooked meat around it.

For a medium rare result, cook for a few minutes longer or until slightly springy to the touch. The steak will be very moist and have a slightly thicker edge of cooked meat and a paler red center.

For a medium steak, cook for another two minutes each side. The meat should be firm to the touch with only a little pinkness in the center and a crisp brown outside. It should still be quite juicy inside.

Well done steak needs a little more time and the meat will be firm to the touch, with a rich brown outside and an evenly cooked center.

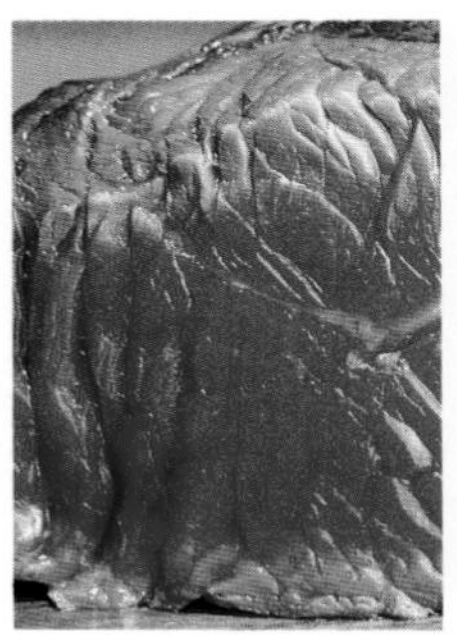

Rare

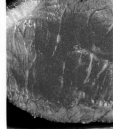

Medium rare

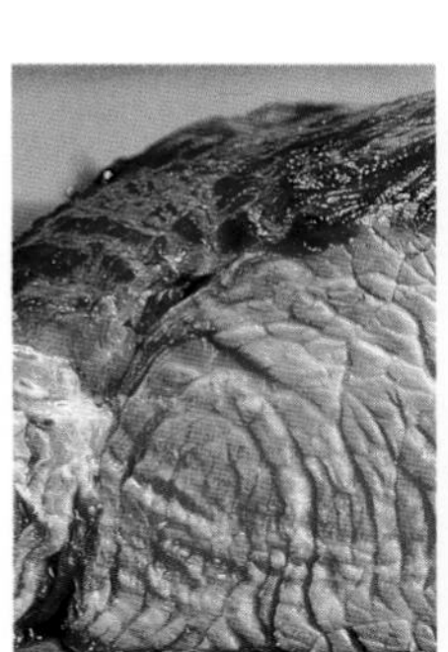

Medium

Well done

Breakfast Skewers with Quick Tomato Sauce

Serve this dish with scrambled eggs and English muffins for a hearty breakfast.

PREPARATION TIME:
25 MINUTES
COOKING TIME:
35 MINUTES
SERVES 4

4 all beef sausages
16 small button mushrooms
4 slices bacon
4 lamb kidneys
2 tablespoons butter, melted
4 large tomatoes, halved

QUICK TOMATO SAUCE
1 tablespoon oil
1 small onion, finely chopped
3 medium tomatoes, peeled, finely chopped
1/4 cup barbecue sauce

1 Prepare and heat the barbecue. Place the sausages in a large pan, cover with cold water and bring slowly to simmering point. Allow to cool. Drain well and cut each sausage into six pieces.

2 Wipe the mushrooms clean with paper towels. Chop the bacon into bite-size pieces. Trim the kidneys, remove the core and cut into quarters.

3 Thread the sausages, bacon, kidneys and mushrooms alternately on presoaked wooden skewers. Place the skewers on a hot lightly oiled barbecue grill, brush with melted butter and cook for 15 minutes, turning occasionally, or until browned and cooked through.

4 Add the tomatoes to the grill, cut-side down, and cook for 5 minutes. Serve skewers with tomatoes and Quick Tomato Sauce.

5 To make Quick Tomato Sauce: Heat the oil in a small pan. Cook the onion over a medium low heat for 5 minutes until soft. Add the tomatoes and sauce. Cook for 10 minutes, stirring occasionally. Serve warm or at room temperature.

Steaks with Lemon Mustard Butter

PREPARATION TIME:
5 MINUTES
COOKING TIME:
6–16 MINUTES
SERVES 6

6 tenderloin steaks, about 5 oz each
1 tablespoon olive oil
2 cloves garlic, crushed
1 teaspoon ground rosemary

LEMON MUSTARD BUTTER
1/2 cup butter
1 tablespoon French mustard
1 tablespoon lemon juice
2 teaspoons grated lemon rind
1 tablespoon finely chopped fresh chives

1 Trim the meat of excess fat and sinew. Flatten the steaks to an even thickness and score the edges to prevent curling. Combine the oil, garlic and rosemary. Rub evenly over each steak.

2 Place the meat on a lightly oiled grill. Cook over a high heat for 2 minutes each side to seal, turning once. For a rare result, cook for another minute each side. For medium and well done results, move meat to a cooler part of the barbecue and cook for another 2–3 minutes each side for medium and 4–6 minutes each side for well done. Serve steaks topped with a slice of Lemon Mustard Butter.

3 To make Lemon Mustard Butter: Cream the butter with the mustard, lemon juice and rind. Stir in the chives. Shape into a log, wrap in plastic wrap and refrigerate until required.

Best-ever Burger with Homemade Barbecue Sauce

The barbecue sauce in this recipe can be made up to a week in advance and stored in the refrigerator.

PREPARATION TIME: 20 MINUTES + 30 MINUTES REFRIGERATION
COOKING TIME: 25 MINUTES
SERVES 6

1 1/2 lb lean ground beef
8 oz sausage meat
1 small onion, finely chopped
1 tablespoon Worcestershire sauce
2 tablespoons ketchup
1 cup fresh bread crumbs
1 egg, lightly beaten
2 large onions, extra, thinly sliced in rings
6 wholemeal hamburger buns or bread rolls
6 small lettuce leaves
1 large tomato, sliced

HOMEMADE BARBECUE SAUCE
2 teaspoons oil
1 small onion, finely chopped
1 tablespoon soft brown sugar
1 tablespoon cider vinegar
1/3 cup ketchup
2 teaspoons Worcestershire sauce
2 teaspoons soy sauce

1 Place the ground beef and sausage meat in a large bowl. Add the onion, sauces, bread crumbs and egg. Using hands, mix until thoroughly combined. Divide the mixture into six equal portions and shape into 3/4 in thick patties. Refrigerate the patties for at least 30 minutes. Prepare and heat the barbecue.
2 Place the patties on a hot lightly oiled barbecue grill. Barbecue over the hottest part of the fire for 8 minutes each side, turning once. While the patties are cooking, fry the onions on an oiled griddle or in a cast iron skillet until golden.
3 To assemble the burgers: Split the hamburger buns in half and place the bases on individual serving plates. Top each base with a lettuce leaf, patty, tomato slice and fried onions. Top with a generous quantity of Homemade Barbecue Sauce. Cover with the remaining bun half.
4 To make the Homemade Barbecue Sauce: Heat the oil in a small pan. Cook the onion for about 5 minutes or until soft. Add the sugar, vinegar and sauces to the pan. Stir to combine and bring to a boil. Reduce the heat and simmer for 3 minutes. Leave to cool.

Hot Dogs with Creamy Slaw

PREPARATION TIME:
20 MINUTES
COOKING TIME:
10 MINUTES
SERVES 6

6 large thick spicy frankfurters
1 tablespoon oil
6 hero rolls or hot dog buns
6 small lettuce leaves

CREAMY SLAW
1 1/3 cups shredded red cabbage
1 1/3 cups shredded green cabbage
2 green onions, finely chopped
1/2 cup whole egg mayonnaise
1 tablespoon German mustard

1 Prepare and heat the barbecue. Make four diagonal cuts in each frankfurter, slicing halfway through. Brush them lightly with oil, then cook on a hot, lightly oiled grill for 7–10 minutes or until cooked through.

2 Split the rolls lengthwise through the center top. Line each roll with a lettuce leaf. Place Creamy Slaw on the lettuce; top with a frankfurter. Serve immediately.

3 To make Creamy Slaw: Place the red and green cabbage and the green onions in a medium bowl and mix together well. Combine the mayonnaise with the mustard and toss with salad to combine thoroughly.

Barbecued Mustard-coated Rib Steaks

Use any fresh herbs you prefer in the Herbed Cream

PREPARATION TIME:
5 MINUTES +
2 HOURS
MARINATING
COOKING TIME:
10–16 MINUTES
SERVES 6

6 rib eye steaks, about 6 oz each, or 6 T-bone steaks
1/3 cup seeded mustard
2 tablespoons bottled salad dressing
1 tablespoon lemon juice
1 tablespoon chopped fresh chives
1 tablespoon honey
1 clove garlic, crushed
dash Tabasco Sauce

HERBED CREAM
2/3 cup sour cream
1 tablespoon finely chopped fresh chives
2 tablespoons finely chopped bottled pimiento

1 Trim the meat of excess fat and sinew. Flatten the steaks to an even thickness and score the edges to prevent curling.
2 Combine the mustard, salad dressing, lemon juice, chives, honey, garlic and Tabasco in a small bowl and whisk for 1 minute or until well combined. Place the meat in a shallow dish and pour the marinade over. Store in the refrigerator, covered with plastic wrap, for 2 hours or overnight, turning occasionally.
3 Place the meat on a lightly oiled grill. Cook over high heat for 2 minutes each side to seal, turning once. For a rare result, cook another 2–3 minutes each side. For medium and well done results, move meat to a cooler part of the barbecue, cook another 2–3 minutes each side for medium and 4–6 minutes each side for well done. Serve steaks with the Herbed Cream.
4 To make Herbed Cream: Mix all the ingredients until well combined; the mixture should be fairly thick.

Spicy Beef and Mint Barbecued Sausages

For a less spicy sausage, leave out the sambal oelek

PREPARATION TIME: 15 MINUTES
COOKING TIME: 10 MINUTES
MAKES 12 SAUSAGES

1 1/2 lb lean ground beef
8 oz sausage meat
2 1/2 tablespoons cornstarch
1 egg, lightly beaten
1 medium onion, finely chopped
2 cloves garlic, crushed
2 tablespoons chopped mint
1 teaspoon sambal oelek or chili paste
1 teaspoon ground cumin
1 teaspoon garam masala
1/2 teaspoon ground cardamom
1/2 cup mango chutney, to serve

1 Combine the ground beef and sausage meat in a bowl and add the cornstarch, egg, onion, garlic, mint, sambal oelek, cumin, garam masala and cardamom; mix well.
2 Divide the mixture into twelve evenly sized portions. Using wet hands, mold each portion into sausage shapes.
3 Place the sausages on a lightly oiled grill. Cook over a medium heat for 10 minutes or until cooked through, turning the sausages occasionally during cooking. Serve with chutney.

Barbecued Mustard-coated Rib Steaks (above). Spicy Beef and Mint Barbecued Sausages

Mustard Beef Kebabs

PREPARATION TIME:
10 MINUTES + STANDING TIME
COOKING TIME:
10 MINUTES
SERVES 4

2 tablespoons coarse grain mustard
1 teaspoon prepared horseradish
2 teaspoons brown sugar
2 tablespoons brandy (or orange juice)
1/2 cup low-fat plain yogurt
1 lb lean top round steak, cut into 1 in cubes
2 medium onions, cut in wedges

1 Combine the mustard, horseradish, sugar, brandy or juice and yogurt. Toss the beef in the yogurt mixture. Let stand, covered, in the refrigerator for at least 30 minutes (or overnight).

2 Thread the meat and onions onto eight wooden or bamboo skewers (soaked in water to prevent burning) and cook on a preheated lightly greased barbecue grill for 5–10 minutes, brushing several times with yogurt mixture. Serve immediately.

Barbecued Chili Beef Burgers with Mustard Butter

This is a tasty variation of an old favorite.

PREPARATION TIME:
25 MINUTES +
2 HOURS
MARINATING
COOKING TIME:
8 MINUTES
MAKES 18

2 lb lean ground beef
3 medium onions
1/4 cup finely chopped parsley
1 1/2 cups packaged bread crumbs
1 tablespoon dried oregano leaves
1 egg, lightly beaten
1 tablespoon milk
1 tablespoon cider vinegar
1 tablespoon tomato paste
2 tablespoons soy sauce
1 tablespoon chili sauce

MUSTARD BUTTER
1/2 cup butter, softened
2 tablespoons sour cream
2 tablespoons German mustard

1 Place the ground beef in a large bowl and add the onions, parsley, bread crumbs, oregano leaves, egg, milk, vinegar, tomato paste and sauces; mix well. Store in refrigerator, covered with plastic wrap, for 2 hours.

2 Divide the mixture into eighteen evenly sized portions; shape each portion into a burger about 3/4 in thick.

3 Place burgers on a preheated lightly oiled grill. Cook over a high heat for 4 minutes each side or until well browned and cooked through. Serve the burgers with salad and dollops of Mustard Butter.

4 To make Mustard Butter: Beat the butter, sour cream and mustard in a small bowl for 2 minutes or until well combined. Let the mixture stand, uncovered, for 20 minutes to allow flavors to blend.

Apricot-glazed Sausages and Onions

PREPARATION TIME: 20 MINUTES
COOKING TIME: 15–20 MINUTES
SERVES 4–6

3 onions
8 thick all beef sausages
1 teaspoon coarse grain mustard
1 cup dried apricot halves
3/4 cup apricot nectar

1 Prepare and heat barbecue. Cut onions in half, slice thinly, and cook on a lightly greased barbecue griddle (or cast iron skillet on the grill) for 5 minutes or until soft. Transfer to a plate to keep warm.
2 Add sausages to the griddle; cook for 5 minutes or until well browned, turning frequently.
3 Slice sausages lengthwise, three-quarters of the way through. Cook, cut-side down, for another 5 minutes or until browned. Add the mustard, apricots and onions to sausages; stir.
4 Add the nectar to the sausage, apricot and onion mixture, a little at a time. Stir until the nectar coats the sausages and begins to thicken. Repeat this process until all the nectar is used. Serve the sausages cut-side up, topped with onion and apricot mixture.

Focaccia and Piquant Steak

PREPARATION TIME:
5 MINUTES +
30 MINUTES
STANDING TIME
COOKING TIME:
15 MINUTES
SERVES 4

1 lb sirloin steak
1/4 teaspoon ground pepper
1 small red onion
1 tablespoon balsamic vinegar
1 tablespoon chopped fresh parsley
1 large red sweet bell pepper
2 pieces focaccia, about 5 x 4 in
butter for spreading
10 lettuce leaves
4 canned anchovy fillets, chopped
1 tablespoon capers, chopped
4 tablespoons mayonnaise
1 tablespoon Dijon mustard

1 Trim the meat of excess fat and sinew and sprinkle with pepper. Cook the meat on a preheated lightly greased grill for 3 minutes on each side or until tender. Cool to room temperature, then slice across the grain evenly into long, thin strips.

2 Slice the onion very thinly and mix with the vinegar and parsley. Let stand for 30 minutes. Halve the red pepper lengthwise and remove the membrane and seeds. Place skin-side down on the hot griddle (or in a cast iron skillet on the grill), cook over high heat for 5 minutes or until skin lifts off and blackens slightly; cool. Remove the skin and slice the pepper thinly.

3 Split the focaccia in half and toast on both sides until brown and crisp. Spread with butter.

4 To assemble, place the lettuce on the focaccia, top with red pepper, meat, anchovies, capers and drained onion and parsley mixture. Finish off with a dollop of the combined mayonnaise and mustard.

Herb Burger

PREPARATION TIME: 20 MINUTES
COOKING TIME: 15–20 MINUTES
MAKES 8

1fi lb lean ground beef or lamb
2 tablespoons chopped fresh basil
1 tablespoon chopped fresh chives
1 tablespoon chopped fresh rosemary
1 tablespoon chopped fresh thyme
2 tablespoons lemon juice
1 cup stale bread crumbs
1 egg
pinch salt
pinch pepper
2 long crusty baguettes
lettuce leaves
2 tomatoes, sliced
ketchup

1 Prepare and heat the barbecue. Place meat in a bowl and combine with the herbs, juice, bread crumbs, egg, salt and pepper. Mix with your hands until well combined. Divide mixture into eight portions.

2 Shape the portions into thick rectangular patties about 6 in long. Cook on an oiled hot barbecue grill for 5–10 minutes each side until well browned and just cooked through.

3 Cut each baguette stick into four sections. Cut each piece in half, horizontally. Top each half with lettuce, tomato, a herb burger and ketchup. Place the remaining half of bread on top. Serve immediately.

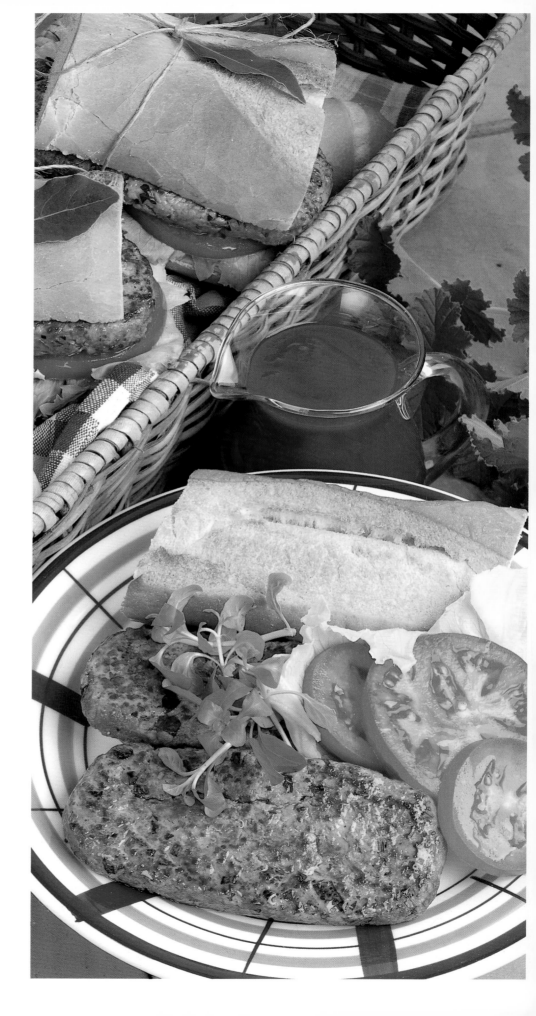

Teriyaki Beef Kebabs

Serve these kebabs with a crisp, green salad.

PREPARATION TIME:
15 MINUTES +
2 HOURS
MARINATING
COOKING TIME:
6–16 MINUTES
SERVES 6

3 lb boneless sirloin steak
1 cup beef stock
1/4 cup teriyaki sauce
2 tablespoons hoisin sauce
2 tablespoons lime juice
1 tablespoon honey
2 green onions, finely chopped
2 cloves garlic, crushed
1 teaspoon finely grated ginger

1 Trim the meat of excess fat and sinew and slice it across the grain evenly into long, thin strips. Thread the meat on skewers, 'weaving' them in place.

2 Combine the stock, sauces, lime juice, honey, green onions, garlic and ginger in a small bowl and whisk for 1 minute or until well combined. Place the skewered meat in a shallow dish and pour marinade over. Store in the refrigerator, covered with plastic wrap, for 2 hours or overnight, turning occasionally. Drain, reserving marinade.

3 Cook the skewered meat on a preheated lightly greased barbecue grill for 2 minutes each side to seal, turning once. For a rare result, cook another 1 minute each side. For medium and well done results, cook another 2–3 minutes each side for medium and 4–6 minutes each side for well done. Brush occasionally with the reserved marinade during cooking.

Beef Satays with Peanut Sauce

PREPARATION TIME:
30 MINUTES +
3 HOURS
MARINATING
COOKING TIME:
10–15 MINUTES
SERVES 4

1 1/2 lb boneless sirloin steak
1/3 cup soy sauce
2 tablespoons oil
2 cloves garlic, crushed
1 teaspoon grated ginger

PEANUT SAUCE
1 cup pineapple juice
1 cup peanut butter
1/2 teaspoon garlic powder
1/2 teaspoon onion powder
2 tablespoons sweet chili sauce
1/4 cup soy sauce

1 Trim the steak of excess fat and sinew. Cut the meat into 1/2 in cubes and thread them onto soaked wooden or bamboo skewers. Place the satays in a shallow, non-metal dish.

2 Combine the soy sauce, oil, garlic and ginger in a small bowl and pour over the satays. Store in the refrigerator, covered with plastic wrap, for several hours or overnight, turning occasionally.

3 Prepare and heat the barbecue 1 hour before cooking. Place the skewers on a hot lightly oiled grill. Barbecue 8–10 minutes or until tender, turning occasionally. Serve with Peanut Sauce.

4 To make Peanut Sauce: Combine juice, peanut butter, garlic and onion powders and sauces in a small pan and stir over medium heat for 5 minutes or until smooth. Serve warm.

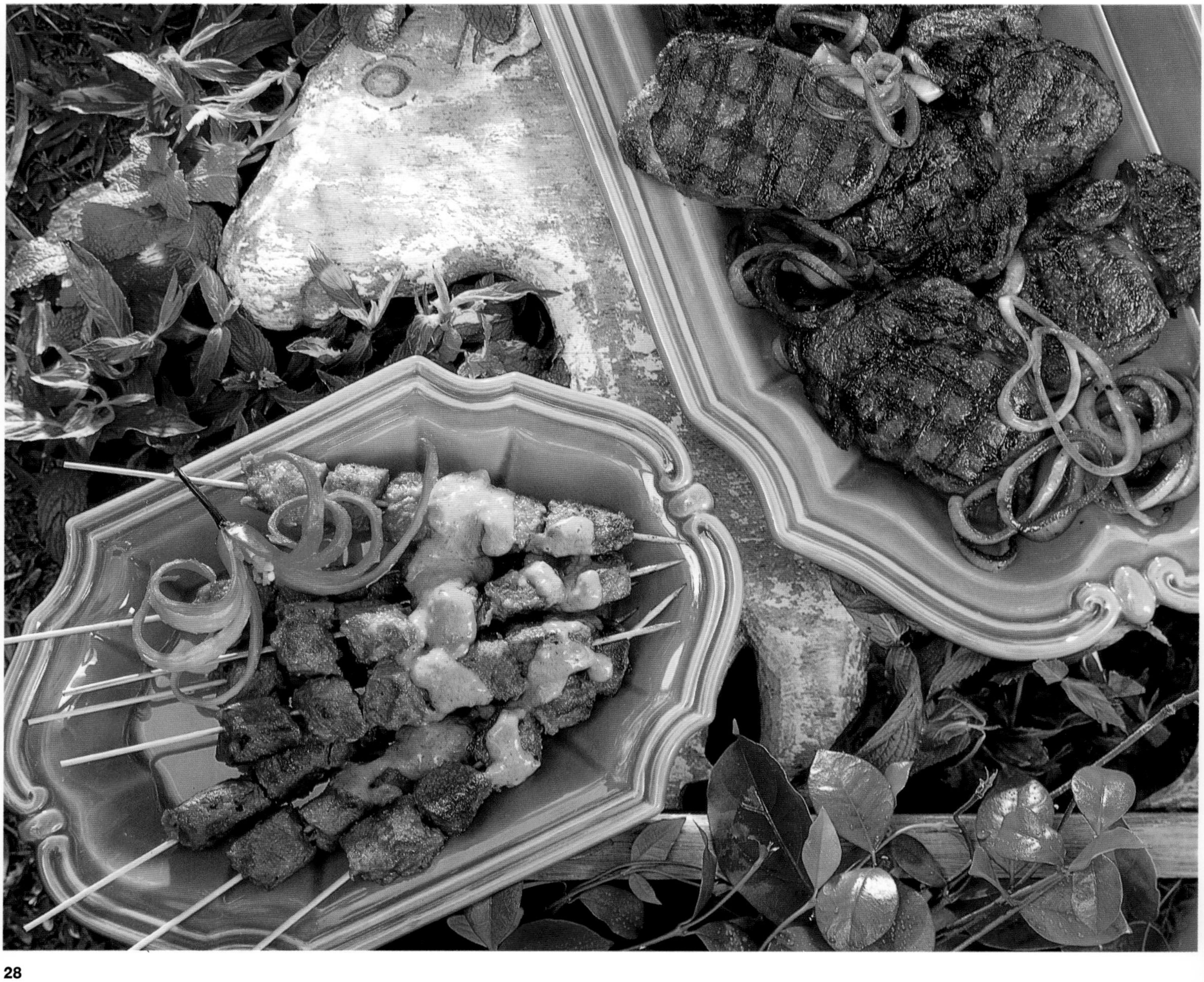

Beef Teriyaki with Onion Rings

PREPARATION TIME:
20 MINUTES + 15 MINUTES MARINATING
COOKING TIME:
15 MINUTES
SERVES 8

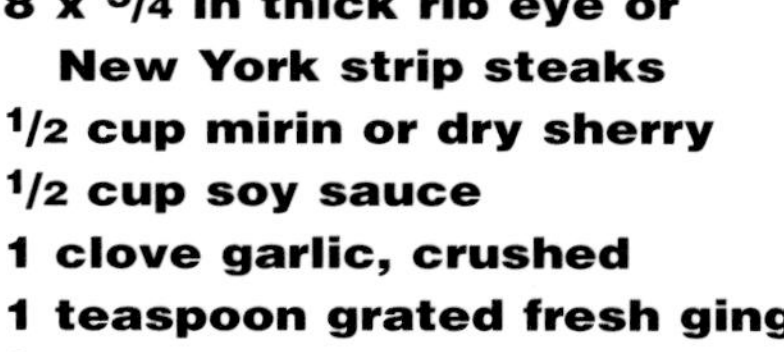

8 x 3/4 in thick rib eye or New York strip steaks
1/2 cup mirin or dry sherry
1/2 cup soy sauce
1 clove garlic, crushed
1 teaspoon grated fresh ginger
1/2 teaspoon ground pepper

ONION RINGS
4 large white onions
2 tablespoons sunflower oil
2 tablespoons beef marinade

1 Marinate the beef in the combined mirin, soy, garlic, ginger and pepper for 15 minutes. Preheat the barbecue griddle (or a cast iron skillet on the grill).
2 Peel the onions and cut into 3/4 in thick slices. Drizzle oil on the griddle. Cook the onion rings until golden, sprinkle with marinade and continue to cook until caramelized — about 5 minutes. Remove to a cooler part of the griddle and keep warm.
3 Oil the preheated grill and cook the beef over a high heat for 5 minutes on one side and 3 minutes on the reverse, cooking for an increased time if a well done steak is preferred. Serve the meat with barbecued onion rings.

Note: Purchase mirin from good delicatessens and Asian food outlets. Dry sherry may be used instead.

Korean Beef Ribs

PREPARATION TIME:
20 MINUTES + 4–6 HOURS MARINATING
COOKING TIME:
15 MINUTES
SERVES 6

4 lb beef short ribs or pork spareribs
1/2 cup soy sauce
1/2 cup water
1 onion, grated
3 cloves garlic, crushed
1 teaspoon grated fresh ginger
1 tablespoon sugar
2 teaspoons oriental sesame oil
2 tablespoons toasted sesame seeds, crushed
1/2 teaspoon ground pepper

Beef Satays with Peanut Sauce (left). Beef Teriyaki with Onion Rings

1 When purchasing the meat, ask the butcher to cut the ribs into 2 in squares. Using a sharp knife, cut through the flesh of each piece to allow the marinade to penetrate.
2 Place the ribs in a pan and cover with water, bring to a boil, cover and simmer for 5 minutes. Drain well. This removes some of the fat.
3 Combine the remaining ingredients in a bowl and add the ribs, mix well, cover and marinate in the refrigerator for 4–6 hours or overnight. Turn the ribs occasionally while marinating, so that the flavors are evenly distributed.
4 Cook the ribs over a hot oiled grill, allowing each side to brown and become crisp. Serve warm.

Note: Most supermarkets have oriental sesame oil (which is made from dark roasted sesame seeds) on their Asian shelves. Or look for it at your local Asian food outlet. Light sesame oil from the health food store will not do.

Burgers with the Works

Serve this classic with French fries and a salad.

PREPARATION TIME: 40 MINUTES
COOKING TIME: 10–15 MINUTES
SERVES 6

$1\frac{1}{2}$ lb lean ground beef
1 onion, finely chopped
1 egg
$\frac{1}{2}$ cup fresh bread crumbs
2 tablespoons tomato paste
1 tablespoon Worcestershire sauce
2 tablespoons chopped fresh parsley
salt and cracked pepper, to taste
3 large onions
2 tablespoons butter
6 slices cheddar cheese
6 eggs, extra
6 slices bacon
6 large hamburger buns, lightly toasted
6 lettuce leaves
2 tomatoes, thinly sliced
6 large slices beets, drained (optional)
6 pineapple rings, drained
ketchup

1 Prepare and heat the barbecue. Combine the beef, onion, egg, bread crumbs, tomato paste, Worcestershire sauce, parsley, salt and pepper in a large bowl. Mix with your hands until well combined.

2 Divide mixture into six portions. Shape each portion into round patties $\frac{3}{4}$ in thick. Cover and set aside.

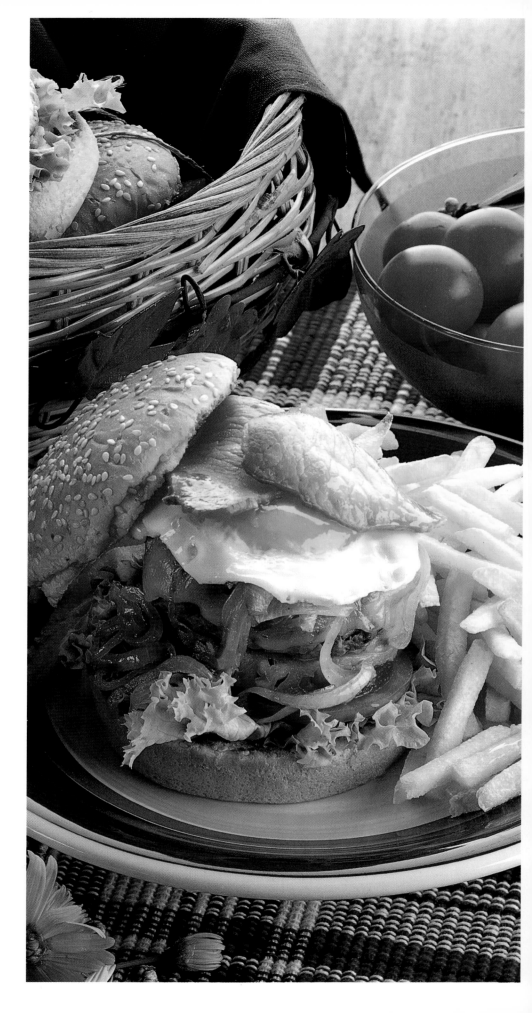

3 Slice the onions into thin rings. Heat the butter on a hot barbecue griddle (or in a cast iron skillet on the grill). Cook the onions, turning often until well browned. Move the onions to a cooler part of the barbecue to keep warm. Brush the preheated barbecue grill liberally with oil. Cook the meat patties for 3–4 minutes each side or until browned and cooked through. Move them to a cooler part of the barbecue or transfer to a plate and keep warm. Place a slice of cheese on each patty. (The heat of the burger will be enough to partially melt the cheese.)

4 Heat a small amount of extra butter in a hot large skillet. Fry the eggs and bacon on the grill or stove until the eggs are cooked through and the bacon is golden and crisp. Remove from heat.

5 To assemble burgers: Place toasted bun bases on individual serving plates. Top each with lettuce, tomato, a beet slice and pineapple. Place cooked meat patty on top, followed by cooked onions, egg, bacon and ketchup. Place remaining bun halves on top.

Steak with Vegetable Relish

The Vegetable Relish is delicious served warm or cold.

PREPARATION TIME:
15 MINUTES + 2 HOURS MARINATING
COOKING TIME:
6–16 MINUTES
SERVES 6

6 sirloin or boneless rib steaks, about 6 oz each
2 tablespoons lemon juice
1 teaspoon dried thyme leaves

VEGETABLE RELISH
2 tablespoons olive oil
1 medium onion, sliced
1 medium red sweet bell pepper, sliced
1/2 teaspoon yellow mustard seeds
1 thin-skinned cucumber, sliced
1 large tomato, peeled, chopped
2 tablespoons cider vinegar
1 tablespoon golden raisins
2 teaspoons soft brown sugar

1 Trim the meat of excess fat and sinew and combine with the lemon juice and thyme. Store in the refrigerator, covered with plastic wrap, for 2 hours or overnight, turning occasionally.

2 Place the meat on a preheated lightly oiled grill. Cook over a high heat for 2 minutes each side to seal, turning once. For a rare result, cook another minute each side. For medium and well done results, move the meat to a cooler part of the barbecue and cook another 2–3 minutes each side for medium and for 4–6 minutes each side for well done. Serve with Vegetable Relish.

3 To make Vegetable Relish: Heat oil in a small pan. Add the onion and stir over a high heat for 2 minutes or until well browned and soft. Add the red pepper and mustard seeds to the pan and stir over a medium heat for 2 minutes. Add the cucumber, tomato, vinegar, raisins and sugar. Bring to a boil, reduce heat to a simmer. Cook for 15 minutes, uncovered, stirring occasionally.

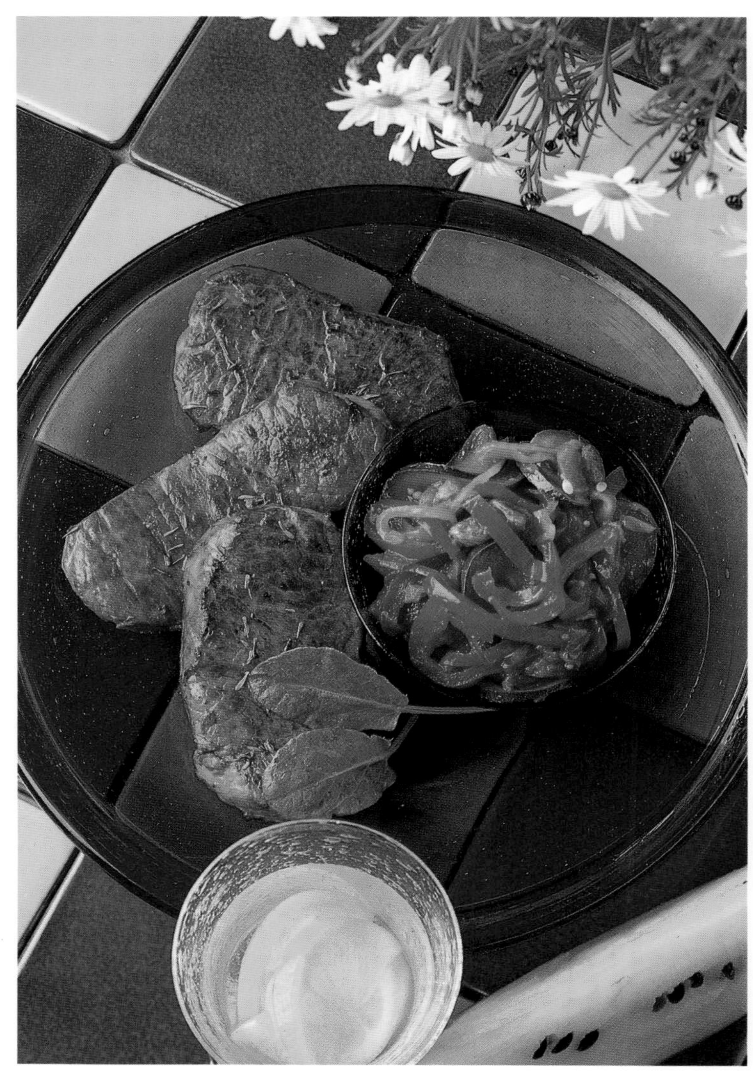

Whole Roast of Beef with Mustard Coating

PREPARATION TIME: 1 HOUR 5 MINUTES + 15 MINUTES STANDING
COOKING TIME: 40 MINUTES
SERVES 6–8

4 lb rib eye or boneless rib roast
1/4 cup brandy

MUSTARD COATING
1/3 cup coarse grain mustard
1/4 cup whipping cream
3/4 cup ground black pepper

1 Prepare the Weber (kettle) barbecue for indirect cooking at moderate heat (normal fire). Trim the meat of excess fat and sinew.
2 Tie the meat securely with string at regular intervals to retain its shape. Brush it all over with the brandy and allow to stand for 1 hour.
3 To make Mustard Coating: Combine the mustard, cream and pepper in a small bowl. Spread evenly over the top and sides of the meat.
4 Place the meat on a large greased sheet of foil. Grasp the corners of the foil and pinch securely to form a tray. (This will hold in the juices.) Place the lid on the barbecue and cook for 30–40 minutes for medium rare. Stand for 10–15 minutes before carving into thick slices. Serve warm with barbecued vegetables.

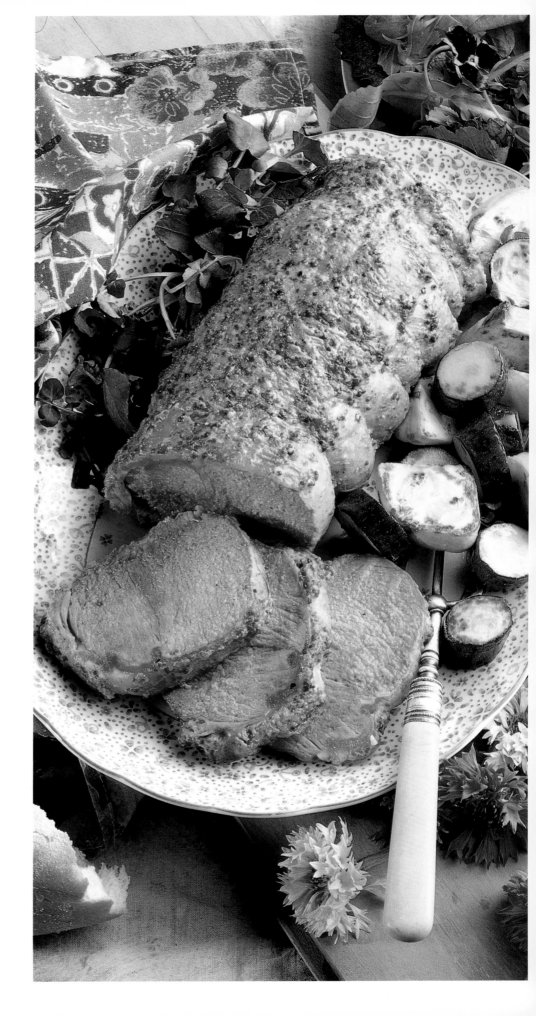

Tangy Beef Ribs

Ribs are ideal finger food — make sure you have plenty of napkins available!

PREPARATION TIME:
20 MINUTES + 3 HOURS MARINATING
COOKING TIME:
15–20 MINUTES
SERVES 4

2 lb beef short ribs
1/2 cup ketchup
2 tablespoons Worcestershire sauce
2 tablespoons soft brown sugar
1 teaspoon paprika
1/4 teaspoon chili powder
1 clove garlic, crushed

1 Chop the ribs into individual serving pieces, if necessary. Bring a large pan of water to a boil. Cook the ribs in boiling water for 5 minutes; drain.

2 Combine the ketchup, Worcestershire sauce, sugar, paprika, chili powder and garlic in a large bowl and mix well. Add ribs to sauce. Cover and marinate, in the refrigerator, for several hours or overnight. Prepare and heat the barbecue 1 hour before cooking.

3 Cook the ribs on a hot lightly greased barbecue grill for 10–15 minutes, brushing frequently with marinade, or until the ribs are well browned and cooked through. Serve with barbecued vegetables or slices of grilled fresh pineapple.

Thai Beef Salad

The herbs in this salad give it a lovely fresh flavor. Fresh kaffir lime leaves, if you can get them, make it really special.

PREPARATION TIME: 10 MINUTES
COOKING TIME: 3–5 MINUTES
SERVES 4–6

1 lb boneless sirloin steak

DRESSING
1 clove garlic, crushed
2 teaspoons palm sugar or brown sugar
1 tablespoon Thai fish sauce
1 tablespoon white vinegar
2 teaspoons grated lemon or lime rind
2 tablespoons lime juice

SALAD
2 green onions, sliced
1 small red sweet bell pepper, diced
2 small seedless cucumbers, thickly sliced
1/2 cup finely chopped cilantro leaves and stems
1/2 cup shredded mint
1/2 cup shredded basil
1 stem of lemongrass, thinly sliced, or 2 teaspoons grated lemon rind
1 fresh red chile, finely shredded
4 fresh kaffir lime leaves, cut into threads (optional)

1 Trim any excess fat from the steak.
2 To make the Dressing: Combine all the ingredients in a screw top jar and shake well.
3 To make the Salad: Combine all the prepared salad ingredients in a large bowl, cover tightly with plastic wrap and chill until serving time.
4 To cook the meat: Sear over a high heat on a lightly oiled barbecue grill. Cook to your taste. Best results with this salad are with moist, juicy rare to medium rare steak. Remove from the barbecue, allow to rest for 10 minutes and slice thinly. Combine the meat slices with the salad and dressing and toss well to distribute the flavors. Serve immediately.

Note: You can use very tender citrus leaves (either lemon or Tahitian lime) instead of fresh kaffir lime leaves, though the fragrance is not quite the same. Fish sauce (nam pla) is available in Thai markets.

Moroccan Beef Koftas

These may be cooked on an open-style barbecue or a kettle barbecue. Allow for slightly longer cooking time if using an open-style barbecue.

PREPARATION TIME: 15 MINUTES
COOKING TIME: 8 MINUTES
SERVES 6

1 1/2 lb very lean ground beef
1 egg
1/2 cup finely chopped cilantro or fresh parsley
salt and pepper, to taste
2 teaspoons ground coriander
2 teaspoons ground cumin
1 teaspoon chili powder
2 teaspoons ground sweet paprika
1/2 teaspoon ground turmeric
1 medium onion, grated
1/2 teaspoon ground cinnamon

1 Combine all the ingredients together and form into sausage shapes around skewers, or shape into patties.
2 Heat the kettle barbecue on medium-high. Lightly oil the grill.
3 Place the skewered koftas on the grill and cook for 4 minutes each side, or until cooked through. Serve with lavosh (Armenian flat bread) or pita bread, and raw onion rings.

Note: Turmeric, a member of the onion family, is an orange-yellow colored spice used to add color and flavor. Like all spices and herbs, store in an airtight container away from direct sunlight.

Thai Beef Salad (above). Moroccan Beef Koftas

Roast Beef with Pecan Sauce

With a kettle or hooded barbecue, you can prepare a wonderful roast. Serve with jacket baked potatoes hot from the coals, and barbecued corn cobs.

PREPARATION TIME:
25 MINUTES + 30 MINUTES STANDING
COOKING TIME:
1fi HOURS
SERVES 8

ROAST
- **5 lb rib eye or boneless rib roast**
- **1 medium onion, grated**
- **1 clove garlic, crushed**
- **1/2 teaspoon ground pepper**
- **1 teaspoon ground dried oregano**

SAUCE
- **1/2 cup pecans, toasted (see note)**
- **1 cup water**
- **2 teaspoons beef bouillon granules**
- **1/4 teaspoon ground pepper**
- **2 tablespoons unsalted butter**
- **2 tablespoons flour**
- **1 cup soaked hickory wood chips (optional)**

1 Slash the rib meat, mix all the ingredients together and spread over roast. Allow to stand for 30 minutes while making the sauce.
2 To make the sauce: Place the toasted pecans in a blender container together with water, bouillon and pepper. Blend to a paste.
3 Melt the butter in a small pan, add the flour and mix to a paste. Cook, stirring occasionally, for 5–6 minutes or until golden. Remove from heat and add the pecan mixture gradually. Return to the heat and stir until the mixture simmers and thickens.
4 To cook the roast: Heat the barbecue kettle, place beef on a rack in a dish, with 1 1/2 cups water. Place on the grill rack, cover and cook for about 1 1/2 hours, basting every 30 minutes with the sauce. The time allowed should result in a rare roast. For medium or well done results, allow extra cooking time. If using hickory chips, add the chips to the barbecue during the final 1/2 hour of cooking time.
5 When done to your preference, remove the roast to a serving dish and serve with the remaining sauce and jacket potatoes.

Note: To toast pecans: Place on a baking sheet and heat in a 350°F oven for 10 minutes or until crisp. Shake occasionally to avoid burning.

Beef Balls in Barbecue Sauce

These tasty beef morsels are great with fresh bread rolls and salad. If preferred, place two or three onto short bamboo skewers and cook, turning the skewers occasionally. For a quick appetizer, place on cocktail picks and serve with extra barbecue sauce as a dip.

PREPARATION TIME:
15 MINUTES
COOKING TIME:
6 MINUTES
SERVES 6

- **1 lb very lean ground beef**
- **1 egg**
- **1 medium onion, finely chopped**
- **1 clove garlic, crushed**
- **1 teaspoon grated fresh ginger**
- **salt and pepper, to taste**
- **1 cup bottled barbecue sauce (see note)**

1 Place the beef, egg, onion, garlic, ginger, salt and pepper in a bowl. Combine thoroughly by hand. Take a tablespoon of the meat mixture and roll into large meatballs.
2 Place on a well oiled, hot barbecue grill and cook for 5–6 minutes, turning and moving them around occasionally.
3 Brush the meatballs liberally with barbecue basting sauce 1 minute before the end of cooking. Serve immediately with the remaining barbecue sauce.

Note: Bottled barbecue sauce is available in most supermarkets. It has a mild hickory smoked flavor. If not available, use your favorite homemade barbecue sauce.

Beef Balls in Barbecue Sauce (above). Roast Beef with Pecan Sauce

MUNDIAL
INOX

Steak in Red Wine

Substitute 2 tablespoons of fresh oregano for dried oregano, if you wish.

PREPARATION TIME:
10 MINUTES +
3 HOURS
MARINATING
COOKING TIME:
5–10 MINUTES
SERVES 4

1 1/2 lb boneless sirloin steak
1 cup good red wine
2 teaspoons garlic salt
1 tablespoon dried oregano leaves
cracked black pepper, to taste

1 Cut the steak into large, evenly sized serving pieces and trim meat of excess fat and sinew.

2 Combine the wine, salt, oregano leaves and pepper in a large, shallow non-metal dish. Add steaks, turning to coat, then cover and refrigerate for several hours or overnight. Prepare and heat the barbecue 1 hour before cooking.

3 Drain steaks, reserving marinade. Cook the steaks on a hot lightly greased barbecue grill for 3–4 minutes each side or until cooked as desired, brushing with the wine mixture frequently. Serve immediately.

Hint: Choose a basting brush with pure bristles. Nylon bristles can melt in the heat and introduce an unpleasant flavor to cooked foods.

Barbecued Beef with Sesame and Ginger

PREPARATION TIME:
15 MINUTES +
2 HOURS
MARINATING
COOKING TIME:
25 MINUTES
SERVES 4–6

1 lb piece beef tenderloin (filet mignon)
1/4 cup sesame oil
1/4 cup soy sauce
2 cloves garlic, crushed
2 tablespoons grated fresh ginger
1 tablespoon lemon juice
2 tablespoons chopped green onions
1/4 cup firmly packed soft brown sugar

1 Trim the beef of any excess fat or sinew.
2 Combine the sesame oil, soy sauce, garlic, ginger, lemon juice, green onions and brown sugar in a non-metallic bowl. Add the beef and coat well with the marinade. Cover and refrigerate for 2 hours, or overnight if possible.
3 Preheat a lightly oiled barbecue grill. When very hot, add the beef and brown on all sides until the meat is sealed. Remove, wrap in foil and cook on the barbecue, turning occasionally, for another 15–20 minutes, depending on how rare or well done you like your meat.
4 Allow the beef to stand for 10 minutes before slicing. Serve with a fresh mixed salad.

Note: Individual steaks can be used and cooked on the barbecue grill; however, there is no need to wrap them in foil. The marinade is delicious as a sauce for the beef. Boil in a small pan for about 5 minutes and drizzle over the beef just before serving.

Steak with Onion Marmalade

PREPARATION TIME:
20 MINUTES
COOKING TIME:
1 HOUR
SERVES 4

4 thick rib eye steaks
black pepper, freshly ground

ONION MARMALADE
2 tablespoons butter
2 red onions, thinly sliced
2 tablespoons soft brown sugar
1 tablespoon balsamic vinegar

1 Trim any fat from the steaks, then sprinkle liberally with freshly ground black pepper. Cover and refrigerate until ready to cook.

2 To make the Onion Marmalade: Heat the butter in a heavy-based pan. Add the onions and cook, stirring occasionally, for about 10 minutes over low heat, or until the onions are soft but not brown. Stir in the brown sugar and balsamic vinegar and continue to cook for about 30 minutes, stirring frequently. The mixture will become thick and glossy.

3 Place the steaks on a lightly oiled preheated barbecue grill and cook for 3 minutes each side to seal, turning once only. For rare steaks, cook for another minute. For medium, cook for another few minutes and for well done, about 5 minutes. Serve at once with the Onion Marmalade and a fresh green salad.

Beef with Fennel Beans and Parsnip Purée

PREPARATION TIME: 15 MINUTES
TOTAL COOKING TIME: 25 MINUTES
SERVES 4

PARSNIP PUREE
4 parsnips
2 tablespoons butter
1 tablespoon whipping cream

FENNEL BEANS
1/4 cup butter
1–2 cloves garlic, crushed
1 small fresh red chile, seeded and chopped
1 medium fennel bulb, thinly sliced
10 oz can cannellini beans, drained and rinsed
10 oz can chickpeas, drained and rinsed
1/4 cup chopped fresh parsley

4 rib eye steaks

1 To make the Parsnip Purée: Cut the peeled parsnips into pieces and cook in salted boiling water for 6–8 minutes, or until they are tender. Drain well, then purée in a food processor until just smooth. Return to the hot pan and beat in the butter and cream with a wooden spoon. Season to taste with salt and freshly ground black pepper. Set aside and keep the purée warm until ready to serve.

2 To make the Fennel Beans: Melt the butter in a heavy-based skillet and add the garlic, chile and fennel. Cook for 5 minutes over medium heat, stirring frequently, until the fennel softens. Stir in the beans and chickpeas and continue to cook for another 3–4 minutes before adding the parsley. Set aside and keep warm.

3 Preheat a lightly oiled barbecue grill. Brush the steaks with a small amount of olive oil and cook them over a medium to high heat, turning once, until they are tender and done to your liking. Arrange the steaks on warm plates and serve immediately with the Parsnip Purée and the Fennel Beans.

Note: Pork chops or medallions are also suitable for this recipe.

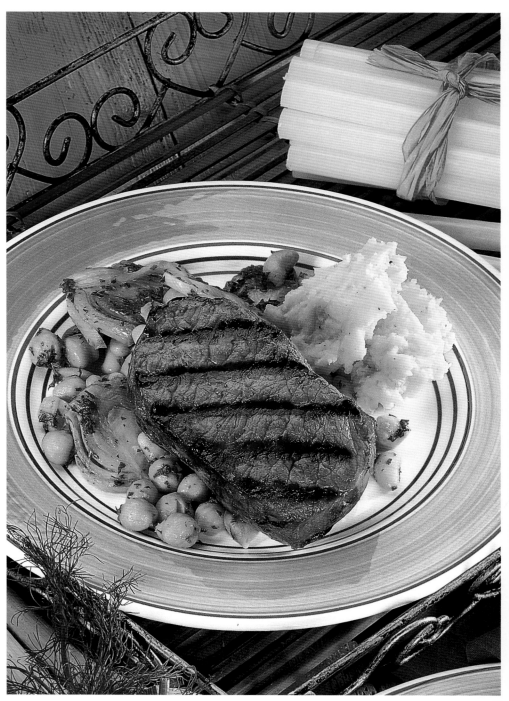

T-Bone Steak with Sweet Onions

PREPARATION TIME:
10 MINUTES
COOKING TIME:
20 MINUTES
SERVES 4

4 tablespoons oil
6 onions, sliced into rings
3 tablespoons barbecue sauce
4 T-bone steaks

1 Heat 2 tablespoons of the oil on a preheated barbecue griddle (or a cast iron skillet on the grill). Add the onions and barbecue sauce and cook for 10 minutes, or until very soft and brown. Remove to a cooler part of the barbecue to keep warm.

2 Brush the T-bone steaks with the remaining oil and add to the hot grill. Cook over a high heat, turning once or twice, until tender and cooked to your liking. Arrange the steaks on warm plates, spoon over some of the sweet onions and serve immediately.

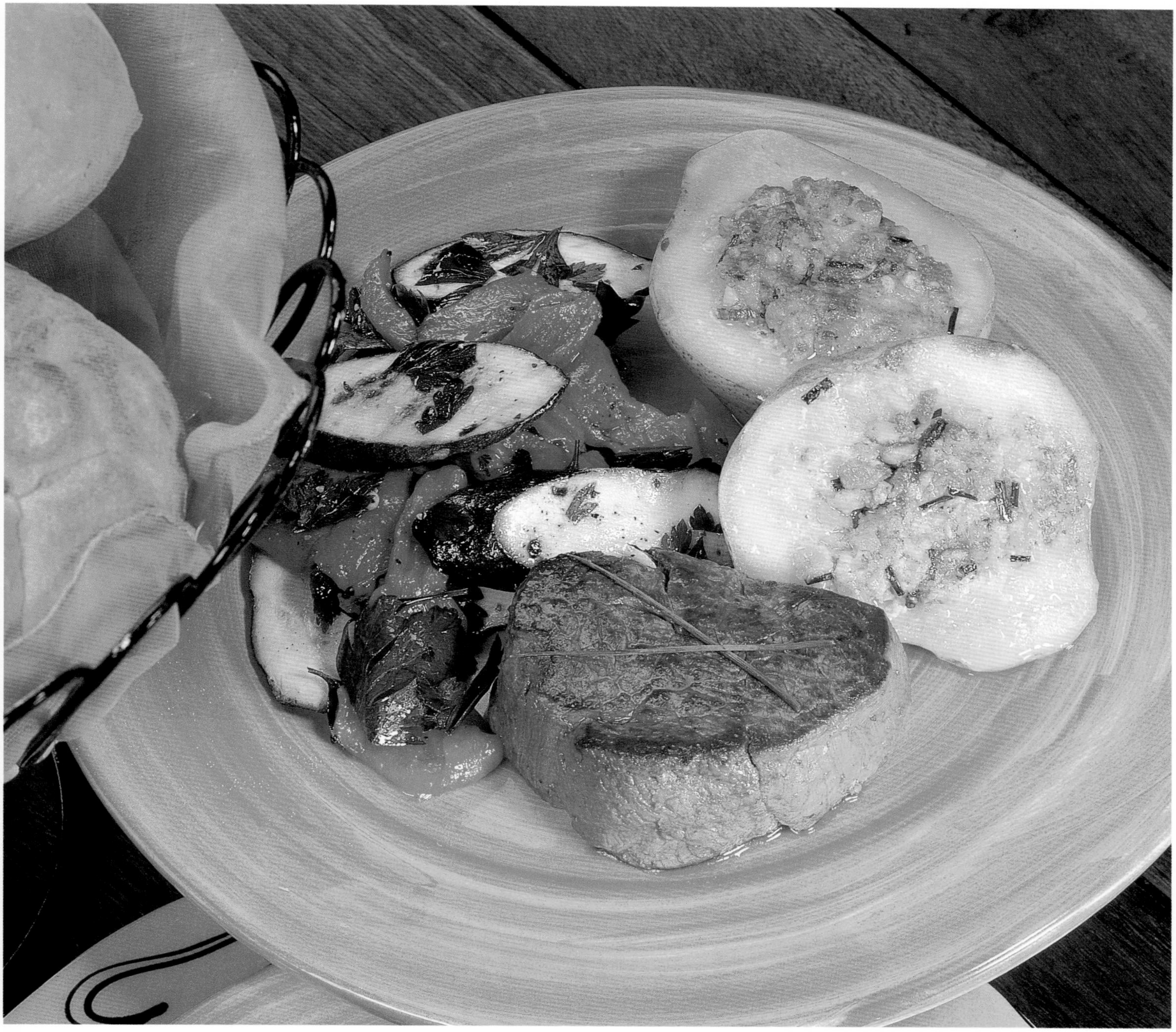

Filet Mignon with Stuffed Pears

PREPARATION TIME:
25 MINUTES
COOKING TIME:
15 MINUTES
SERVES 4

4 medium-firm pears
3 oz mild, soft blue cheese
2 slices sugar-cured ham, finely chopped
1 tablespoon finely chopped fresh chives
2 tablespoons chopped mixed nuts
4 filet mignon steaks

1 Cut each pear in half and remove the core and a little of the flesh to make a deep dip in the middle.
2 In a bowl, mix together the cheese, ham, chives and nuts. Pack the mixture firmly into the pear halves and round off the tops.
3 Preheat a barbecue grill and brush with a little oil. Add the steaks and cook over high heat until tender and done to your liking. Keep warm.
4 Add the pears to the grill, filling-side up, and cook for 2–3 minutes. Cover loosely with foil and steam for another 2 minutes. Serve with the steaks.

Steak with Red Pepper Relish and Creamy Mash

PREPARATION TIME: 30 MINUTES
TOTAL COOKING TIME: 50 MINUTES
SERVES 4

4 thick New York strip steaks
2–3 cloves garlic, crushed
2 teaspoons olive oil

RED PEPPER RELISH
1 large red sweet bell pepper
1 large yellow sweet bell pepper
1 tablespoon balsamic vinegar
1 teaspoon soft brown sugar

CREAMY MASH
1/ lb potatoes
2 tablespoons whipping cream
2 tablespoons butter

1 Trim the steaks of any excess fat or sinew. Combine the garlic and olive oil, coat the steaks with the mixture and then cover and refrigerate.

2 To make the Red Pepper Relish: Halve the peppers, remove the seeds and cut into strips. Heat some olive oil on a barbecue griddle (or in a cast iron skillet on the grill), add the pepper strips and cook over low heat, stirring frequently, for about 20 minutes. Partially cover the griddle or pan during this cooking time and take care not to burn. Stir in the balsamic vinegar and brown sugar and continue to cook for another 10 minutes. Remove to a cooler part of the barbecue and keep warm.

3 To make the Creamy Mash: Cut the peeled potatoes into cubes. Bring a pan of salted water to a boil, add the potatoes and boil for 10–15 minutes, or until just tender. Drain, then mash with a fork or potato masher. Beat in the cream and butter and season with some salt and freshly ground black pepper.

4 Add the steaks to the oiled hot grill. For rare steaks, cook for 2–3 minutes each side. For medium and well done steaks, cook for another 3–4 minutes each side for medium and 5–6 minutes each side for well done. Arrange on warm plates and serve with the Creamy Mash and the Red Pepper Relish.

Hot Peppered Steaks with Horseradish Sauce

PREPARATION TIME: 15 MINUTES
COOKING TIME: 10 MINUTES
SERVES 4

4 medium-sized boneless sirloin steaks
1/4 cup seasoned, cracked pepper

HORSERADISH SAUCE
2 tablespoons brandy
1/4 cup beef stock
1/3 cup whipping cream
1 tablespoon horseradish cream
1/2 teaspoon sugar
salt and pepper, to taste

1 Prepare and heat the barbecue, and lightly grease the grill. Trim the meat of excess fat and sinew and coat both sides with pepper, pressing it firmly into the meat.

2 Cook the meat over a high heat for 2 minutes each side to seal, turning once. For a rare result, cook another minute each side. For medium and well done results, move the meat to a cooler part of the barbecue and cook another 2–3 minutes each side for medium and 4–6 minutes each side for well done. Serve with Horseradish Sauce.

3 To make Horseradish Sauce: Combine the brandy and stock in a pan. Bring to a boil, reduce heat. Add the cream, horseradish and sugar and stir until heated through. Season to taste.

Herbed Lamb

This is best cooked on a kettle barbecue. If using an open-style barbecue, allow extra time for cooking.

PREPARATION TIME:
15 MINUTES + 30 MINUTES MARINATING
COOKING TIME:
8 MINUTES
SERVES 4–6

12 Frenched lamb rib chops

MARINADE
1 clove garlic, crushed
salt and pepper, to taste
1 medium onion, grated
2 tablespoons finely chopped fresh oregano
2 tablespoons lemon juice
4 tablespoons olive oil
1 cup hickory or cherry wood chips, soaked (optional)

1 Make sure the lamb is well trimmed by removing fat and sinew. Score the edges of the chops to prevent them from curling.
2 To make the marinade: Combine all the ingredients in a large shallow non-metal dish and add the chops. Turn the chops over in the marinade and let stand for 30 minutes, turning once.
3 Place the chops on a preheated lightly greased barbecue grill, add water-soaked wood chips to the glowing coals, if using, and cook over a medium heat, hood down, for 4 minutes. Turn and continue to cook for 3 minutes to give a medium rare result and continue to cook if well done is preferred. Serve with a crisp green salad or barbecued vegetables.

Lamb Loin with Ginger (above). Herbed Lamb

Lamb Loin with Ginger

PREPARATION TIME:
20 MINUTES +
30 MINUTES
MARINATING
COOKING TIME:
10 MINUTES
SERVES 6

3 loin fillets from boned lamb loin roasts

MARINADE
2 cloves garlic, crushed
2 teaspoons grated fresh ginger
2 green onions, finely chopped
1 tablespoon Korean chili paste
2 tablespoons toasted sesame seeds, crushed
1 teaspoon ground pepper
1 tablespoon water
2 teaspoons oriental sesame oil

1 Use a sharp knife to remove the silvery sinew from the outside of each lamb loin muscle. Split the muscle almost in half lengthwise, leaving them joined, and open them out so they are flat.
2 To make the marinade: Combine all the ingredients thoroughly. Pour over the lamb, mix and allow to marinate for 30 minutes or overnight in the refrigerator.
3 Cook on a preheated lightly oiled barbecue grill, over a medium high heat for 3 minutes on each side or until done. Serve sliced with your favorite salad.

Note: Adjust the quantity of chili paste to suit your taste.

Lamb Kebabs with Golden Pilaf

PREPARATION TIME:
25 MINUTES
COOKING TIME:
30 MINUTES
MAKES 8

1 1/2 lb lean ground lamb
1 small onion, finely chopped
2 tablespoons finely chopped cilantro
1 tablespoon ground cumin
1 teaspoon grated lemon rind

GOLDEN PILAF
3 tablespoons oil
1 teaspoon turmeric
1 medium onion, sliced
2 cups Basmati or jasmine rice
4 cups vegetable broth

1 Place the lamb, onion, cilantro, cumin and lemon rind in a large mixing bowl and combine thoroughly. Divide the mixture into eight equal portions and form into sausage shapes around large metal or soaked wooden skewers. Refrigerate until required.
2 To make Golden Pilaf: Heat the oil in a large pan. Add the turmeric and onion and stir over a medium heat for 2 minutes or until the onion is soft. Add the rice and continue stirring for 1 minute, until grains of rice are coated in oil.
3 Add the broth and cover the pan with a tight-fitting lid. Bring slowly to a boil, stirring once. Reduce heat and simmer, covered, for 10 minutes or until almost all the water is absorbed. Remove from the heat and stand covered for 5 minutes or until the water is absorbed and the rice is just tender. Stir the rice with a fork to separate the grains before serving.
4 Place the kebabs on a preheated lightly greased barbecue grill. Cook for 12 minutes, turning occasionally to brown all over. Serve on a bed of Golden Pilaf.

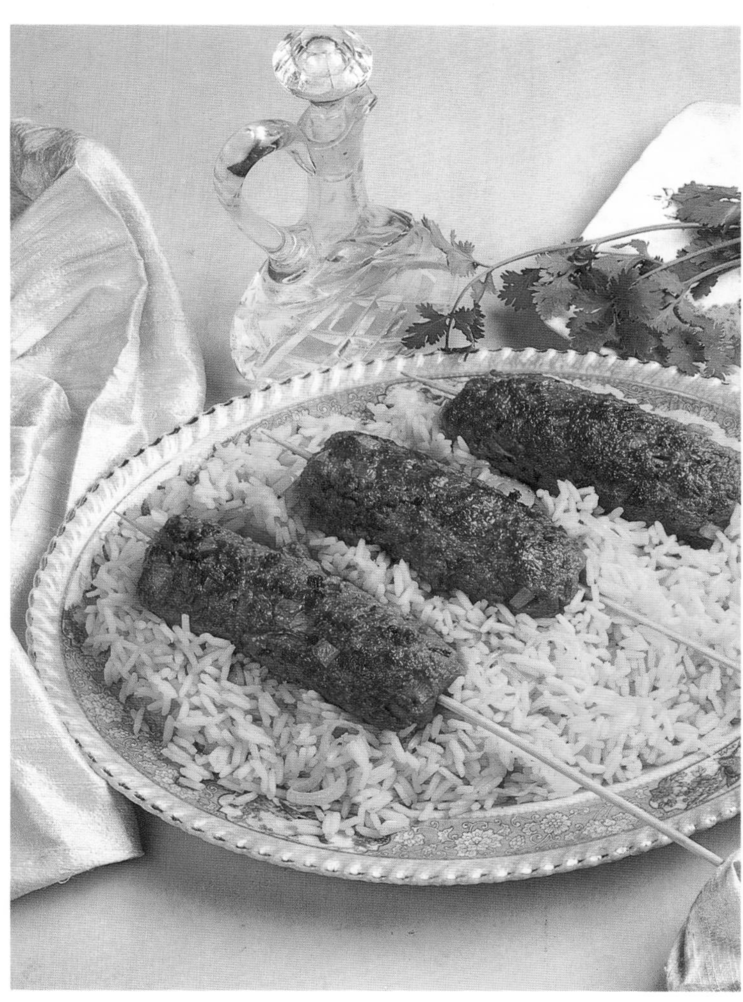

Spicy Rotisserie Leg of Lamb

PREPARATION TIME:
10 MINUTES + 1 HOUR MARINATING
COOKING TIME:
1fi HOURS
SERVES 8

4 lb leg of lamb

MARINADE
2 teaspoons ground turmeric
1 teaspoon ground sweet paprika
salt and pepper, to taste
2 large cloves garlic, crushed
1 teaspoon grated fresh ginger
3 tablespoons plain yogurt
1 teaspoon ground cardamom

1 Trim off the excess fat and score the leg of lamb with shallow diagonal cuts $1\frac{1}{4}$ in apart on both sides.
2 To make the marinade: Combine all the ingredients and spread over the lamb, making sure to fill the criss-cross cuts. Marinate for 1 hour or overnight in the refrigerator.
3 Heat covered barbecue. Skewer the lamb and attach to the rotisserie, taking care to balance the leg of lamb so the weight is evenly distributed or the rotisserie will not turn smoothly. Cook $1\frac{1}{2}$ hours over a low heat until done to your liking. Baste with the remaining marinade every 15 minutes.

Barbecued Spicy Lamb Koftas

Serve these koftas with barbecued vegetables such as eggplant and sweet peppers.

PREPARATION TIME:
10 MINUTES +
1 HOUR STANDING
COOKING TIME:
10 MINUTES
SERVES 6

1 lb lean ground lamb
1 medium onion, finely chopped
1 clove garlic, crushed
2 tablespoons chopped fresh mint
1 teaspoon ground coriander
1 teaspoon ground cardamom
1/4 teaspoon curry powder
pinch cayenne pepper
1/2 cup dry bread crumbs
1 egg, lightly beaten
1 cup dry bread crumbs, extra

YOGURT DRESSING
2/3 cup plain yogurt
1 tablespoon chopped cilantro
2 teaspoons chopped fresh mint
1/2 teaspoon grated lemon rind

1 Place the lamb in a medium bowl and add the onion, garlic, herbs, spices and bread crumbs. Mix together well using your hands. Divide the meat mixture into twelve even portions. Mold into sausage shapes around oiled, metal skewers.
2 Brush lightly with egg; roll in extra bread crumbs to coat evenly. Store in the refrigerator, covered with plastic wrap, for 1 hour or overnight.
3 Place skewers on a lightly greased barbecue grill. Cook over a medium heat for 10 minutes or until cooked through, turning occasionally. Serve with Yogurt Dressing.
4 To make Yogurt Dressing: Beat all the ingredients in a small bowl until well combined. Refrigerate.

Fragrant Leg of Lamb

This recipe is best cooked on a kettle barbecue.

PREPARATION TIME: 15 MINUTES
COOKING TIME: 1 HOUR 30 MINUTES
SERVES 6

4 lb leg of lamb
4 cloves garlic
6–8 sprigs rosemary
2 tablespoons olive oil
2 tablespoons freshly ground black pepper

1 Prepare the Weber (kettle) barbecue for indirect cooking at moderate heat (normal fire). Place a drip tray on the bottom grate.

2 Trim the meat of excess fat and sinew. Cut narrow, deep slits all over top and sides of meat.

3 Cut the garlic cloves in half lengthwise. Put the garlic and rosemary sprigs into slits. Brush all over with oil and sprinkle with black pepper.

4 Place the lamb on the barbecue grill over a drip tray, cover and cook for 1 hour 30 minutes for medium rare meat. Brush with olive oil occasionally. Stand lamb in a warm place, covered with foil for 10–15 minutes before carving.

Fragrant Leg of Lamb. Baked Vegetables (see page 179)

Oriental Lamb

PREPARATION TIME:
20 MINUTES + 30 MINUTES MARINATING
COOKING TIME:
10 MINUTES
SERVES 6

6 tenderloin fillets from boned lamb rib roasts

MARINADE
1 clove garlic, crushed
1 teaspoon grated fresh ginger
1 small onion, peeled and coarsely chopped
1 tablespoon fresh curry leaves (see note)
1/4 teaspoon ground turmeric
salt and pepper, to taste
1 tablespoon lemon juice
1 tablespoon water
1 teaspoon oriental sesame oil

1 Trim the lamb fillets and remove all the silvery sinews using a sharp knife. Split each of the fillets in half lengthwise starting at the tip and leaving it joined at the thick end.

2 To make the marinade: Combine all the ingredients in a blender until smooth. If a blender is not available, grate the onion and finely chop the curry leaves. Combine all the ingredients in a small bowl. Pour the marinade over the lamb, mix and allow to marinate for 30 minutes.

3 Thread the meat onto metal skewers ribbon fashion. Cook on a preheated lightly oiled barbecue grill over a medium high heat for 5 minutes each side or until done. Serve with your favorite salad.

Note: Fresh curry leaves can be found in Asian food stores. If not available, substitute fresh oregano or marjoram leaves. The taste is just as delicious.

Barbecued Lamb Shanks

Try this recipe with other cuts of meat on the bone, such as pork chops, osso bucco, pieces of ox tail and chicken drumsticks.

PREPARATION TIME: 5 MINUTES + OVERNIGHT MARINATING
COOKING TIME: 45 MINUTES
SERVES 6

2 cloves garlic, crushed
1/3 cup olive oil
6 lamb shanks
salt and pepper, to taste

1 Combine the garlic and oil in a small bowl, cover and marinate, at room temperature, overnight.
2 Prepare the Weber (kettle) barbecue for indirect cooking at moderate heat (normal fire). Place a drip tray under the grill rack.
3 Trim the shanks of excess fat and sinew. Brush the garlic oil generously over the shanks and sprinkle with salt and pepper.
4 Place the lamb shanks on the grill, cover with a lid and roast for 35–45 minutes or until the meat is tender when pierced with a fork. Serve with barbecued vegetables, such as sweet peppers, and thick slices of charbroiled potato, scattered with herbs.

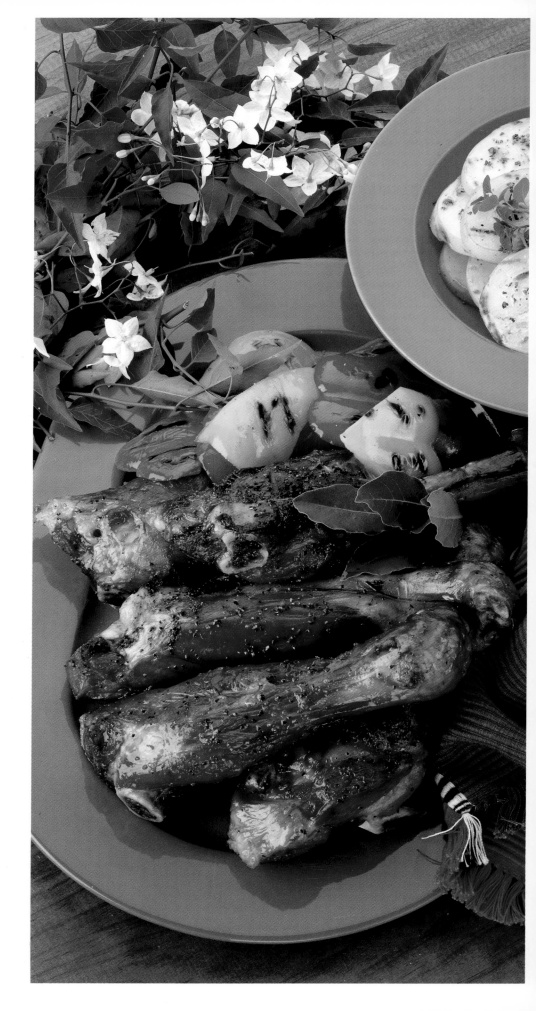

Barbecued Lamb with Chermoula

Marinate this dish overnight for best results.

PREPARATION TIME:
25 MINUTES + 3 HOURS MARINATING
COOKING TIME:
1 HOUR
SERVES 6

1 medium onion, grated
2 cloves garlic, crushed
4 tablespoons chopped flat-leaved parsley
4 tablespoons chopped cilantro
1/2 teaspoon ground cumin
1/2 teaspoon ground saffron
1/2 teaspoon harissa sauce (see note)
1/2 cup olive oil
2 tablespoons lemon juice
1 x 4 lb leg of lamb

1 To make Chermoula: Mix the onion, garlic, flat-leaved parsley, cilantro, cumin, saffron, harissa, olive oil and lemon juice together; stand for 1 hour.
2 Starting at the thicker end of the leg of lamb, cut down and around the bone. Scrape away as much meat as possible. Remove bone. Cut down into, not through, the thickest part of the meat; open out flat.
3 Spread the Chermoula mixture onto both sides of the lamb and marinate for at least 3 hours.
4 Prepare the kettle barbecue for indirect cooking. Place a drip tray on the bottom grate. Place the lamb on the grill rack, cover and cook for 1 hour for a medium rare result. Brush with oil frequently during cooking. Stand the lamb for 10–15 minutes before carving. Cut in thick slices across the grain and serve.

Note: Harissa is a fiery condiment widely used in Morocco. The basic ingredients are red chiles, cayenne, olive oil and garlic. It is delicious served with poached eggs or sausages. Look for it in Middle-Eastern markets.

Lamb Chops Indienne

PREPARATION TIME:
10 MINUTES +
1 HOUR
MARINATING
COOKING TIME:
6–8 MINUTES
SERVES 6

12 Frenched lamb rib chops, excess fat removed

MARINADE
2 teaspoons curry powder
1 teaspoon garam masala
1 teaspoon garlic powder
2 teaspoons onion powder
1 tablespoon white vinegar
salt, to taste
1/4 cup water
2 tablespoons oil

1 To make the marinade: Combine all the ingredients and spread evenly over the lamb chops. Allow the meat to marinate for 1 hour or overnight in refrigerator.
2 Heat the barbecue to medium and place the marinated lamb chops on an oiled grill. Cook for 5 minutes, turn and cook for another 3 minutes. Cook longer according to taste if required. Serve with mango chutney.

Note: Garam masala can be purchased in supermarkets and Indian food stores.

Lamb Kebabs

A real change from roasts and chops, and quick to cook, too, either grilled or barbecued.

PREPARATION TIME:
20 MINUTES +
3 HOURS
MARINATING
COOKING TIME:
8–10 MINUTES
SERVES 4–6

2 lb lean boneless lamb
1 clove garlic, crushed
1 teaspoon salt
1/2 teaspoon black pepper
1 teaspoon finely grated fresh ginger
1/2 teaspoon ground turmeric
1 teaspoon ground coriander
1 teaspoon ground cumin
1 tablespoon lemon juice
1 tablespoon sesame oil
1 tablespoon peanut oil

1 Cut the lamb into large cubes and place in a bowl.
2 Combine all the other ingredients and mix well. Pour over the lamb and stir thoroughly, making sure all pieces of lamb are coated with marinade. Cover and refrigerate overnight, if possible, or for at least 3 hours.
3 Thread five pieces of lamb on each skewer (make sure you soak the skewers beforehand) and cook over glowing coals. Cubes of lamb should be crusty brown all over. Serve hot with rice or flat breads.

Butterflied Leg of Lamb

Ask the butcher to bone and butterfly the leg of lamb to make the preparation of this dish much easier.

PREPARATION TIME:
20 MINUTES + 30 MINUTES MARINATING
COOKING TIME:
25 MINUTES
SERVES 6–8

3 lb leg of lamb, boned and butterflied

MARINADE
2 teaspoons ground dried mint
2 cloves garlic, crushed
1 tablespoon olive oil
1 tablespoon preserved green peppercorns, mashed (see note)
salt and pepper, to taste

1 Trim off excess fat and lay the boned leg of lamb on a flat surface. Score the inside, criss-cross fashion. Turn the lamb and repeat with the other side.
2 To make the marinade: Combine all the ingredients and rub into the scored surfaces of the lamb. Allow the meat to marinate, covered, for at least 30 minutes or overnight.
3 Place the lamb on a lightly oiled preheated barbecue grill and cook for 20–25 minutes, turning once during cooking for a rare result. Increase the cooking time if you prefer lamb well done. Allow the meat to stand for 15 minutes before slicing.

Note: Preserved green peppercorns are available at delicatessens and some supermarkets. Store the remaining peppercorns and brine in an airtight jar, refrigerated. To reduce flare-ups, place a foil tray directly under the lamb to catch melted fat.

Smoked Leg of Lamb

This recipe calls for a kettle or covered barbecue. If cooked by any other method, it will not have quite the same wonderful results.

PREPARATION TIME:
10 MINUTES +
1 HOUR MARINATING
COOKING TIME:
1fi HOURS
SERVES 6–8

3 lb leg of lamb, excess fat removed
3 cups mesquite or hickory chips, soaked (optional)

MARINADE
2 teaspoons ground sweet paprika
1/2 teaspoon ground pepper
salt, to taste
1 teaspoon ground dried mint flakes
3 cloves garlic, crushed
1 teaspoon ground cumin
1 tablespoon ground rice
2–3 tablespoons water

1 Put the mesquite or hickory chips, if using, to soak in cold water before starting preparation of the food.
2 To make the marinade: Combine all the ingredients. Score the lamb with shallow diagonal slashes to form diamond shapes and spread with the marinade, making sure it gets into all the slashes. Cover and let stand for 1 hour or overnight in the refrigerator.
3 Heat the barbecue, skewer the lamb securely and attach to the rotisserie.
4 Roast with the hood down on a low heat for about 1 1/2 hours, basting with the leftover marinade. Add two handfuls of soaked chips to the glowing coals every 30 minutes, if using.
5 When the meat is done to your liking, remove the rotisserie spit from the barbecue and let the meat stand for 10 minutes before serving. Serve the smoked leg of lamb with vegetables of your choice, or spiced rice.

Note: Marinated meats should be at room temperature before barbecuing to allow for even cooking, and for the meat to absorb extra flavor. If not, the outside may be overcooked while the inside is still raw.

Spicy Lamb Kebabs

Fresh grated ginger adds a distinctive flavor to this recipe.

PREPARATION TIME:
30 MINUTES +
OVERNIGHT MARINATING
COOKING TIME:
10 MINUTES
SERVES 6

3 lb leg of lamb, boned

MARINADE
2 teaspoons grated fresh ginger
2 cloves garlic, crushed
salt and pepper, to taste
1 tablespoon ground coriander
2 teaspoons ground cumin
2 teaspoons ground turmeric
1/2 teaspoon ground nutmeg
1/2 teaspoon ground cardamom
1 teaspoon white vinegar
2 tablespoons peanut oil

1 Trim any excess fat from the lamb and cut into 1 in cubes.
2 To make the marinade: Combine all the ingredients in a medium-sized bowl.
3 Add the lamb, and stir to coat with spice mix. Cover and refrigerate overnight.
4 Thread each skewer with four to five pieces of lamb and barbecue on a lightly oiled preheated barbecue grill. Cook until well browned, turning gradually. Serve with pita bread or rice and a sauce of finely chopped cucumber and yogurt.

Smoked Leg of Lamb (above). Spicy Lamb Kebabs

Spicy Grilled Lamb

A boneless lamb loin, fat-trimmed, is a delicately flavored, fat-free portion of lamb that could also be used in this recipe.

PREPARATION TIME:
20 MINUTES +
30 MINUTES
MARINATING
COOKING TIME:
10 MINUTES
SERVES 6

6 lamb sirloin chops (round bone)

MARINADE
1 clove garlic, crushed
1 teaspoon grated fresh ginger (see note)
1 tablespoon lemon juice
1 tablespoon water
1/2 cup chopped cilantro leaves
1 small onion, coarsely chopped
1/4 teaspoon ground pepper
1 teaspoon mild curry powder
1/2 teaspoon garam masala
salt and pepper, to taste

1 Place the lamb in a shallow dish.
2 To make the marinade: Combine all the ingredients in a blender or food processor until smooth and pour over the lamb. Allow to marinate for 30 minutes. (If a food processor or blender is unavailable, finely chop the cilantro, grate the onion and combine the marinade ingredients in a small bowl.)
3 Cook over a medium high heat on a barbecue grill for 5 minutes each side or until rosy pink inside, brown outside. If using lamb loins, cut into thick diagonal slices to serve.

Note: If you don't often use fresh ginger, peel and slice a small root, place in a clean jar and cover with dry sherry. It will keep in the refrigerator for months. The sherry can also be used in Asian-style dishes.

Spicy Grilled Lamb (above). Tandoori-style Lamb

Tandoori-style Lamb

A tandoori is an earthern oven using charcoal as a fire source. This Mongol-initiated style of cooking is adaptable for poultry, meats, fish and even vegetable dishes. Cook this dish on a kettle barbecue.

PREPARATION TIME: 10 MINUTES + 1 HOUR MARINATING
COOKING TIME: 12 MINUTES
SERVES 4

12 Frenched lamb rib chops

MARINADE
1 clove garlic, crushed
1 teaspoon grated fresh ginger
1/2 teaspoon ground pepper
1 teaspoon ground turmeric
1 teaspoon ground sweet paprika
1 teaspoon garam masala
1/4 cup plain yogurt

1 Trim the rib chops of any excess fat. Then score the edges of the meat to prevent the meat from curling when barbecued.
2 To make the marinade: Make a paste with all the other ingredients and coat the chops with marinade. Set aside for 1 hour.
3 Preheat the barbecue and cook on the oiled grill for 6 minutes each side.

Spiced Lamb with Cucumber Salsa

The 'coolness' of the salsa complements the spiciness of the lamb perfectly. Try this combination cold, in crusty rolls.

PREPARATION TIME: 15 MINUTES + 2 HOURS MARINATING
COOKING TIME: 30–40 MINUTES
SERVES 6

3 lb leg of lamb, boned
2/3 cup plain yogurt
1 medium onion, chopped
1 teaspoon grated ginger
1 teaspoon ground cumin
1 teaspoon ground coriander
1 teaspoon poppy seeds
1 teaspoon ground turmeric
1/2 teaspoon garam masala
1/4 teaspoon ground nutmeg

CUCUMBER SALSA
1 thin-skinned cucumber, cut into 1/2 in cubes
1 small tomato, cut into 1/2 in cubes
1 small red onion, thinly sliced
grated rind and juice of 1 lime
1 tablespoon chopped cilantro
1 tablespoon chopped fresh basil
1 teaspoon soft brown sugar

Trim the meat of excess fat and sinew. Flatten out ıe leg.

Combine the yogurt, onion, ginger, cumin, ɔriander, poppy seeds, turmeric, garam masala and ıutmeg in a food processor or blender and process for) seconds or until smooth.

Place meat in a large dish. Spread the yogurt ıixture over the meat and turn the lamb until well ɔated. Store in the refrigerator, covered with plastic rap, for 2 hours or overnight. Bring to room ɛmperature before cooking.

Place the meat on a preheated lightly greased grill. ;ook for 30 minutes over medium coals, turning nce. Cook another 5 minutes for a medium result ıd another 10 minutes for well done. Serve sliced ith Cucumber Salsa.

To make Cucumber Salsa: Combine the ıgredients in a bowl; mix well.

Lamb Rib Chops with Rosemary Marinade

This dish is ideal for a barbecue picnic.

REPARATION ME:
5 MINUTES +
MINUTES
ARINATING
OOKING TIME:
-8 MINUTES
ERVES 4

12 Frenched lamb rib chops, well trimmed
1/4 cup olive oil
2 tablespoons chopped fresh rosemary
1 1/2 teaspoons cracked black pepper
1 bunch fresh rosemary, extra

1 Prepare and heat the barbecue. Trim the chops of excess fat and sinew. Place the chops in a shallow, non-metal dish and brush with half the oil.

2 Scatter half the chopped rosemary and pepper on the meat and set aside for 20 minutes. Turn the meat over and brush with the remaining oil, scatter over remaining rosemary and pepper. Tie the extra bunch of rosemary to the handle of a wooden spoon.

3 Arrange the chops on a hot lightly greased grill. Cook 2–3 minutes each side. As the chops cook, bat them frequently with the rosemary spoon. This will release flavorsome oils into the meat. When the chops are almost done, remove the rosemary from the spoon and drop it on the fire where it will flare up briefly and infuse rosemary smoke into the chops.

Lamb with Mixed Mushrooms

PREPARATION TIME:
30 MINUTES
COOKING TIME:
20 MINUTES
SERVES 4

$1^1/_2$ lb lamb leg center slices
$^1/_4$ cup butter
1 red onion, chopped
4 green onions, cut into short lengths
1–2 cloves garlic, crushed
12 oz mixed mushrooms, thickly sliced
$^1/_4$ cup sherry
$^1/_3$ cup chopped fresh parsley

1 Lightly coat the lamb with some olive oil, then sprinkle liberally with freshly ground black pepper. Cover and refrigerate until ready to use.

2 Preheat a lightly oiled grill. Add the lamb and cook over high heat for about 4 minutes each side, taking care not to overcook. The lamb should be cooked through, but still slightly pink inside. Allow to rest for a few minutes before slicing off the bone into strips.

3 Meanwhile, preheat a cast iron skillet on the grill and melt the butter. Add the onion, green onions and garlic and cook for 2–3 minutes, or until softened but not browned. Add the mushrooms and cook over moderate heat, tossing frequently, for about 5 minutes, or until tender and golden brown. Pour in the sherry and sprinkle the parsley over the top. Arrange the lamb strips on warm plates and serve with the mixed mushrooms.

Lamb Pita

PREPARATION TIME:
0 MINUTES +
5 MINUTES
MARINATING
COOKING TIME:
MINUTES
SERVES 4

12 oz lamb center slices
2 teaspoons finely grated lemon rind
1 tablespoon finely chopped fresh oregano
2 cloves garlic, finely chopped
2 tablespoons olive oil
1 red onion, thinly sliced
4 small pita breads
1/2 cup hummus
1/2 cup plain yogurt
1 small short, thin cucumber, thinly sliced
1 small red fresh chile, seeds removed, finely chopped
snow pea sprouts

1 Trim the lamb of excess fat and cut into thin strips. In a bowl, combine the lemon rind, oregano, garlic, olive oil and some freshly ground pepper. Add the lamb and refrigerate for 15 minutes.

2 Preheat a lightly oiled barbecue griddle (or cast iron skillet on the grill) until extremely hot. Cook the lamb and onion for 2–3 minutes, turning to brown the meat quickly and soften the onion. Remove and keep warm. Place the pita breads on the grill and warm both sides.

3 Spread each round of bread with a little of the hummus and yogurt. Add the barbecued lamb and onions and sprinkle with the cucumber, chile and a few snow pea sprouts. Serve immediately.

Note: Tenderloin can be used instead of the center slice. Ask the butcher to remove the fat and bone from a loin roast to provide the muscle in one strip.

Lamb with Salsa Verde and Polenta

PREPARATION TIME: 40 MINUTES + 20 MINUTES SETTING
COOKING TIME: 35 MINUTES
SERVES 4

SALSA VERDE
1 cup fresh parsley, lower stalks removed
1 cup fresh basil leaves
1 cup fresh mint leaves
1/2 cup fresh dill
2 tablespoons capers
1–2 cloves garlic
1 tablespoon superfine sugar
1 teaspoon grated lemon rind
1 tablespoon lemon juice
1 slice white bread
2–3 canned anchovy fillets
1/3 cup olive oil

POLENTA WEDGES
2 1/4 cups chicken broth
1 cup polenta (cornmeal)
1/4 cup butter
1/2 cup whipping cream
extra melted butter, for brushing

12 Frenched lamb rib chops, well trimmed

1 To make Salsa Verde: Place the parsley, basil, mint, dill, capers, garlic, sugar, lemon rind and juice, bread and drained anchovies in a food processor and finely chop. With the motor running, gradually add the oil and blend the mixture until smooth.

2 To make the Polenta Wedges: Heat the broth in a large pan until boiling. Gradually add the polenta, stirring constantly over low heat for 20 minutes until the polenta leaves the side of the pan. Stir in the butter and cream and season with salt and ground pepper. Grease a 3 in deep, 9 in round cake pan or spring form, spoon in the polenta and smooth the surface. Set in the refrigerator for 20 minutes.

3 Turn the polenta out of the pan, cut into wedges and brush all over with the melted butter. Lightly oil a preheated barbecue grill and cook the wedges for 2–3 minutes each side, or until brown. Remove and keep warm.

4 Place the lamb on the grill and brown for about 2 minutes each side, or until cooked through but still just pink inside. Serve with the Salsa Verde and Polenta Wedges.

Lamb Loin with Eggplant, Tomato and Pesto

PREPARATION TIME:
30 MINUTES
COOKING TIME:
25 MINUTES
SERVES 4

PESTO
2 cups fresh basil leaves
2 cloves garlic, crushed
1/3 cup pine nuts
3/4 cup olive oil
3/4 cup grated Parmesan

1 medium eggplant
4 plum tomatoes, halved
2 boneless lamb loin roasts, trimmed of fat
1/4 cup crumbled goats cheese

1 To make the Pesto: Place the basil leaves, garlic and pine nuts in a food processor and finely chop. With the motor running slowly, gradually, pour in the olive oil. Add the Parmesan and process the mixture briefly.

2 Cut the eggplant into thick slices and brush with some olive oil. Preheat a barbecue grill and cook the eggplant, brushing with a little more oil, for 3–4 minutes each side, or until golden brown and softened. Remove and keep warm. Add the tomatoes and cook, brushing with olive oil, until soft. Remove and keep warm.

3 Sprinkle each lamb loin liberally with freshly ground black pepper. Wipe clean the preheated grill and lightly oil. Cook the lamb for 3–4 minutes, turning to brown on all sides, until the lamb is cooked through but still pink inside. Cut the loins into diagonal slices and arrange on four plates. Arrange the tomato on top of the eggplant and top with a little pesto. Sprinkle the goats cheese over the top and serve with the lamb.

Note: Instead of using basil to make the pesto, you could use cilantro or mint, or a mixture of them both. If you prefer a milder taste, use ricotta or feta rather than goats cheese (chèvre).

Moroccan Lamb with Pistachio Couscous

PREPARATION TIME: 40 MINUTES + 2 HOURS MARINATING
COOKING TIME: 15–20 MINUTES
SERVES 4

MOROCCAN MARINADE
1/4 cup olive oil
1 tablespoon lemon juice
2 teaspoons honey
1–2 cloves garlic, crushed
1 teaspoon ground cumin
1/2 teaspoon ground turmeric
1/2 teaspoon ground cinnamon
1/4 teaspoon cayenne pepper

2 boneless lamb loin roasts, trimmed of fat and sinew
pinch saffron
1 1/2 cups hot chicken broth
1 1/4 cups couscous
1 tablespoon olive oil
1 red onion, chopped
1 fresh red chile, seeded and chopped
2 cloves garlic, crushed
1/2 cup dried currants
2/3 cup shelled pistachios
grated rind of 1 lemon
grated rind of 1 orange
1/4 cup chopped fresh mint

1 To make the Moroccan Marinade: Mix together all the ingredients in a bowl, pour over the lamb loins to coat, and cover and refrigerate for 2 hours.

2 Add the saffron powder or threads to the hot broth and pour over the couscous in a bowl. Set aside for 10 minutes, then stir to break up any lumps.

3 Heat the oil in a skillet, add the onion, chile and garlic and cook for about 3 minutes. Add the currants and pistachios and continue to cook for another 5 minutes. Mix in the lemon and orange rind and the mint. Stir the mixture through the couscous.

4 Preheat a lightly oiled barbecue grill and add the drained lamb. Cook, turning once, over high heat until browned all over. Then continue to cook for another 2–3 minutes, turning frequently. Remove and slice the lamb on the diagonal. Serve with the couscous.

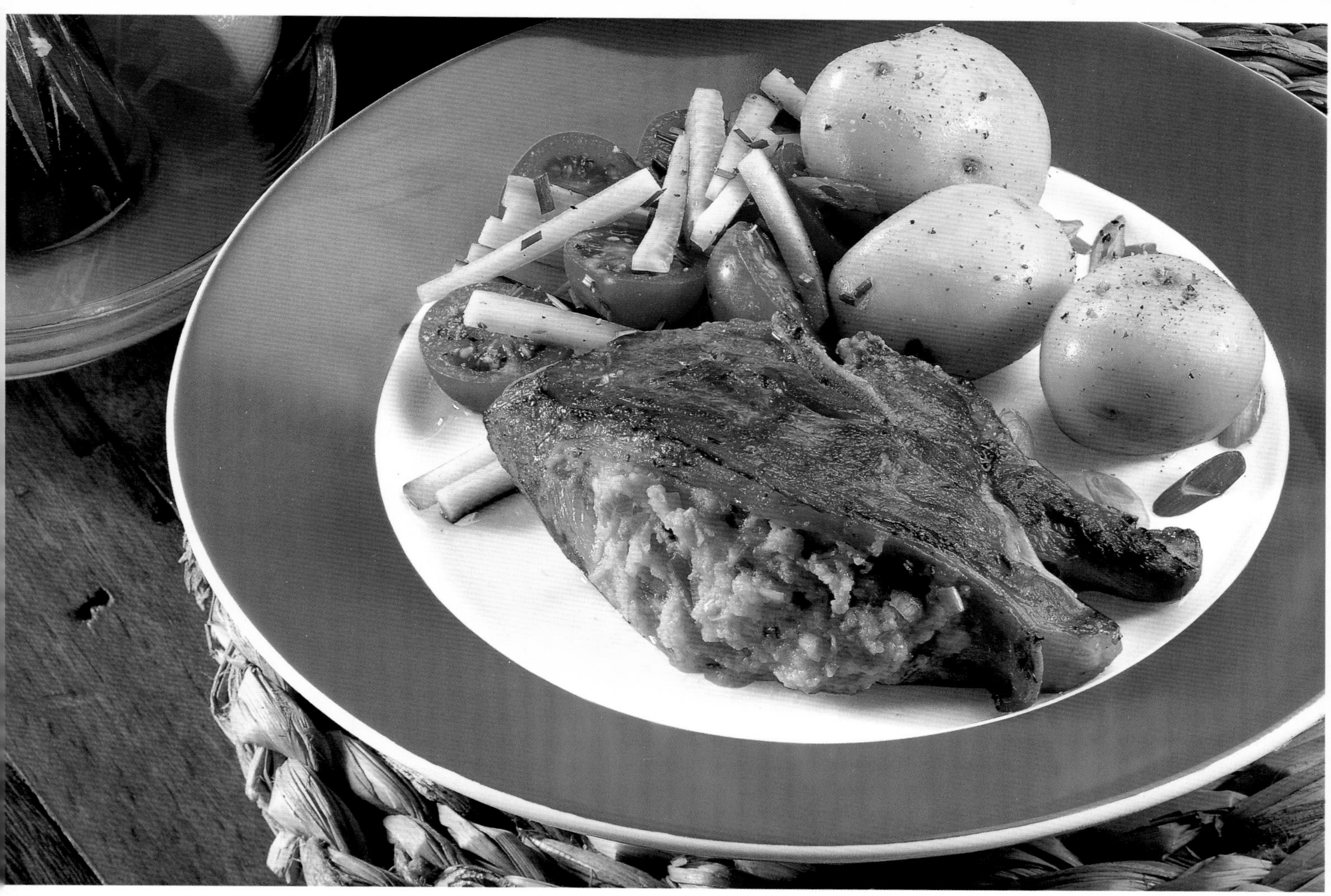

Lamb Chops with Citrus Pockets

PREPARATION TIME:
25 MINUTES
COOKING TIME:
15 MINUTES
SERVES 4

4 thick lamb leg sirloin or shoulder arm chops, about 8 oz each
2 tablespoons lemon juice

FILLING
3 green onions, finely chopped
1 stalk celery, finely chopped
1 tablespoon grated fresh ginger
3/4 cup fresh bread crumbs
2 tablespoons orange juice
2 teaspoons finely grated orange rind
1 teaspoon finely chopped fresh rosemary

1 Cut a deep, long pocket into the side of each of the lamb chops through the fat.

2 To make the Filling: Combine in a bowl the green onions, celery, ginger, bread crumbs, orange juice and rind, and the rosemary. Spoon the mixture into the lamb pockets.

3 Preheat a lightly oiled barbecue grill and cook the chops over high heat, turning once, for 15 minutes, or until the lamb is cooked through but still pink in the center. Drizzle with the lemon juice and serve with boiled potatoes and a salad.

Lamb Satays with Chili Peanut Sauce

Why not let your guests cook their own satays?

PREPARATION TIME: 25 MINUTES + 1 HOUR MARINATING
COOKING TIME: 15 MINUTES
SERVES 4

1 1/4 lb boneless lamb sirloin
2 cloves garlic, crushed
1/2 teaspoon ground black pepper
2 tablespoons finely chopped lemongrass
2 tablespoons soy sauce
2 teaspoons sugar
1/4 teaspoon ground turmeric

CHILI PEANUT SAUCE
1 1/2 cups unsalted roasted peanuts
2 tablespoons vegetable oil
1 medium onion, coarsely chopped
1 clove garlic, roughly chopped
1 tablespoon sambal oelek or chili paste
1 tablespoon soft brown sugar
1 tablespoon kecap manis (Indonesian sweet soy sauce) or soy sauce
1 teaspoon grated fresh ginger
1 1/2 teaspoons ground coriander
1 cup canned coconut cream or coconut milk
1/4 teaspoon ground turmeric
salt and pepper, to taste

1 Trim the lamb of excess fat and sinew and cut into thin strips. Thread onto soaked wooden skewers, bunching the strips along three-quarters of the length. Place the satays in a shallow, non-metal dish.

2 Combine the garlic, pepper, lemongrass, soy sauce, sugar and turmeric in a small bowl and mix well. Brush the marinade over the skewered meat and set aside for 1 hour. Prepare and heat the barbecue.

3 To make the Chili Peanut Sauce: Process the peanuts in a food processor for 10 seconds or until coarsely ground. Heat the oil in a small pan. Add the onion and garlic and cook over a medium heat for 3–4 minutes or until translucent. Add the sambal oelek, sugar, kecap manis, ginger and coriander. Cook, stirring, for 2 minutes.

4 Add the coconut cream, turmeric and processed peanuts. Reduce the heat and cook for 3 minutes or until thickened; season with salt and pepper. Remove from the heat.

5 Place the mixture in a food processor. Process for 20 seconds or until almost smooth. Spoon into individual serving dishes to cool.

6 Barbecue the satays on a hot lightly greased grill for 2–3 minutes each side or until browned.

Lamb Chops with Pineapple Salsa

PREPARATION TIME:
20 MINUTES
COOKING TIME:
10 MINUTES
SERVES 6

12 lamb loin chops
2 tablespoons oil
1 teaspoon cracked black pepper

PINEAPPLE SALSA
1/2 ripe pineapple (or 1 3/4 cups drained canned pineapple)
1 large red onion
1 fresh red chile
1 tablespoon cider or rice vinegar
1 teaspoon sugar
salt and black pepper, to taste
2 tablespoons chopped mint

1 Prepare and heat the barbecue. Trim the meat of excess fat and sinew. Brush with oil and season with pepper.

2 To make Pineapple Salsa: Peel the pineapple and remove the core and eyes. Cut into 1/2 in cubes. Peel the onion and finely chop. Slit open the chile, scrape out the seeds and chop the chile flesh finely. Combine the pineapple, onion and chile in a medium bowl and mix lightly. Add the vinegar, sugar, salt, pepper and mint; mix well.

3 Place the lamb chops on a lightly greased barbecue grill. Cook for 2–3 minutes each side, turning once, until just tender. Serve with Pineapple Salsa, baked potatoes and a green salad.

Ginger-Orange Pork Chops

PREPARATION TIME: 15 MINUTES + 3 HOURS MARINATING
COOKING TIME: 20 MINUTES
SERVES 6

6 pork loin butterfly chops (6 oz each)
1 cup green ginger wine or sherry
1/2 cup orange marmalade
2 tablespoons oil
1 tablespoon grated fresh ginger

1 Trim the pork of fat and sinew. Place in a shallow non-metal dish.
2 Combine the wine, marmalade, oil and ginger in a small bowl and mix well. Pour the marinade over the meat. Store, covered with plastic wrap, in the refrigerator for several hours or overnight, turning occasionally. Prepare and heat the barbecue 1 hour before cooking. Drain the pork chops and reserve the marinade.
3 Place the pork on a hot lightly oiled barbecue grill. Cook for 5 minutes each side or until tender, turning once.
4 While meat is cooking, place the reserved marinade in a small pan. Bring to a boil, reduce heat and simmer for 5 minutes until the marinade has reduced and thickened slightly. Pour over the pork steaks immediately.

Note: Look for green ginger wine at gourmet delis or liquor stores.

Pork Loin Chops with Apple Chutney

Try the Apple Chutney served with a cheese platter. It also goes well with cold meats.

PREPARATION TIME:
20 MINUTES +
3 HOURS
MARINATING
COOKING TIME:
25 MINUTES
SERVES 6

6 pork loin rib chops
2/3 cup white wine
2 tablespoons oil
2 tablespoons honey
1 1/2 teaspoons ground cumin
2 cloves garlic, crushed

APPLE CHUTNEY
3 medium green apples
1/2 cup apple juice
1/2 cup fruit chutney
1 tablespoon butter

1 Trim the pork chops of excess fat and sinew and place in a shallow, non-metal dish.
2 Combine wine, oil, honey, cumin and garlic in a small bowl and mix well. Pour the marinade over the chops. Store, covered with plastic wrap, in the refrigerator for several hours or overnight, turning occasionally. Prepare and heat the barbecue 1 hour before cooking.
3 Place the chops on a hot lightly oiled barbecue grill. Cook for 8 minutes each side or until tender, turning once. Serve immediately with Apple Chutney.
4 To make Apple Chutney: Peel the apples and cut them into small cubes. Place them in a small pan and cover with apple juice. Bring to a boil, reduce heat and simmer, covered, for 7 minutes or until completely soft. Add the chutney and butter and stir to combine. Serve warm.

Pork Loin Chops with Apple Chutney (above). Ginger-Orange Pork Chops

Skewered Ginger Pork

Ginger and pork are a great combination and this recipe brings the two together in a delightful dish.

PREPARATION TIME:
20 MINUTES +
1 HOUR
MARINATING
COOKING TIME:
10 MINUTES
SERVES 6

1 lb boneless pork fillets
2 tablespoons grated fresh ginger
1/2 teaspoon ground pepper
1 teaspoon oriental sesame oil
1 tablespoon lemon juice
1 small onion, grated
salt and pepper, to taste

1 Cube the pork, combine the remaining ingredients and marinate the pork for 1 hour.
2 Skewer the pork and barbecue on a hot grill for 5 minutes each side or until cooked to personal taste. Serve with a salad and hot bread rolls, and garnish with lime halves if desired.

Pork Ribs with a Chili Watermelon Sauce

PREPARATION TIME:
20 MINUTES
COOKING TIME:
1 HOUR
10 MINUTES
SERVES 4

- **2 lb pork spareribs**
- **1/4 cup orange juice**
- **6 oz (about 1 cup) watermelon flesh, seeds removed**
- **2 cloves garlic, finely chopped**
- **2 fresh red or green chiles, chopped**
- **1/4 cup tomato paste**
- **1 teaspoon soy sauce**

1 Preheat the oven to 400°F. Place the ribs on a rack over a baking dish and brush all over with the orange juice. Cook for 1 hour, turning once.

2 Lightly mash the watermelon with a fork and combine with the garlic, chiles, tomato paste and soy sauce. Preheat a lightly oiled barbecue grill and cook the ribs for about 7 minutes, basting with some of the watermelon sauce.

3 Serve the spareribs drizzled with the remaining watermelon sauce.

Note: Baking the meat before grilling produces more succulent spareribs.

Pork with Apple and Onion Wedges

PREPARATION TIME: 25 MINUTES
COOKING TIME: 15 MINUTES
SERVES 4

12 oz boneless top loin pork roast
12 pitted prunes
2 green apples, unpeeled, cored, and cut into wedges
2 red onions, cut into wedges
1/4 cup butter, melted
2 teaspoons superfine sugar
1/2 cup whipping cream
2 tablespoons brandy
1 tablespoon chopped fresh chives

1 Trim the pork of any excess fat and sinew and cut into four evenly sized portions. Make a slit with a knife through the center of each portion and push 3 prunes into each one. Brush the pork and the apple and onion wedges with the melted butter and sprinkle just the apples and onions with the sugar.

2 Lightly oil a deep-sided preheated cast iron skillet or barbecue griddle. Brown the pork evenly on each side. Add the apples and onions (depending on the size of the pan or griddle, it may be necessary to cook these in batches). Cook, turning frequently, for 5–7 minutes, or until the pork is cooked through and the apples and onions are softened. Remove the pork, apples and onions from the heat and keep warm.

3 Mix together the cream, brandy and chives in a bowl. If you are using a skillet with deep sides, add the mixture to the pan over a hot grill. Alternatively, pour into a saucepan on top of the stove or barbecue grill. Simmer for about 3 minutes, or until slightly thickened and reduced. Season to taste with salt and freshly ground black pepper.

4 Slice the meat on the diagonal, arrange on warm plates and pour on the sauce. Add the apples and onion wedges and serve with a green salad.

Pork and Sun-dried Tomato Burgers

PREPARATION TIME:
20 MINUTES +
15 MINUTES
REFRIGERATION
COOKING TIME:
15 MINUTES
SERVES 4

12 oz lean ground mixed pork and veal
2/3 cup sun-dried tomatoes, chopped
3 green onions, finely chopped
2 tablespoons chopped fresh basil
1 red sweet bell pepper, seeded and sliced
1 tablespoon balsamic vinegar

1 Combine the pork and veal, sun-dried tomatoes, green onions, basil and salt and pepper in a bowl. Knead for 2 minutes, or until the meat becomes a little sticky. Form into four patties and refrigerate for 15 minutes.

2 Mix the red pepper with a little olive oil. Cook on a preheated barbecue griddle (or in a cast iron skillet on the grill), tossing well and drizzling with the balsamic vinegar until just softened. Remove to a cooler area of the barbecue and keep warm.

3 Brush the patties with olive oil and cook on the hot oiled grill for 4–5 minutes on each side, or until browned and cooked through. Serve with the red pepper slices.

Honey Pork with Bok Choy

PREPARATION TIME:
25 MINUTES +
1 HOUR MARINATING
COOKING TIME:
25 MINUTES
SERVES 4

MARINADE
2 tablespoons soy sauce
1 tablespoon oil
1 tablespoon kecap manis or soy sauce
1 tablespoon honey
1 tablespoon oyster sauce

2 pork tenderloins, about 12 oz each, well trimmed
2 tablespoons oil
2 cloves garlic, crushed
2 teaspoons grated fresh ginger
6 oz (about 2 1/4 cups) shiitake mushrooms, sliced
6 baby bok choy, halved
1/4 cup chicken broth
3 oz instant (2-minute) noodles
1/3 cup cilantro leaves

1 To make the marinade: Combine the ingredients and marinate the pork for 1 hour in the refrigerator. Drain, reserving the marinade.
2 Preheat a lightly oiled barbecue grill and brown the pork over high heat for 2 minutes. Continue to cook, turning occasionally, for about 5 minutes. Remove and keep warm.
3 Heat the oil in a skillet over the stove or barbecue grill. Cook the garlic and ginger for 2 minutes, then add the mushrooms and cook for 3 minutes. Add the bok choy, reserved marinade and broth. Simmer, stirring, for 5 minutes.
4 Cook the instant noodles, without the flavor sachet, according to the manufacturer's instructions. Drain and add to the vegetables. Slice the pork and place on top of the noodles and vegetables, and sprinkle with the cilantro.

Note: Kecap manis is also known as Indonesian soy sauce. Bok choy is also known as Chinese white cabbage.

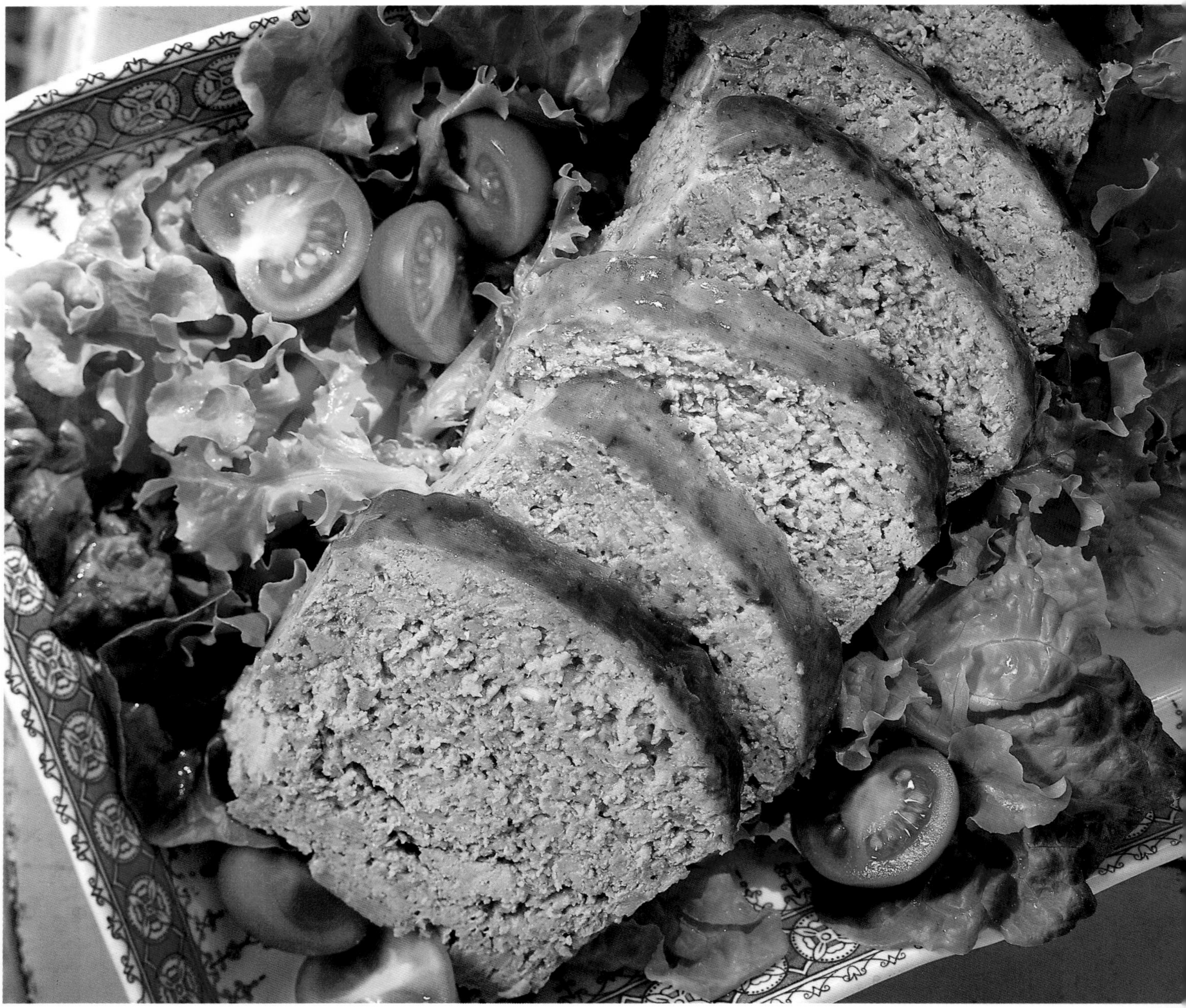

Piquant Meatloaf

PREPARATION TIME:
10 MINUTES
COOKING TIME:
1 HOUR
SERVES 6–8

$2\frac{1}{4}$ lb lean ground mixed pork and veal
$\frac{3}{4}$ cup bottled plum sauce
1 medium onion, grated
$\frac{1}{2}$ cup chopped cilantro
2 cloves garlic, crushed
salt and pepper, to taste
2 eggs, lightly beaten
1 cup fresh bread crumbs

BASTING MIXTURE
2 teaspoons chicken bouillon granules
2 tablespoons hot water

1 Combine the pork and veal in a bowl with the remaining meatloaf ingredients.
2 Place the mixture in an $8\frac{1}{2}$ x $5\frac{1}{2}$ x $2\frac{3}{4}$ in lightly greased or non-stick loaf pan.
3 Preheat the barbecue and place the loaf pan on a rack over the grill. Cook with the hood down for 1 hour, basting the meatloaf every 15 minutes with combined chicken bouillon granules and hot water.
4 Serve sliced with a crisp green salad.

Note: Bottled plum sauce can be purchased from supermarkets and Asian stores. Use barbecue sauce as a substitute.

Sweet and Sour Pork Kebabs

Chili garlic sauce is available from Asian food shops and some supermarkets.

PREPARATION TIME:
30 MINUTES +
3 HOURS
MARINATING
COOKING TIME:
20 MINUTES
SERVES 6

2 1/4 lb boneless pork loin
1 large red sweet bell pepper
1 large green sweet bell pepper
16 oz can pineapple pieces
1 cup orange juice
1/4 cup white vinegar
2 tablespoons soft brown sugar
2 teaspoons chili garlic sauce
2 teaspoons cornstarch

1 Trim the pork of excess fat and sinew and cut meat into 1 in cubes. Cut both bell peppers into 3/4 in squares. Drain pineapple and reserve juice. Thread the meat, alternately with the peppers and pineapple, onto soaked wooden skewers.

2 Combine the reserved pineapple juice with orange juice, vinegar, sugar and sauce. Place the kebabs in a shallow non-metal dish and pour half the juice mixture over. Refrigerate, covered with plastic wrap, for 3 hours or overnight, turning occasionally. Prepare and heat barbecue 1 hour before cooking.

3 To make the Sweet and Sour Sauce: Place the remaining marinade in a small pan. Mix the cornstarch with a tablespoon of the marinade in a small bowl until smooth; add to pan. Stir over a medium heat until the mixture boils and thickens, then transfer to a small serving bowl. Cover surface with plastic wrap and allow to cool.

4 Place the kebabs on a hot lightly oiled barbecue grill and cook for 15 minutes, turning occasionally, until tender. Serve kebabs with Sweet and Sour Sauce.

Pork and Veal Pita Burgers

PREPARATION TIME:
10 MINUTES
COOKING TIME:
8 MINUTES
SERVES 4–6

1 lb lean ground mixed pork and veal
1 large onion, grated
salt and pepper, to taste
1 teaspoon ground oregano leaves
1 clove garlic, crushed
1 teaspoon hot chili sauce
1/3 cup fresh bread crumbs

1 Combine all the ingredients, mix well and divide into six. Shape the portions into flat, round patties and place on an oiled hamburger frame.

2 Barbecue on a medium high heat on the grill plate for 4 minutes, turn over and cook for another 4 minutes. Serve the burgers on pita bread with a mixed salad, sour cream and pickled sour cucumbers.

Note: Make sure that all of the burgers are the same size to allow for even cooking.

Stars and Stripes Barbecue Ribs

PREPARATION TIME:
30 MINUTES + OVERNIGHT MARINATING
COOKING TIME:
15 MINUTES
SERVES 6–8

3 1/2 lb pork spareribs

SAUCE
1 teaspoon dry mustard, or prepared English mustard
1 teaspoon ground sweet paprika
1/2 teaspoon ground oregano
1/2 teaspoon ground cumin
1/4 cup peanut oil
2 cloves garlic, crushed
1 teaspoon Tabasco sauce
1 cup ketchup
2 tablespoons Worcestershire sauce
1/3 cup tomato paste
1/3 cup brown sugar
1 tablespoon cider vinegar

1 To make the sauce: Mix the mustard and dry spices with oil in a medium pan. Blend in the sauce and remaining ingredients. Cook, stirring, over a medium heat for 5 minutes until combined. Cool before refrigerating. Store half in a clean glass jar for later use.

2 Coat the ribs with the remaining sauce and marinate overnight. Cook on a medium hot

barbecue grill, turning frequently, until well done.

Note: This marinade and the sauce are equally good with beef spareribs or short ribs. However, if using beef ribs they should be simmered until tender and drained before marinating and barbecuing.

Pork and Veal Pita Burgers (above). Stars and Stripes Barbecue Ribs

Honey Soy Sausages

PREPARATION TIME: 15 MINUTES + OVERNIGHT MARINATING
COOKING TIME: 5–6 MINUTES
SERVES 4–6

8–10 thick pork or beef sausages
1 1/4 in piece fresh ginger
1/3 cup honey
1/3 cup soy sauce
1 clove garlic, crushed
1 tablespoon sweet sherry
2 sprigs fresh thyme

1 Place the sausages in a large bowl or shallow non-metal dish. Peel the ginger and grate it finely. Combine the honey, soy sauce, ginger, garlic, sherry and thyme in a bowl; mix well.
2 Pour the marinade over the sausages. Cover and refrigerate overnight to allow the flavors to be absorbed.
3 Prepare and heat the barbecue 1 hour before cooking. Lightly grease the barbecue grill. Cook the sausages 5–6 minutes, away from the hottest part of the fire, brushing occasionally with marinade. Turn the sausages frequently to prevent the marinade burning (it should form a thick, slightly sticky glaze around the sausages).

Pork Butterfly Chops with Olive Tapenade

Tapenade is ideal with meats such as pork which have mild, subtle flavors.

PREPARATION TIME: 20 MINUTES
COOKING TIME: 10 MINUTES
SERVES 4

4 x 6 oz boneless loin pork butterfly chops
2 tablespoons olive oil
1 tablespoon lemon juice
1 tablespoon fresh thyme leaves
1/4 teaspoon ground black pepper

OLIVE TAPENADE
2 tablespoons olive oil
1/2 small onion, finely chopped
1 clove garlic, crushed
3/4 cup pitted black olives, finely chopped
2 canned anchovies, finely chopped
1 small, ripe tomato, peeled, seeded and chopped
2 teaspoons balsamic vinegar
1 medium fresh red chile, finely chopped
1 tablespoon chopped fresh basil leaves

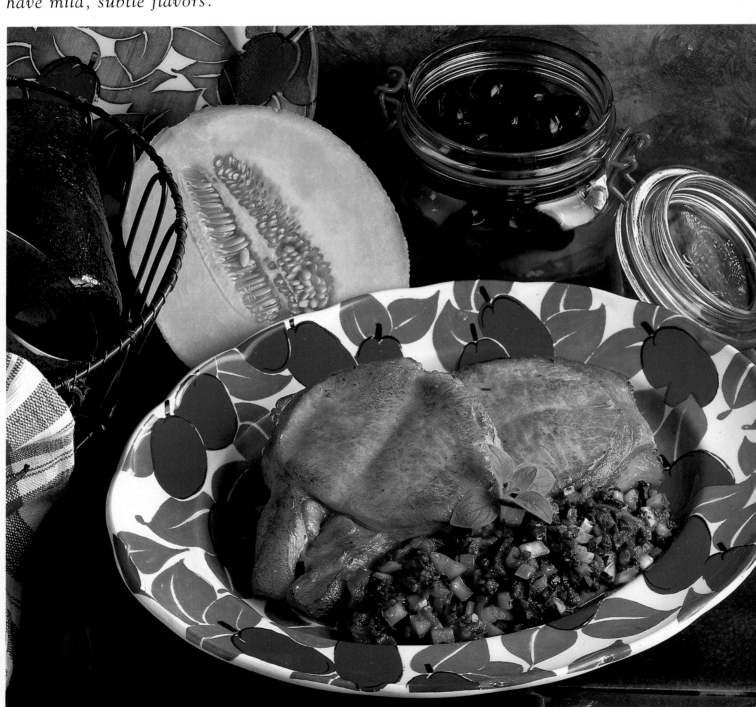

1 Trim the pork butterfly chops of excess fat and sinew.
2 Combine the oil, lemon juice, thyme and pepper and brush over the meat.
3 Place the meat on a lightly oiled barbecue grill. Cook over a medium heat for 5 minutes on each side or until tender. Serve with Olive Tapenade.
4 To make Olive Tapenade: Heat the oil in a small pan, add the onion and garlic, and stir until the onion is tender. Add the olives, anchovies, tomato, vinegar, chile and basil and stir 1 minute to combine. Serve hot or cold.

Orange and Ginger-glazed Ham

Leftover ham can be sliced and served with fried eggs, or with grilled tomatoes. Cubed ham is delicious in fried rice. The ham bone can be used for stock or as the basis of pea soup.

PREPARATION TIME:
25 MINUTES
COOKING TIME:
1 HOUR 30 MINUTES
SERVES 20

12–14 lb ham on the bone
1/4 cup orange juice
3/4 cup orange marmalade
1 tablespoon grated fresh ginger
2 teaspoons mustard powder
2 tablespoons soft brown sugar
whole cloves (about 30)

1 Prepare a Weber (kettle) barbecue for indirect cooking at moderate heat (normal fire).
2 Remove the rind by running your thumb around the edge of the ham, under the rind. Begin pulling from the widest edge. When the rind has been removed to within 4 in of the shank end, cut through the rind around the shank. Using a sharp knife, remove excess fat from the ham and discard. (Reserve the rind for crackling, if desired. Rub the rind with salt and barbecue for 40 minutes.)
3 Using a sharp knife score the top of the ham with deep diagonal cuts. Score diagonally the other way, forming a diamond pattern. Place the ham on the barbecue; put on the lid and cook for 45 minutes.
4 Place the juice, marmalade, ginger, mustard and sugar in a small pan. Stir over a medium heat until combined; set aside to cool.
5 Remove the lid from the barbecue and carefully press cloves into the top of the ham (approximately one clove per diamond); brush all over with the marmalade mixture.
6 Cover the barbecue and cook for another 45 minutes. Serve garnished with clove-studded orange slices. Ham can be served warm or cold.

Poultry

There is a great range of poultry cuts to choose from these days, and all of them — chicken thighs and breasts, leg and thigh quarters, wings and drumsticks — are ideal for the barbecue. Quail, too, are small and tender — perfect for barbecue cooking — allow at least one bird per person.

When buying chicken, appearances are important. The flesh of a fresh chicken should be moist, with no dry spots, and the breasts should be plump. If blood or juices are visible in the bottom of plastic packaging, it may mean that the chicken has been on display for longer than is ideal. If offered on special, you should cook the chicken the same day.

Keep uncooked chicken in the coldest part of the refrigerator and cook within two days of purchase. A whole chicken should be removed from its wrappings, washed, patted dry and jointed, depending on how it is to be cooked. Wrap the pieces again in clean plastic wrap or foil and store in the refrigerator. Make sure that a frozen chicken is allowed to thaw completely in the refrigerator (don't remove the wrapping; the skin may dry out and toughen). Poultry is highly susceptible to bacterial growth at room temperature, so never try speeding up the defrosting process by leaving the bird out on the kitchen counter as it may result in food poisoning.

Poultry lends itself wonderfully to marinating — the various flavors will permeate the flesh, and the acid content in ingredients like lemon juice, wine or vinegar will increase its tenderness. For thicker cuts like boned skinless breasts or drumsticks, slash the flesh in several places to allow the flavors of the marinade to be better absorbed. Baste the meat with the marinade occasionally during cooking to prevent it drying out.

Mango Chicken

Buy mangoes that are firm to soft. They may be green, yellow, or bright orange with a rosy blush, depending upon the variety.

PREPARATION TIME:
20 MINUTES
COOKING TIME:
30 MINUTES
SERVES 6

2 onions
2 tablespoons oil
1 clove garlic, crushed
6 boned chicken breast halves
salt and pepper, to taste
3 medium nearly ripe mangoes or 16 oz can mangoes
watercress, to garnish

GLAZE
1/2 cup reserved mango juice or puréed fresh mangoes
1 tablespoon honey
2 teaspoons chicken bouillon granules
1 clove garlic, crushed
1 teaspoon cornstarch
cold water

1 Thinly slice the onions. Heat the oil and cook onions and garlic over a low heat until golden brown. Remove from heat.
2 Place the breast halves skin-side down onto a board or work surface. Flatten each out to enclose filling. Season each with salt and pepper to taste. Place equal portions of the onion and garlic over the surface of the chicken.
3 Drain the mangoes and reserve the juice for the glaze. If using fresh mangoes, you must peel the fruit and cut close to the sides of the seed to get two full slices from each mango. Slice off the remaining flesh and purée in a blender.
4 Arrange the mango slices on the chicken breasts. Fold the chicken breasts over to enclose the mango slices and onions. Secure with cocktail picks or metal skewers.
5 To make the glaze: Combine the mango purée or juice, honey, chicken bouillon and garlic in a small pan, cook over low heat until thoroughly combined. Add cornstarch mixed smoothly with a tablespoon of cold water to the glaze. Stir over a low heat until thickened.
6 Cook chicken on a lightly oiled barbecue grill over medium heat for 15 minutes. Turn and cook for another 10 minutes or until the chicken is done. Brush with the glaze during the last few minutes of cooking. Serve with the remaining sauce on a platter garnished with watercress.

Garlic and Ginger Chicken

PREPARATION TIME:
15 MINUTES + 30 MINUTES MARINATING
COOKING TIME:
50 MINUTES
SERVES 6–8

3 lb chicken

MARINADE
1/4 cup lemon juice
1/4 cup olive oil
1 tablespoon grated fresh ginger
2 cloves garlic, crushed
2 teaspoons mild curry powder
salt and pepper, to taste

GARLIC SAUCE
2 cloves garlic, crushed
3/4 cup mayonnaise
1 teaspoon mild curry powder
1/2 teaspoon white pepper

1 Rinse the chicken, pat dry with paper towels. Place on a shallow dish.
2 To make marinade: Combine all the ingredients in a bowl and pour over the chicken. Allow to marinate for 30 minutes or overnight in the refrigerator, turning occasionally.
3 To make Garlic Sauce: Combine all the ingredients and store covered in the refrigerator until required.
4 Preheat the barbecue. Remove the chicken from the marinade and skewer onto rotisserie. Cook the chicken for approximately 50 minutes on the rotisserie. The chicken should be tender inside and crisp golden brown on the outside. Serve immediately with Garlic Sauce.

Mango Chicken (above). Garlic and Ginger Chicken

Saffron Chicken

Saffron is the world's most expensive spice and has a wonderful flavor. Buy it from a reputable dealer (such as a chef's supplier) or look for a well-known brand name.

PREPARATION TIME:
15 MINUTES + 30 MINUTES MARINATING
COOKING TIME:
25 MINUTES
SERVES 8

8 boneless chicken breast halves

MARINADE
1/4 teaspoon saffron powder (see note)
2 tablespoons hot water
1 tablespoon lime juice
1 teaspoon ground sweet paprika
1/2 teaspoon ground pepper
1 clove garlic, crushed
2 tablespoons olive oil
1 teaspoon onion powder
1 tablespoon chicken bouillon granules
1/4 cup sour cream
1 teaspoon cornstarch
1/2 cup milk

1 Lightly score the breast halves, and pat dry with paper towels. Place in a shallow dish. Dissolve the saffron in the hot water and combine with lime juice, paprika, pepper, garlic, olive oil and onion powder.
2 Pour over the chicken and turn to coat in the marinade. Allow the chicken to stand for 30 minutes.
3 Remove the chicken from marinade and cook on a preheated barbecue grill over low heat for 8–10 minutes each side, or until the chicken is tender and golden, turning once during the cooking.
4 Place the remaining marinade in a small pan with the chicken bouillon and sour cream. Combine the cornstarch and milk, stir into the sauce and heat until thickened. Season to taste with pepper. Serve this sauce with the chicken.

Note: If purchasing saffron strands (most brands are sold in strand form), lightly toast half a teaspoon of the strands in a dry pan, shaking the pan to prevent burning. Empty onto a small saucer and when cool and crisp, crush with the back of a spoon.

Marinated Chicken Satay

Chicken Satay can also be served as a first course.

PREPARATION TIME:
15 MINUTES + 1 HOUR MARINATING
COOKING TIME:
6 MINUTES
SERVES 6

1 lb boned, skinless chicken breasts or thighs

MARINADE AND SAUCE
1 large onion, grated
2 tablespoons lemon or lime juice
2 cloves garlic, crushed
2 teaspoons grated fresh ginger
2 teaspoons sambal oelek or crushed chiles
1/3 cup soy sauce
2 tablespoons brown sugar
1 tablespoon sesame oil
3/4 cup coconut milk
1/2 cup chunky peanut butter
2 tablespoons toasted sesame seeds

1 Cut the chicken into bite-size squares. Combine the onion, lemon juice, garlic, ginger, sambal oelek, soy sauce, brown sugar and sesame oil. Pour over the prepared chicken and stir to coat all the pieces thoroughly. Allow to marinate for 1 hour in the refrigerator. Meanwhile, soak the bamboo skewers in cold water.
2 Remove the chicken pieces from the marinade and thread onto twelve soaked bamboo skewers, leaving a portion of the skewer free for handling. Barbecue the satays on a preheated grill for about 6 minutes, turning until they are browned. Brush with a little extra oil if necessary.
3 Pour the remaining marinade into a pan and place on the edge of the barbecue. Add the coconut milk and peanut butter, stir until the mixture boils and thickens. Serve satays, sprinkled with sesame seeds, on a platter. Accompany with steamed rice and serve with satay sauce.

Saffron Chicken (above). Marinated Chicken Satay. Spicy Chicken Wings (right)

Spicy Chicken Wings

PREPARATION TIME:
10 MINUTES +
1 HOUR
MARINATING
COOKING TIME:
20–25 MINUTES
SERVES 6

12 chicken wings
2 tablespoons mild curry powder
2 cloves garlic, crushed
1 tablespoon oil
2 tablespoons lemon juice
1/2 teaspoon white pepper
1/4 cup water
1 tablespoon chicken bouillon granules

1 Remove the tips from the chicken wings, rinse and pat dry with paper towels. Score through the skin and flesh with a sharp knife.
2 Combine the remaining ingredients, mixing well.
3 Pour the marinade over the prepared wings. Mix to coat well.
4 Grill on a lightly oiled preheated barbecue over medium heat for 12 minutes, turn and continue cooking until tender and golden brown.

Barbecued Quail with Garlic and Sour Cream

These small birds make good eating, especially when well cooked over a barbecue.

PREPARATION TIME:
15 MINUTES +
30 MINUTES
MARINATING
COOKING TIME:
40 MINUTES
SERVES 6

12 quail

MARINADE
1/2 cup olive oil
1/3 cup dry white wine
1/3 cup chopped green onions
1/2 cup chopped fresh herbs
2 cloves garlic, crushed

6 whole heads of garlic

SOUR CREAM SAUCE
1 cup sour cream
2 tablespoons finely chopped green onions
salt and white pepper, to taste
lime or lemon juice, to taste

1 Place the quail on a board, breast-side down. Cut through the back with poultry shears to butterfly and discard backbone.
2 To make the marinade: Combine the olive oil, white wine, green onions, fresh herbs and garlic. Pour over the quail and allow to marinate for 30 minutes.
3 Wrap the garlic heads in a double layer of heavy-duty or quilted foil.
4 Place the wrapped garlic directly onto the coals — not flames — of the fire, or place on top of the grill. Cook for 30–40 minutes. This long, slow cooking mellows the flavor of the garlic.
5 Remove the quail from the marinade and barbecue on a lightly oiled grill for 12–15 minutes. Turn occasionally and brush with the marinade during cooking.
6 To make Sour Cream Sauce: Combine the sour cream and green onions and season with salt, pepper, and juice to taste. Serve the barbecued quail with the knobs of garlic and Sour Cream Sauce.

Chicken and Shrimp Kebabs

This recipe is a less expensive version of lobster and steak — 'Surf 'n'Turf', as it is known.

PREPARATION TIME:
25 MINUTES +
30 MINUTES
MARINATING
COOKING TIME:
20 MINUTES
SERVES 6

12 oz boned, skinless chicken breast halves
1 lb large uncooked shrimp
16 oz can apricot halves, in natural juice
16 oz can pineapple rings
2 teaspoons grated fresh ginger
2 tablespoons olive oil
salt and white pepper, to taste
2 teaspoons cornstarch
1 tablespoon water
1 teaspoon grated fresh ginger, extra
2 green onions, finely sliced

1 Cut the chicken into large pieces. Shell and devein the shrimp. Drain the apricot halves and pineapple slices, reserving the juice. Cut the pineapple slices into quarters. Thread the prepared chicken, shrimp and fruit alternately onto soaked bamboo or metal skewers.
2 Combine 1 cup reserved pineapple juice with grated ginger, olive oil, salt and pepper. Pour the mixture over the kebabs and allow to marinate for 30 minutes.
3 Remove from the marinade and barbecue on a hot grill for 5 minutes each side or until the chicken is tender and shrimp have turned pink. Meanwhile, heat the remaining marinade in a pan on the edge of the grill, thicken with combined cornstarch and water, add the extra grated ginger and green onions and allow to boil until the sauce thickens. Serve Chicken and Shrimp Kebabs immediately.

Barbecued Quail with Garlic and Sour Cream (above). Chicken and Shrimp Kebabs (right). Glazed Chicken Quarters

Glazed Chicken Quarters

PREPARATION TIME: 20 MINUTES + 30 MINUTES MARINATING
COOKING TIME: 30 MINUTES
SERVES 6

16 oz can pineapple slices
6 chicken leg and thigh quarters

MARINADE
2 tablespoons oil
1/2 cup ketchup
1 tablespoon cider vinegar
1 tablespoon barbecue sauce
1 tablespoon brown sugar
1/4 cup reserved pineapple juice
1 clove garlic, crushed
salt and pepper, to taste

1 Drain the pineapple slices and reserve the juice.

2 To make the marinade: Combine the oil, ketchup, vinegar, barbecue sauce, sugar, pineapple juice, garlic, salt and pepper in a small pan over a low heat. Brush the marinade over the surface of the chicken and allow to marinate for 30 minutes, or longer in the refrigerator if a strong flavor is required.

3 Remove the chicken and cook on a preheated lightly oiled barbecue grill for 30–35 minutes or until tender and the juices run clear. Turn often and brush with remaining marinade towards the end of cooking. Cook the pineapple rings along with the chicken during the last 5 minutes, brushing with the marinade.

Oriental Chicken Kebabs

A delicious meal served with a salad and crisp French bread.

PREPARATION TIME: 30 MINUTES + 30 MINUTES MARINATING
COOKING TIME: 10 MINUTES
SERVES 4

1 tablespoon light soy sauce
1 tablespoon white wine
2 teaspoons coarse grain mustard
2 teaspoons snipped chives
1 teaspoon oil
1 clove garlic, crushed
1 teaspoon grated fresh ginger
4 boned, skinless chicken breast halves, cut into chunks
bamboo skewers, soaked in water
12 button mushrooms
12 cherry tomatoes
1 onion, cut into eighths
1 green sweet bell pepper, seeded and cubed
3 canned, unsweetened pineapple rings, quartered

1 Combine the soy sauce, wine, mustard, chives, oil, garlic and ginger in a glass or ceramic bowl. Add the chicken. Marinate for 30 minutes, turning the chicken frequently.

2 Thread the chicken onto skewers, alternating the meat with the mushrooms, tomatoes, onion, green pepper and pineapple.

3 Cook skewers on a preheated lightly greased barbecue grill for 5–10 minutes, turning frequently and basting occasionally.

Kashmiri Chicken Roast

This chicken is flavorsome cooked on a kettle rotisserie barbecue.

PREPARATION TIME: 20 MINUTES + 30 MINUTES MARINATING
COOKING TIME: 1 HOUR 10 MINUTES
SERVES 4–6

3½ lb chicken

MARINADE
¼ teaspoon ground saffron
2 tablespoons hot water
2 teaspoons ground fenugreek leaves
2 cloves garlic, crushed
1 teaspoon grated fresh ginger
½ teaspoon chili powder
2 teaspoons garam masala
½ teaspoon turmeric
½ teaspoon ground pepper
4 tablespoons blanched almonds or ¼ cup ground almonds
½ cup chopped cilantro
1 tablespoon ghee or unsalted butter
½ cup warm water

1 Remove the skin from the chicken and lightly score the flesh criss-cross fashion.
2 To make the marinade: Dissolve the saffron in hot water and combine with the remaining ingredients. Use the marinade to coat the entire chicken, both inside and out. Place onto a rotisserie bar.
3 Heat the kettle barbecue to high, arrange the skewered chicken in place and roast for 20 minutes.
4 Lower the heat to medium and cook another 30 minutes. Baste the chicken with the remaining marinade. Raise the heat and cook a final 10 minutes. Let rest, covered, for 10 minutes before carving. Serve with salad and flat bread, chapatis or naan.

Chicken with Orange and Mustard Glaze

PREPARATION TIME:
15 MINUTES
COOKING TIME:
15 MINUTES
SERVES 8

8 chicken breast halves on the bone
salt and pepper, to taste

SAUCE
1/2 cup chicken broth
3/4 cup marmalade
1 tablespoon coarse grain mustard
1 tablespoon French mustard

1 Trim the chicken and pat dry with paper towels. Season lightly with salt and pepper on both sides.
2 To make the sauce: Place all ingredients in a small heavy-gauge pan and place on the barbecue grill to heat through.
3 Cook the chicken breasts on a hot, oiled grill for 10–15 minutes, brushing with a little sauce from time to time during the last 5 minutes of cooking.
4 Serve the remaining sauce with the cooked chicken.

Indonesian Chicken

PREPARATION TIME:
20 MINUTES +
1 HOUR
MARINATING
COOKING TIME:
45 MINUTES
SERVES 6–8

3 lb chicken

MARINADE
2 cloves garlic, crushed
1 medium onion, chopped
1 teaspoon chopped fresh ginger
3 fresh red chiles, chopped
1 teaspoon turmeric
salt and pepper, to taste
1 teaspoon grated lemon rind
1 teaspoon ground coriander
1/2 cup coconut milk
4 kaffir lime leaves
1 tablespoon brown sugar
2 tablespoons white vinegar
1 1/2 cups coconut milk, extra
1 cup water

1 Split the chicken in half, through the breastbone and down the back and remove the backbone.
2 To make the marinade: Blend the garlic, onion, ginger, chiles, turmeric, salt, pepper, lemon rind, coriander and coconut milk. Marinate the chicken in half the mixture for 1 hour and remove.
3 In a wok, heat the remaining marinade, lime leaves, brown sugar, vinegar, extra coconut milk and water. Cook for 2–3 minutes. Add the marinated chicken

and simmer for 15 minutes, basting while cooking. Turn over and cook another 15 minutes.

4 Remove the chicken from the wok. Place on a barbecue and cook until browned and firm to the touch.

5 Serve the remaining marinade as a sauce. Sprinkle with chopped cilantro.

Chicken with Orange and Mustard Glaze (above). Indonesian Chicken

Southern-style Drumsticks

PREPARATION TIME:
15 MINUTES +
4 HOURS
MARINATING
COOKING TIME:
25 MINUTES
SERVES 4

8 drumsticks
1/2 cup buttermilk
2 cloves garlic, crushed
1 teaspoon ground cumin
1/4 teaspoon cayenne pepper
1/4 teaspoon salt
1/4 teaspoon black pepper
2 cobs of corn, halved
4 teaspoons butter
4 drops Tabasco sauce

1 Trim the chicken of excess fat and sinew.

2 Place the drumsticks in a shallow glass or ceramic dish. Combine the buttermilk, garlic, cumin, cayenne pepper, salt and black pepper and pour over the chicken. Cover with plastic wrap and refrigerate for 4 hours, turning occasionally. Drain the chicken.

3 Place the drumsticks on a lightly oiled barbecue grill. Grill over a medium heat for 25 minutes, turning occasionally, until the chicken is tender and cooked through. Serve immediately, with cooked corn cobs.

4 Cook the corn in a large pan of boiling water for 10 minutes. Drain and place on individual pieces of aluminum foil. Melt the butter; add Tabasco and brush liberally onto the corn. Wrap in foil and place on the grill for 10 minutes, turning occasionally.

Thai-Style Thighs

PREPARATION TIME:
15 MINUTES +
1 HOUR
MARINATING
COOKING TIME:
12 MINUTES
SERVES 6

1 lb skinless chicken thighs

MARINADE:

1/4 cup pepper cilantro paste (see note)
1 clove garlic, crushed
1/2 teaspoon turmeric
1/2 teaspoon chili powder or to taste
1 tablespoon water
2 teaspoons chicken bouillon granules
1 tablespoon peanut oil

1 Cut each thigh in half, lightly score criss-cross and set aside.

2 To make the marinade: Combine all the ingredients, mix well and marinate chicken for 1 hour or longer in the refrigerator.

3 Heat the barbecue grill and barbecue the chicken pieces for 6 minutes each side, or until done to your liking. Serve with salad.

Note: Pepper Cilantro Paste: Pound, in a mortar and pestle, 1/4 cup chopped cilantro, 2 cloves garlic and 1 teaspoon whole black peppercorns.

Opposite: Garlic Chicken (left), Chicken Koftas

Garlic Chicken

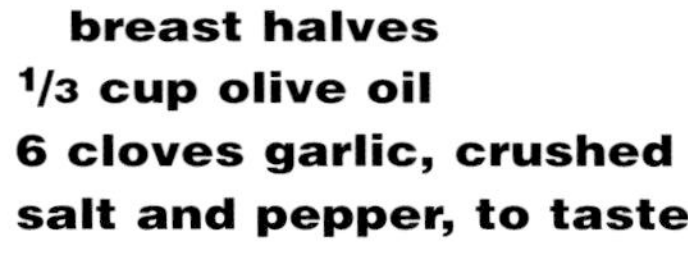

PREPARATION TIME:
10 MINUTES +
1 HOUR
MARINATING
COOKING TIME:
5–10 MINUTES
SERVES 8

8 boned, skinless chicken breast halves
1/3 cup olive oil
6 cloves garlic, crushed
salt and pepper, to taste

1 Trim all visible fat from chicken; dry and score the smooth surface. In a baking dish, combine the oil, garlic and seasonings. Add chicken and spoon the garlic oil over. Cover and refrigerate overnight, or marinate at room temperature for 1 hour.
2 Heat the barbecue grill rack and cook chicken over a medium heat until firm to the touch.

Chicken Koftas

PREPARATION TIME:
20 MINUTES
COOKING TIME:
8 MINUTES
SERVES 8

1 lb ground minced chicken
1/4 teaspoon black pepper
1 tablespoon chopped cilantro
1 egg, lightly beaten
1 clove garlic, crushed
1 teaspoon salt
1 cup cornflake crumbs
2 teaspoons chili sauce

1 Mix all ingredients together and form into eight long koftas on flat metal or soaked bamboo sticks.
2 Place on a grill over a heated barbecue. Cover and cook 8 minutes, turning frequently to avoid charring. Cook to golden brown and serve between hot split hero rolls or baguettes with salad and a rich tomato sauce (see page 237).

Chicken in a Thyme Cream Sauce

PREPARATION TIME:
15 MINUTES
COOKING TIME:
10 MINUTES
SERVES 4

4 boned, skinless chicken breast halves, about 6 oz each
1/4 cup all-purpose flour
2 tablespoons olive oil
1 tablespoon chopped fresh lemon thyme
2 teaspoons dry sherry
1/3 cup whipping cream

1 Trim the chicken of any excess fat and sinew and toss in the flour.

2 Place a deep-sided cast iron skillet on the preheated barbecue grill, heat through and brush with the olive oil. Cook the chicken for about 5 minutes on each side, or until golden brown, then sprinkle with the lemon thyme. Turn the chicken over, brush with the sherry and pour in about half the cream. Cook for another 2–3 minutes before turning the chicken over again and drizzling with the remaining cream. Season to taste with salt and pepper and serve.

Chicken and Kidney Kebabs

PREPARATION TIME:
15 MINUTES + 20 MINUTES MARINATING
COOKING TIME:
5–10 MINUTES
SERVES 4

8 oz lamb kidneys
3 cloves garlic, finely chopped
2 bay leaves, torn into small pieces
1/4 cup olive oil
8 oz boned, skinless chicken breast halves
5 oz double smoked, cooked ham
2 small onions
2 tablespoons dry sherry

1 Place eight bamboo skewers in water to soak. Trim the kidneys of any sinew or fat and cut into bite-size pieces. Combine the garlic, bay leaves and olive oil. Add the kidneys, cover and marinate in the refrigerator for about 20 minutes.
2 Cut the chicken and ham into bite-size pieces and the onions into small wedges.
3 Drain the kidneys and reserve the marinade. Thread the pieces of onion, kidney, chicken and ham alternately onto the bamboo skewers.
4 Lightly oil a preheated barbecue grill and cook the kebabs for about 5–10 minutes, brushing lightly with the reserved marinade and sherry as they cook and turning them regularly. When golden brown, remove from the grill and serve with rice or mashed potatoes.

Note: If you prefer, chicken livers may be used in place of lamb kidneys.

Chicken with Couscous and Sweet Potato

PREPARATION TIME: 45 MINUTES
COOKING TIME: 55 MINUTES
SERVES 4

- **4 boned, skinless chicken breast halves**
- **2 cloves garlic, crushed**
- **2 teaspoons olive oil**
- **12 oz sweet potatoes, peeled and cut into cubes**
- **1 red onion, cut into wedges**
- **1 small red sweet bell pepper, seeded and sliced**
- **1 1/4 cups couscous**
- **1 1/2 cups chicken broth or water**
- **10 oz can (about 1 1/4 cups) chickpeas, drained and rinsed**
- **3 green onions, finely chopped**
- **2 tablespoons chopped fresh mint**

HARISSA DRESSING

- **1/3 cup olive oil**
- **2 tablespoons lime juice**
- **2 teaspoons harissa sauce**
- **1 clove garlic, crushed**

1 Trim the chicken of any excess fat and sinew and brush with the combined garlic and oil. Cover and refrigerate. Preheat the oven to 375°F. Spread the sweet potatoes, onion and red pepper in a single layer in a baking dish and brush with a little olive oil. Bake for 45 minutes, stirring occasionally. Remove from the oven and keep warm.

2 To make the Harissa Dressing: Combine the dressing ingredients in a jar and shake well.

3 Place the couscous in a large bowl, boil the broth or water and then pour over. Allow to stand for 5 minutes, then stir in the chickpeas, green onion and mint. Pour half the dressing over and stir until the couscous is an even color.

4 Preheat a lightly oiled barbecue grill. Add the chicken and cook for 4–5 minutes each side, or until tender.

5 Cut each breast half into slices. Pile the couscous onto plates, top with the sweet potato mixture and drizzle with the remaining dressing. Arrange the chicken slices on top. Season to taste with salt and cracked pepper.

Mirin and Sake Chicken

PREPARATION TIME:
10 MINUTES + 15 MINUTES MARINATING
COOKING TIME:
20 MINUTES
SERVES 4

4 large boned, skinless chicken breast halves
2 tablespoons mirin
2 tablespoons sake
1 tablespoon oil
2 in piece fresh ginger, very finely sliced
1 tablespoon soy sauce

1 Trim the chicken of excess fat and sinew and place in a non-metallic dish. Combine the mirin, sake and oil and pour over the chicken. Refrigerate for 15 minutes, then drain, reserving the marinade.
2 Preheat a lightly oiled barbecue grill. Add the chicken and cook for about 5 minutes each side, or until golden brown and tender. Remove and keep warm. Cook the ginger in a little extra oil in a pan on the grill or stove top until soft. Add remaining marinade and boil for about 7 minutes.
3 Drizzle the soy sauce over the chicken and top with the ginger. Serve immediately.

Chicken Burger with Tarragon Mayonnaise

PREPARATION TIME:
25 MINUTES
COOKING TIME:
20 MINUTES
SERVES 6

2¼ lb ground chicken
1 small onion, finely chopped
2 teaspoons lemon rind
2 tablespoons sour cream
1 cup fresh bread crumbs
6 onion bread rolls

TARRAGON MAYONNAISE
1 egg yolk
1 tablespoon tarragon vinegar
½ teaspoon French mustard
1 cup olive oil
salt and white pepper, to taste

1 Prepare and heat the barbecue.

2 Place the chicken in a mixing bowl. Add the onion, rind, sour cream and bread crumbs. Using your hands, mix until thoroughly combined. Divide the mixture into six equal portions and shape into ¾ in thick patties.

3 Place the patties on a hot lightly oiled barbecue grill. Cook for 7 minutes each side, turning once. Serve on an onion roll with salad fillings and Tarragon Mayonnaise.

4 To make Tarragon Mayonnaise: Place egg yolk, half the vinegar and the mustard in a small mixing bowl. Whisk together for 1 minute until light and creamy. Add the oil about 1 teaspoon at a time, whisking constantly until the mixture thickens. Increase the flow of oil to a thin stream and continue whisking until all the oil has been incorporated. Stir in the remaining vinegar and salt and white pepper.

Chicken Breast with Flaming Sauce

PREPARATION TIME:
15 MINUTES
COOKING TIME:
12 MINUTES
SERVES 4

4 boned, skinless chicken breast halves
chives, for garnish

SAUCE
3 medium-sized ripe tomatoes
2 teaspoons olive oil
1 small onion, coarsely chopped
1 clove garlic, crushed
1 tablespoon paprika
$^1/_2$ teaspoon dried thyme
1 large red sweet bell pepper, sliced

1 Pour boiling water over the tomatoes, stand for 1 minute then plunge them into cold water. Remove skins and dice tomatoes coarsely.

2 Heat oil and cook the onion, covered, for 2–3 minutes. Add the garlic, paprika and thyme and cook another 1 minute. Add the red pepper and tomatoes and cook for 10 minutes or until soft. Purée the mixture until smooth.

3 While the sauce is cooking, place the chicken on a preheated lightly greased barbecue grill. Cook over a medium heat for 6–8 minutes or until the chicken is just cooked, turning once. Serve the chicken breasts on top of the sauce and garnish each serve with a few whole chives.

Chicken Teriyaki

Serve these kebabs with steamed rice or Japanese-style egg noodles and stir-fried vegetables.

PREPARATION TIME:
20 MINUTES + 2 HOURS MARINATING
COOKING TIME:
6 MINUTES
MAKES 12

- **1 1/2 lb boned, skinless chicken breast halves**
- **1/4 cup soy sauce**
- **2 tablespoons mirin (optional)**
- **2 tablespoons sherry**
- **2 tablespoons soft brown sugar**
- **2 teaspoons grated fresh ginger**
- **2 tablespoons oil**

1 Trim the chicken of excess fat and sinew and cut into long, thin strips. Soak twelve bamboo skewers in water to prevent burning.
2 Place the chicken in a shallow glass or ceramic dish. Combine the soy sauce, mirin, sherry, brown sugar and ginger. Stir to dissolve the sugar, then pour over the chicken. Cover and refrigerate for up to 2 hours, turning occasionally. Drain.
3 Thread the chicken onto skewers ribbon fashion.
4 Brush the kebabs with oil and place on a lightly oiled grill. Cook over medium high heat for 6 minutes or until tender, turning and brushing with oil occasionally.

Cranberry Wings

These make a great appetizer or snack to nibble on.

PREPARATION TIME:
20 MINUTES + 2 HOURS MARINATING
COOKING TIME:
30 MINUTES
SERVES 6

- **3 lb chicken wings**
- **freshly ground black pepper**
- **3/4 cup orange marmalade**
- **1/2 cup bottled cranberry sauce**
- **1/2 cup spicy red barbecue sauce**
- **1/3 cup white vinegar**

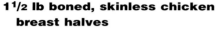

1 In a glass or ceramic container, combine the chicken wings, pepper, marmalade, cranberry sauce, barbecue sauce and vinegar. Stir to coat the wings in the sauce mixture. Refrigerate, covered, for about 2 hours or overnight. Drain, reserving the marinade.
2 Barbecue the wings on a preheated lightly greased grill, turning them occasionally, for 15–20 minutes. Continue cooking, basting wings with the sauce mixture until cooked through and well glazed, about 10 minutes more.

Tarragon Lemon Chicken

Mix any selection of your favorite herbs and spices with the butter and use for basting. This chicken dish is delicious served hot or cold.

PREPARATION TIME:
20 MINUTES
COOKING TIME:
20 MINUTES
SERVES 4

- **1/3 cup unsalted butter**
- **2 tablespoons finely chopped chives**
- **1 tablespoon finely chopped cilantro**
- **1 tablespoon lemon juice**
- **1/2 teaspoon dried tarragon leaves**
- **1/4 teaspoon paprika**
- **8 boned chicken thighs**
- **freshly ground pepper**

1 Place the butter in a small pan over a low heat, stirring until melted, and add the chives, cilantro, lemon juice, tarragon and paprika.
2 Sprinkle the chicken with pepper. Barbecue over medium low coals on a preheated lightly greased grill until tender and golden, turning and basting frequently with the butter mixture, for about 15–20 minutes. Serve chicken with a seasonal salad and potatoes.

Chicken Teriyaki (above). Tarragon Lemon Chicken. Cranberry Wings

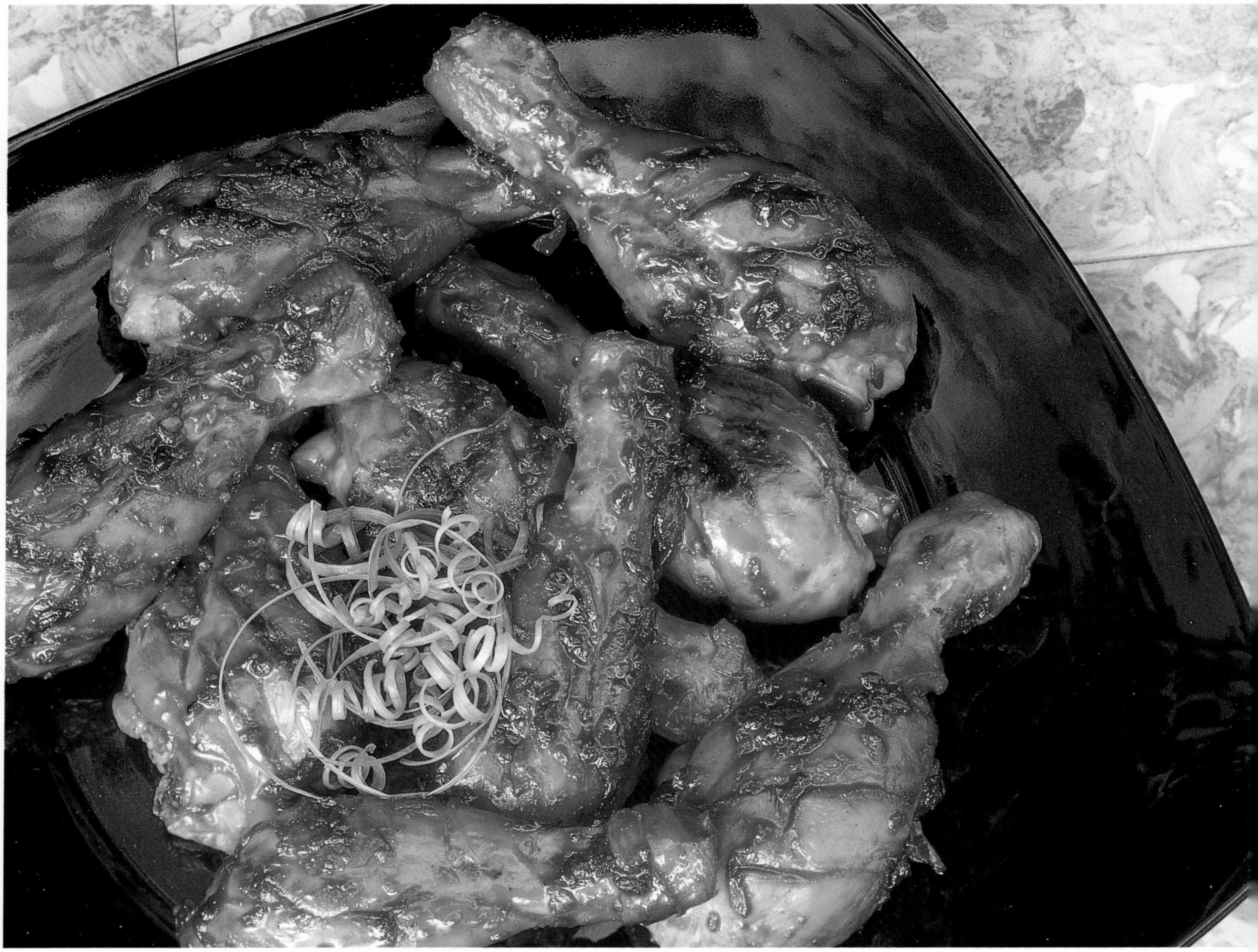

Honey Soy Chicken Drumsticks

Add a little chili sauce for those who prefer it hotter. This is best cooked on a kettle barbecue.

PREPARATION TIME:
15 MINUTES +
1 HOUR
MARINATING
COOKING TIME:
25–30 MINUTES
SERVES 6

1/3 cup soy sauce
2 cloves garlic, crushed
1 small onion, grated
1/2 teaspoon white pepper
1 tablespoon honey
1/4 cup green ginger wine or sherry
12 chicken drumsticks

1 Combine the soy sauce, garlic, onion, pepper, honey and ginger wine or sherry in a small pan, stir over a low heat until the honey softens and the ingredients are thoroughly mixed.

2 Remove the skin from the drumsticks and score through the flesh at 3/4 in intervals. Pour the marinade over the prepared chicken and allow to marinate for 1 hour.

3 Remove the drumsticks from the marinade and barbecue over a preheated, oiled grill with the hood down for 20–25 minutes, turning occasionally until the chicken is tender and the juices are clear. Brush two or three times with the remaining marinade towards the end of cooking. Serve the drumsticks with salad.

Note: If using an open barbecue, allow extra time for cooking.

Lemon Honey Chicken

This recipe is best suited to a kettle barbecue. Try the cooked garlic cloves spread on crusty toast with a little olive oil, salt and pepper.

PREPARATION TIME:
10 MINUTES
COOKING TIME:
1 HOUR 30 MINUTES
SERVES 4–6

3 1/2–4 lb chicken
salt
1/2 teaspoon cracked pepper
1 whole bulb garlic
small bunch fresh lemon thyme
1 teaspoon salt, extra
1 1/2 teaspoons grated lemon rind
1 teaspoon honey
2 tablespoons olive oil
4 teaspoons butter, melted

1 Light barbecue using 4 lb of charcoal briquettes and about eight firestarters. Allow 40 minutes for coals to be fully alight. Coals should be arranged under either side of the grill, not directly beneath.

2 Remove giblets and any large fat deposits from chicken. Wipe chicken and pat dry with paper towels. Season cavity with salt and pepper, to taste.

3 Using a sharp knife, cut off the top of the garlic bulb. Push the whole bulb of garlic, unpeeled, and the bunch of lemon thyme into the cavity. Close the cavity with several cocktail picks or a skewer.

4 Rub the skin with combined salt, rind, honey, oil and butter. Place on the barbecue over a drip tray. Cook for 1 hour, brushing occasionally with oil mixture to keep the skin moist. Test if chicken is done by inserting a skewer into the thigh. If the juice runs clear, the chicken is cooked.

5 Stand the chicken away from the heat for about 5–6 minutes before carving. Carefully separate garlic cloves and serve with the chicken.

Bacon-wrapped Chicken Parcels

PREPARATION TIME: 10 MINUTES
COOKING TIME: 10 MINUTES
SERVES 3

6 boned, skinless chicken breast halves
2 tablespoons olive oil
2 tablespoons lime juice
1/4 teaspoon ground coriander
salt and freshly ground black pepper, to taste
1/3 cup fruit chutney
1/4 cup chopped pecan nuts
6 slices bacon

1 Trim the chicken of excess fat and sinew. Place the oil, juice, coriander, salt and pepper in a small bowl and mix well.
2 Using a sharp knife, cut a pocket in the thickest section of each breast half.
3 Combine the chutney and nuts in a small bowl. Spoon 1 tablespoon of chutney mixture into each chicken breast pocket.
4 Turn the tapered end of the breast to the underside. Wrap a bacon slice firmly around each breast to enclose the filling. Secure bacon with a cocktail pick.
5 Place chicken parcels onto a lightly oiled grill. Cook over a medium heat for 5 minutes each side or until well browned and cooked through, turning once.
6 Brush parcels with the lime juice mixture several times during cooking. Pour any leftover mixture over the cooked chicken just before serving.

Chicken Parcels with Honey Mustard Glaze

'REPARATION
IME:
5 MINUTES
:OOKING TIME:
0–25 MINUTES
;ERVES 6–8

8 boned chicken thighs
16 pitted prunes
8 green onions, halved
2 tablespoons flaked almonds
4 slices bacon, halved lengthwise

HONEY MUSTARD GLAZE
1 tablespoon brown sugar
1 tablespoon Dijon mustard
1 tablespoon honey
1 tablespoon butter, melted
freshly ground black pepper

1 Open out each chicken thigh and place 2 prunes, ? pieces of green onion and a few flaked almonds on :ach one.
2 Roll up the thighs, wrap a piece of bacon around :ach one and secure with cocktail picks.
3 Barbecue parcels on a preheated lightly greased ›arbecue grill until cooked, about 20 minutes. Baste 'requently with glaze.
4 To prepare Honey Mustard Glaze: Blend all ngredients together in a small bowl.

Smoked Chicken Breasts

This is a dish just made for a Weber (or kettle) barbecue. Serve it with chili noodles.

PREPARATION TIME:
5 MINUTES
COOKING TIME:
25 MINUTES
SERVES 4

4 boned, skinless chicken breast halves
1 tablespoon olive oil
seasoned pepper, to taste
hickory or mesquite chips, for smoking

1 Prepare the Weber (kettle) barbecue for indirect cooking at moderate heat (normal fire). Trim the chicken of excess fat and sinew.
2 Brush the chicken with oil and sprinkle with the seasoned pepper.
3 Spoon a pile of smoking chips (about 25) over the coals in each charcoal rail.
4 Cover the barbecue and cook the chicken for 15 minutes. Test with a sharp knife. If the juices do not run clear, cook another 5–10 minutes until cooked.

Note: Chicken is best smoked just before serving.

Chicken Burger with Tangy Garlic Mayonnaise

PREPARATION TIME:
20 MINUTES +
3 HOURS MARINATING
COOKING TIME: 15 MINUTES
SERVES 4

4 boned, skinless chicken breast halves
1/2 cup lime juice
1 tablespoon sweet chili sauce
4 slices bacon
4 hamburger buns
4 lettuce leaves
1 large tomato, sliced

GARLIC MAYONNAISE
2 egg yolks
2 cloves garlic, crushed
1 tablespoon Dijon mustard
1 tablespoon lemon juice
1/2 cup olive oil

1 Place the chicken breast halves in a shallow, non-metal dish and pierce with a skewer several times.
2 Combine the lime juice and the chili sauce, and then pour over the chicken. Cover and marinate the chicken for 3 hours or overnight.
3 Prepare and light the barbecue 1 hour before cooking. Cut the bacon in half crosswise.
4 Place the chicken and the bacon on a hot lightly greased barbecue grill. Cook the bacon for about 5 minutes or until crisp. Cook the chicken for another 5–10 minutes or until well browned and cooked through, turning once.
5 Cut the hamburger buns in half and toast each side until lightly browned. Top the bases of the buns with lettuce, tomato, chicken and bacon. Top with Garlic Mayonnaise and finish with the remaining bun top.
6 To make Garlic Mayonnaise: Place the egg yolks, crushed garlic, mustard and lemon juice in a food processor or blender. Process until smooth. With the motor constantly running, add the oil in a thin, steady stream. Process until the mayonnaise reaches a thick consistency. Refrigerate, covered, until required.

Chicken with Orange-Chive Butter

PREPARATION TIME:
20 MINUTES +
2 HOURS
MARINATING
COOKING TIME:
20 MINUTES
SERVES 4

8 chicken thighs
1/2 cup orange juice
1 teaspoon ground black pepper
2 teaspoons sesame oil

ORANGE-CHIVE BUTTER
1/3 cup butter
1 teaspoon finely grated orange rind
1 teaspoon finely chopped chives
1 tablespoon orange marmalade
salt, to taste

1 Trim the chicken of excess fat and sinew.
2 Place the chicken in a shallow glass or ceramic dish.
3 Combine juice, pepper and oil in a small bowl and pour over chicken. Cover with plastic wrap and refrigerate for 2 hours, turning occasionally. Drain chicken and reserve marinade. Place chicken on a preheated lightly greased barbecue grill and cook for 10 minutes each side, brushing occasionally with reserved marinade. Serve immediately with slices of Orange-Chive Butter.
4 To make Orange-Chive Butter: Allow the butter to soften slightly at room temperature. Place in a small mixing bowl and beat with a wooden spoon for 1 minute until creamy. Add the remaining ingredients and mix until well combined.
5 Place the butter on a sheet of plastic wrap and form into a log shape. Roll up tightly and refrigerate until required. Serve sliced.

Chicken Kebabs with Curry Mayonnaise

Serve these kebabs with rice and fried pappadams, or wrapped in lavosh or pita bread.

PREPARATION TIME: 25 MINUTES + 30 MINUTES MARINATING
COOKING TIME: 10 MINUTES
SERVES 4

- **1 1/4 lb boned, skinless chicken breast halves**
- **4 large green onions**
- **1 small red sweet bell pepper**
- **1 small green sweet bell pepper**
- **1/4 cup olive oil**
- **1 teaspoon freshly ground black pepper**
- **1/2 teaspoon ground turmeric**
- **1 1/2 teaspoons ground coriander**

CURRY MAYONNAISE

- **3/4 cup whole egg mayonnaise**
- **1 tablespoon hot curry powder**
- **1/4 cup sour cream**
- **1 tablespoon sweet fruit or mango chutney, mashed**
- **1/4 cup finely chopped, peeled cucumber**
- **1/2 teaspoon toasted cumin seeds**
- **1 tablespoon finely chopped fresh mint**
- **1 teaspoon finely chopped mint, extra**

1 Prepare and heat the barbecue. Trim chicken of excess fat and sinew. Cut chicken into 1 1/4 in cubes.
2 Trim the green onions, cut white stems and the thicker parts of green stems into 1 1/4 in lengths; discard tops. Cut the red and green peppers into 1 1/4 in squares.
3 Thread the chicken, green onions and red and green peppers onto skewers, using at least two pieces of each. Arrange the kebabs, side by side, in a shallow, non-metal dish. Combine the oil, pepper, turmeric and coriander in a bowl. Pour over the kebabs and set aside for 30 minutes at room temperature.
4 To make Curry Mayonnaise: Combine the mayonnaise, curry powder, sour cream, chutney, cucumber, cumin seeds and mint in a bowl and mix well. Spoon into a dish or sauceboat for serving. Sprinkle mayonnaise with extra chopped mint.
5 Place kebabs on a hot, lightly oiled barbecue grill. Cook for 2–3 minutes each side or until cooked through and tender. Serve Curry Mayonnaise separately.

Curry, Coconut and Lime Drumsticks

A deliciously different way to serve a barbecue favorite — as an appetizer, first course, or with jasmine rice.

PREPARATION TIME:
10 MINUTES + 3 HOURS MARINATING
COOKING TIME:
16 MINUTES
SERVES 4

8 chicken drumsticks
2 tablespoons curry paste
1 teaspoon grated lime rind
2 tablespoons lime juice
2/3 cup coconut cream
1 tablespoon honey
salt, to taste
2 tablespoons unsweetened, grated dry coconut
1 tablespoon grated lime rind, extra

1 Secure the skin of drumsticks to joint with cocktail picks.
2 Make three deep cuts into the thickest section of the drumstick.
3 Combine the curry paste, lime rind and juice, coconut cream, honey and salt in a large bowl. Add the chicken and mix to coat well. Store, covered, in refrigerator 3 hours or overnight, stirring occasionally. Drain; reserve the marinade.
4 Place drumsticks on a preheated lightly greased barbecue grill. Cook for 8 minutes each side or until cooked through, brushing occasionally with reserved marinade. Discard the cocktail picks.
5 Combine the coconut and extra lime rind, sprinkle over the chicken. Serve hot.

Chili Chicken with Salsa

Salsa can be made a day ahead and stored in the refrigerator. Serve it at room temperature.

PREPARATION TIME:
10 MINUTES +
3 HOURS
MARINATING
COOKING TIME:
10 MINUTES
SERVES 4

8 boned chicken thighs
1/2 cup lemon juice
1/2 teaspoon bottled crushed chile (sambal oelek)
2 tablespoons oil
2 teaspoons sesame oil
2 tablespoons soy sauce
2 tablespoons honey
1 clove garlic, crushed
2 green onions, chopped
2 tablespoons finely chopped cilantro
salt, to taste

SALSA
1 small green cucumber, chopped
1 small red onion, finely chopped
1 medium tomato, chopped
2 tablespoons olive oil
1 tablespoon white wine vinegar
1/4 teaspoon superfine sugar
1/4 cup cilantro leaves

1 Trim the chicken of excess fat and sinew.
2 Combine the juice, chile, oils, soy sauce, honey, garlic, green onions, cilantro and salt in a large bowl and mix well.
3 Add the chicken and stir to combine. Cover with plastic wrap. Refrigerate for 3 hours or overnight, stirring occasionally.
4 Drain chicken and reserve the marinade. Place chicken on lightly oiled grill. Cook over medium heat for 5 minutes each side or until tender and cooked through. Brush with the reserved marinade in the last minutes of cooking. Serve hot with Salsa.
5 To make Salsa: Combine all ingredients in a bowl and mix well.

Tandoori Chicken on Skewers

Drumsticks can also be marinated in tandoori mixture. Cook whole, as directed, turning often.

PREPARATION TIME:
15 MINUTES +
3 HOURS
MARINATING
COOKING TIME:
8 MINUTES
MAKES ABOUT 16

6 boned, skinless chicken breast halves
2 teaspoons turmeric
1 teaspoon sweet paprika
1 teaspoon garam masala
1/2 teaspoon ground cardamom
1 teaspoon ground coriander
1 small onion, grated
1 clove garlic, crushed
2 teaspoons lemon juice
2 teaspoons sugar
salt, to taste
1 cup plain yogurt
red food coloring (optional)

1 Soak bamboo skewers for several hours in water. Trim the chicken of excess fat and sinew.
2 Combine the turmeric, paprika, garam masala, cardamom, coriander, onion, garlic, lemon juice, sugar, salt and yogurt in a large mixing bowl and mix until well combined, stirring in a few drops of red food coloring if desired.
3 Cut chicken into long strips, 3/4 in wide. Add to the marinade and mix until chicken is well coated. Store, covered with plastic wrap, in the refrigerator for 3 hours or overnight, stirring occasionally. Drain and reserve marinade.
4 Thread the chicken onto skewers. Place skewers on lightly greased grill. Cook over medium high heat for 8 minutes or until tender and well browned, turning often and brushing with reserved marinade several times during cooking.

Tandoori Chicken on Skewers (above). Chili Chicken with Salsa

Honey-glazed Chicken Breasts

For a distinctive taste to this dish, use honey with a strong, dark flavor such as lavender or rosemary.

PREPARATION TIME: 6 MINUTES + 20 MINUTES MARINATING
COOKING TIME: 10 MINUTES
SERVES 6

6 boned, skinless chicken breast halves
1/4 cup butter, softened
1/4 cup honey
1/4 cup barbecue sauce
2 teaspoons coarse grain mustard

1 Trim the chicken of excess fat and sinew and remove the skin.
2 Use a sharp knife to make three or four diagonal slashes across one side of each chicken breast. Prepare and heat barbecue.
3 Combine the butter, honey, barbecue sauce and mustard in a small bowl. Spread half of the marinade thickly over the slashed side of the chicken and cover. Set the remaining marinade aside. Stand the chicken at room temperature for 20 minutes.
4 Place the chicken breasts, slashed-side up, on a hot lightly greased grill. Cook for 2–3 minutes each side or until tender. Brush with the reserved marinade several times during cooking. Serve hot with buttered ribbon noodles.

Chicken Fajitas

Tomato salsa is available from supermarkets.

PREPARATION TIME:
35 MINUTES + 3 HOURS MARINATING
COOKING TIME:
10 MINUTES
SERVES 4

4 boned, skinless chicken breast halves
2 tablespoons olive oil
1/4 cup lime juice
2 cloves garlic, crushed
1 teaspoon ground cumin
1/4 cup chopped cilantro
8 flour tortillas
1 tablespoon olive oil, extra
2 medium onions, sliced
2 medium green sweet bell peppers, cut in thin strips
1 cup finely shredded cheddar cheese
1 large avocado, sliced
1 cup bottled tomato salsa

1 Trim the chicken of fat and sinew and cut it into thin strips. Place in a shallow non-metal dish.

2 Combine the oil, juice, garlic, cumin and cilantro in a bowl and mix well. Pour over the chicken. Store, covered, in the refrigerator for several hours or overnight. Prepare and heat the barbecue 1 hour before cooking.

3 Wrap the tortillas in foil and place on a cool part of the barbecue grill for 10 minutes to warm through. Heat the oil on a barbecue griddle (or in a cast iron skillet on the grill). Cook the onions and green peppers for 5 minutes or until soft. Push over to a cooler part of the griddle or pan to keep warm.

4 Add the chicken and marinade to the griddle and cook 5 minutes until just tender. Transfer the chicken, vegetables and wrapped tortillas to a serving platter. Make up individual fajitas by placing chicken, cooked onions and green peppers, shredded cheese and avocado over flat tortillas. Top with salsa, or serve on the side. Roll up to enclose filling.

Chicken Thighs with Corn Relish

PREPARATION TIME: 20 MINUTES
COOKING TIME: 25 MINUTES
SERVES 4

- **8 boned chicken thighs with skin on**
- **1 tablespoon olive oil**
- **1 small clove garlic, crushed**
- **1/4 teaspoon ground turmeric**
- **1/2 teaspoon salt**

CORN RELISH

- **1 cup frozen or canned corn kernels**
- **1 tablespoon olive oil**
- **1 fresh red chile, seeded and chopped**
- **1 small green sweet bell pepper, finely chopped**
- **1 medium onion, finely chopped**
- **1/3 cup white vinegar**
- **1/4 cup sugar**
- **1 teaspoon seeded mustard**
- **1/2 cup water**
- **1 tablespoon cornstarch**
- **1 teaspoon paprika**
- **1 teaspoon finely chopped cilantro leaves**
- **1 tablespoon olive oil, extra**

1 Prepare and heat the barbecue. Trim the chicken of excess fat and sinew.
2 Pierce the skin of the thighs with the point of a knife. Place the chicken in a large skillet of boiling water. Reduce the heat and simmer for 5 minutes. Remove from pan and drain. Cool. Combine the olive oil, garlic, turmeric and salt and rub over the skin side of the chicken. Set aside.
3 To make Corn Relish: Cook corn in a pan of boiling water for 2–3 minutes or until tender; drain (if using canned corn, drain but do not cook). Heat oil in medium pan. Add the chile, green pepper and onion. Cook over a medium heat until tender. Add the corn, vinegar, sugar and mustard, and cook, stirring, for another 5 minutes. Add blended water and cornstarch. Bring to a boil, reduce heat and stir until thickened. Stir in the paprika, cilantro and remaining extra oil. Remove from the heat; cool.
4 Place the chicken, skin-side up, on a hot lightly greased barbecue grill. Cook for 2 minutes; turn and cook skin-side down for 4 minutes. Continue cooking for another 5–10 minutes, turning frequently, until the chicken is well browned and cooked through. Serve with Corn Relish.

Middle Eastern Baked Chicken

PREPARATION TIME:
30 MINUTES
COOKING TIME:
1 HOUR
15 MINUTES
SERVES 6

3 1/2 lb chicken
1/2 cup boiling water
1/2 cup instant couscous
4 pitted dates, chopped
4 dried apricots, chopped
1 tablespoon lime juice
1 tablespoon olive oil
4 teaspoons butter
1 medium onion, chopped
1–2 cloves garlic, chopped
1 teaspoon salt
1/4 teaspoon cracked black pepper
1 teaspoon ground coriander
2 tablespoons chopped parsley
salt and pepper, extra
1 teaspoon ground cumin
1 tablespoon olive oil, extra

1 Prepare and heat the Weber (kettle) barbecue for indirect cooking. Place the drip tray underneath the top grill.
2 Remove giblets and deposits of fat from chicken. Wipe and pat chicken dry with paper towels.
3 Pour boiling water over couscous and set aside for 15 minutes for couscous to swell and soften. Soak the dates and apricots in lime juice; set aside.
4 Heat the oil and butter in a pan, add onion and garlic; cook 3–4 minutes until translucent. Remove from heat and add the couscous and soaked dried fruit, salt, pepper, coriander and parsley. Mix well. Spoon the stuffing into the chicken cavity and close with cocktail picks or a skewer. Tie the legs together with string.
5 Rub chicken skin all over with combined salt, pepper, cumin and extra oil. Place the chicken in the center of a large piece of greased foil. Gather the edges of the foil and wrap them securely around the chicken.
6 Place the parcel on a barbecue grill over the drip tray. Cover the barbecue and cook for 50 minutes. Open the foil, crimping the edges to form a tray to retain most of the cooking liquids. Cook another 20 minutes or until tender and golden. Remove from the heat and let stand 5–6 minutes before carving.

Buffalo Chicken Wings with Ranch Dressing

A taste of the Wild West in your own backyard.

PREPARATION TIME: 25 MINUTES + 3 HOURS MARINATING
COOKING TIME: 10 MINUTES
SERVES 4

8 large chicken wings
2 teaspoons black pepper
2 teaspoons garlic salt
2 teaspoons onion powder
olive oil, for deep frying
1/2 cup ketchup
2 tablespoons Worcestershire sauce
1 tablespoon butter, melted
2 teaspoons sugar
Tabasco sauce, to taste

RANCH DRESSING
1/2 cup whole egg mayonnaise
1/2 cup sour cream
2 tablespoons lemon juice
2 tablespoons chopped chives
salt and white pepper, to taste

1 Wash the wings thoroughly and pat dry with paper towels. Cut the tips off each wing and discard. Bend each wing back to snap the joint and cut through to create two pieces.
2 Combine the pepper, garlic salt and onion powder. Using your fingers, rub the mixture into each chicken piece.
3 Heat oil to moderately hot in a deep heavy-based skillet. Cook the chicken pieces in batches for 2 minutes. Remove with tongs or a slotted spoon and drain on paper towels.
4 Transfer the chicken to a non-metal bowl or shallow dish. Combine the sauces, butter, sugar and Tabasco, pour over the chicken and stir to coat. Refrigerate, covered, for several hours or overnight. Prepare and heat the barbecue for 1 hour before cooking.
5 Place the chicken on a hot lightly oiled barbecue grill. Cook for 5 minutes, turning the chicken and brushing with marinade. Serve with Ranch Dressing.
6 To make Ranch Dressing: Combine the mayonnaise, cream, juice, chives, salt and pepper in a bowl and mix well.

Thai Chile Chicken

PREPARATION TIME: 20 MINUTES + 1 HOUR MARINATING
COOKING TIME: 20 MINUTES
SERVES 4–6

12 boned chicken thighs
6 cloves garlic
1 teaspoon black peppercorns
3 cilantro roots and stems, coarsely chopped
1/4 teaspoon salt

CHILE GARLIC DIP
4–5 dried red chiles
2 large cloves garlic, chopped
1/4 cup sugar
1/3 cup cider or rice vinegar
pinch salt
1/4 cup boiling water

1 Prepare and heat the barbecue. Trim the chicken of excess fat and sinew.

2 Place the garlic, peppercorns, cilantro and salt in a food processor bowl. Process for 20–30 seconds or until the mixture forms a smooth paste. Place the chicken in a shallow non-metal dish. Spread with the garlic mixture. Stand the chicken at room temperature for 1 hour.

3 To make Chile Garlic Dip: Soak the chiles in hot water for 20 minutes. Drain and chop finely. Place in a mortar with the garlic and sugar. Grind to a smooth paste. Place mixture in a small pan. Add the vinegar, salt and water. Bring to a boil, reduce heat and simmer for 2–3 minutes. Allow to cool.

4 Barbecue the chicken on a hot greased grill 5–10 minutes each side, turning once. Serve with Chile Garlic Dip.

Citrus Chicken Drumsticks

This is a refreshing, tangy dish.

PREPARATION TIME:
20 MINUTES +
3 HOURS
MARINATING
COOKING TIME:
20 MINUTES
SERVES 4

8 chicken drumsticks
1/3 cup orange juice
1/3 cup lemon juice
1 teaspoon grated orange rind
1 teaspoon grated lemon rind
1 teaspoon sesame oil
1 tablespoon olive oil
1 green onion, finely chopped

1 Wash the drumsticks and pat dry with paper towels. Trim any excess fat and score the thickest part of the chicken with a knife. Place in a shallow non-metal dish.

2 Combine the juices, rinds, oils and green onion in a bowl and pour over the chicken. Store, covered with plastic wrap, in the refrigerator for several hours or overnight, turning occasionally. Drain the chicken and reserve the marinade. Prepare and heat the barbecue 1 hour before cooking.

3 Cook the drumsticks on a hot lightly oiled barbecue grill for 15–20 minutes or until tender. Brush occasionally with the reserved marinade. Serve immediately.

Tandoori Weber Chicken

Tandoori chicken requires a slow heat. Do not place chicken on the barbecue while the fire is still very hot.

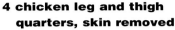

PREPARATION TIME:
5 MINUTES +
HOURS
MARINATING
COOKING TIME:
HOUR
SERVES 4

4 chicken leg and thigh quarters, skin removed
1 teaspoon salt
2 cloves garlic, crushed
1 tablespoon lemon juice
1 cup plain yogurt
1 1/2 teaspoons garam masala
1/2 teaspoon ground black pepper
1/2 teaspoon ground turmeric
2–3 drops red food coloring
20–30 mesquite or hickory chips, for smoking
olive oil, for basting

1 Place the chicken quarters in a non-metal dish; rub them with salt and garlic.
2 Combine the lemon juice, yogurt, garam masala, pepper and turmeric in a bowl. Add food coloring to make the marinade a bright orange-red color. Pour over the chicken, and coat evenly with the back of a spoon. Cover and set aside for 4 hours, turning the chicken every hour and redistributing the marinade. During the last hour of marinating, heat and prepare Weber (kettle) barbecue for indirect cooking.
3 When the barbecue coals are covered with fine white ash, add mesquite or hickory chips to coals. Cover the barbecue and leave until the smoke is well established (about 5 minutes).
4 Brush the barbecue grill with oil. Arrange the chicken on the grill and put the lid on the barbecue. Smoke-cook for 45 minutes to 1 hour or until the chicken is well crisped. Brush chicken with oil several times during cooking. Serve with side salad and onion rings.

Opposite: Citrus Chicken Drumsticks (above). Tandoori Weber Chicken

Spiced Chicken

PREPARATION TIME:
20 MINUTES +
1 HOUR
MARINATING
COOKING TIME:
10 MINUTES
SERVES 6

1/4 teaspoon black pepper
1 tablespoon chopped cilantro
1 clove garlic, crushed
1 teaspoon grated fresh ginger
2 teaspoons curry powder
1/4 teaspoon citric acid
1/4 cup water
2 teaspoons chicken bouillon granules
1 tablespoon peanut oil
1/4 teaspoon salt
1 teaspoon garam masala
1 lb boned, skinless chicken thighs

1 Mix together the pepper, cilantro, garlic, ginger, curry powder, citric acid, water, chicken bouillon, peanut oil, salt and garam masala.
2 Lightly score the chicken, in a criss-cross fashion. Place the chicken in the marinade and marinate for about 1 hour or refrigerate overnight.
3 Preheat the barbecue grill and cook the chicken for 10 minutes over medium heat, turning once, until the chicken is done. Eat with steamed rice or flat bread and a salad.

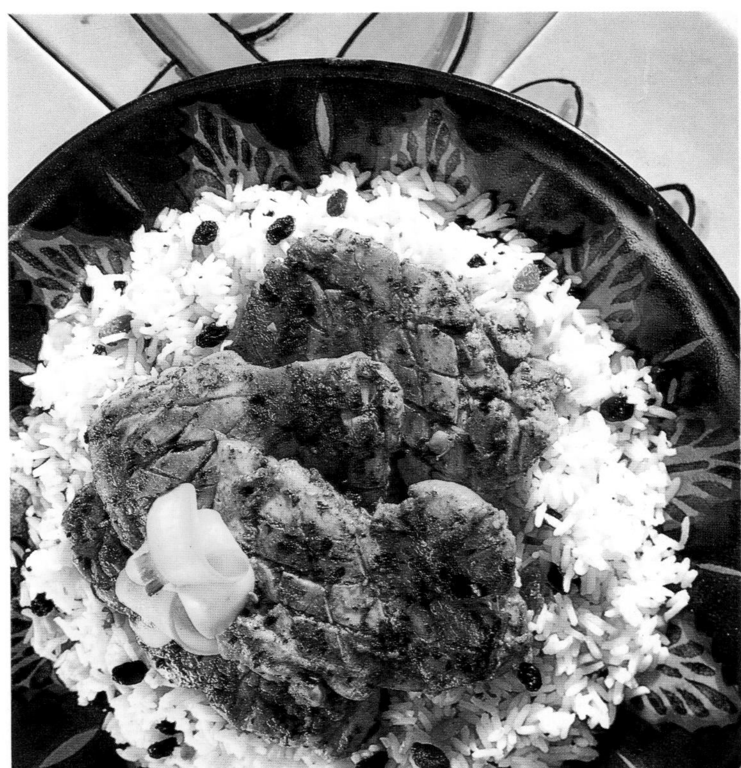

Seafood

There are numerous delicious ways to barbecue seafood. Depending on the variety and size, it may be wrapped in foil and grilled, cooked in a fish basket, marinated and tossed on the barbecue or skewered as kebabs. Remember, though, that seafood should not be marinated for any longer than one hour, otherwise the flesh may become 'powdery'. If the marinade is acidic, for example, if it is based on lemon juice or wine, marinate the seafood for no longer than half an hour.

When barbecuing fish on an electric or gas barbecue, a medium high heat is required. Always remember that cooking times are approximate, so use your own judgment. Be careful to avoid burning fish. Overcooking shellfish will cause it to shrink and toughen. If you are using an open charcoal grill, cook over glowing coals, not flames, and grease the barbecue grill or griddle before cooking, so the seafood doesn't stick.

No matter the type of seafood you're after, one rule always applies: buy from a reputable fish merchant. If the merchant is busy all the time, it's a good indication that stock is turning over regularly. Stay away from the store which has strong fishy odors, as opposed to a fresh, seaside fragrance. When purchasing whole fish, look for bright and bulging eyes. The flesh should be firm and gills bright pink. Ask the fish shop to gut and scale the fish you have selected.

Purchasing fillets can be a little tricky. Often, shops fillet fish left over from the previous day. Look for fillets which are shiny and firm with a good shape and not discolored. If you're not happy with the fillets on display, ask them to fillet the fish you choose. The head and bones can be used for stock, which can be frozen.

Shellfish should not be discolored around the joint and should be firmly closed. The shells should be lustrous and not broken in any way. They should smell of the sea.

Seafood Kebabs

Serve these delicious Seafood Kebabs with a variety of salads and crusty bread.

PREPARATION TIME:
15 MINUTES + 15 MINUTES MARINATING
COOKING TIME:
7 MINUTES
SERVES 6–8

1 1/2 lb firm white fish fillets
18 large uncooked shrimp
18 scallops
1 red sweet bell pepper
1 green sweet bell pepper
1 yellow sweet bell pepper

MARINADE
1/4 cup olive oil
1/4 cup lemon juice
2 teaspoons chopped fresh dill
1/2 teaspoon salt
1/2 teaspoon white pepper
lemon wedges, to serve

1 Remove skin from the fillets if necessary. Cut into 1 1/4 in square pieces. Shell and devein the shrimp. Cut the red, green and yellow peppers into pieces the same size as the fish. Place prepared ingredients in a bowl.
2 To make the marinade: Combine all the ingredients. Pour over the fish and turn to coat. Allow to marinate for 15 minutes.
3 Thread the ingredients alternately onto soaked bamboo skewers or metal skewers.
4 Cook kebabs on a preheated oiled grill until fish turns white and shrimp are pink and opaque. Serve immediately with lemon wedges and a tartare sauce.

Note: Bamboo skewers must be soaked for barbecuing. The longer they soak, the less they'll burn. Wrap foil around the exposed ends to prevent scorching. If using metal skewers, you may need to reduce cooking time slightly as they will conduct the heat. To make a quick Tartare Sauce: Add 1/4 cup chopped gherkin pickles, 1 tablespoon chopped capers, 2 tablespoons chopped red pepper, 2 tablespoons chopped parsley to 1 1/2 cups mayonnaise; mix well. Serve with hot or cold seafoods.

Seafood Kebabs (above). Tandoori Shrimp

Tandoori Shrimp

Although this recipe is not cooked in a tandoor oven, you will be more than happy with the result.

PREPARATION TIME:
20 MINUTES + 15 MINUTES MARINATING
COOKING TIME:
5 MINUTES
SERVES 6 AS AN APPETIZER, 3–4 AS MAIN MEAL

24 large uncooked shrimp
1/2 cup plain yogurt
1/3 cup finely chopped cilantro leaves
2 tablespoons finely chopped mint leaves
salt, to taste
1 tablespoon chopped fresh ginger
2 cloves garlic, crushed
1 teaspoon chili powder
1 teaspoon turmeric
1 teaspoon ground coriander
1 teaspoon garam masala
few drops bright red food coloring (optional)
2 lemons, cut into wedges, to serve

1 Shell and devein the shrimp, leaving only the tail shells on. Rinse and pat dry.
2 Combine yogurt with cilantro, mint and salt. Pour over the shrimp and let stand for 5 minutes.
3 Mix together the remaining ingredients and use to marinate the shrimp for 10 minutes.
4 Thread the shrimp onto metal skewers and grill high above glowing coals for about 5 minutes. Turn the skewers so the shrimp cook evenly. Shrimp are ready when they start to curl and turn opaque. Serve with lemon wedges.

Note: Complement this dish with a tomato onion sambal. Finely chop one medium tomato that has been peeled and seeded, combine with one small finely chopped white or red onion. Add some lime or lemon juice to moisten. Or try the following cool Cucumber and Yogurt Sauce: Peel a large cucumber, cut in half and scoop out the seeds. Finely chop cucumber flesh, sprinkle with a little salt and let stand for 5–6 minutes. Drain off the accumulated liquid. Add cucumber to 1/2 cup plain yogurt and stir in 2 teaspoons chopped mint.

Blackened Fish Fillets

For the best results when barbecuing, choose firm white fish fillets which are an even thickness of about 1/2 in.

PREPARATION TIME:
10 MINUTES + 30 MINUTES MARINATING
COOKING TIME:
5 MINUTES
SERVES 4

4 medium white fish fillets

SEASONING MIXTURE
2 tablespoons ground black pepper
1 tablespoon garlic powder
1 tablespoon onion powder
1 tablespoon dried thyme
1 teaspoon salt
1 tablespoon hot chili powder
1 tablespoon all-purpose flour
2 teaspoons ground dried oregano
Tabasco sauce to taste
1/4 cup olive oil or ghee

1 Pat fish fillets dry with paper towels. To make the seasoning mixture: Combine all ingredients and use to coat fish. Allow to stand for 30 minutes.
2 Heat the grill of an open barbecue and brush the surface with olive oil or ghee.
3 Cook fillets approximately 4–5 minutes each side, turning only once.

Barbecued Lobster

This is probably one of the most expensive recipes in the book but also one of the most enjoyable.

PREPARATION TIME:
20 MINUTES
COOKING TIME:
5 MINUTES
SERVES 6–8

6 small green lobster tails
1/4 cup olive oil
salt, to taste
1/4 cup lemon juice
1 tablespoon chopped fresh dill
ground pepper, to taste
lemon wedges, to serve

1 Cut the lobster tails in half lengthwise and slit the underside of the tails with the point of a sharp knife to allow access to the flesh. Combine the olive oil, salt, lemon juice, dill and pepper to taste.
2 Brush the marinade onto the lobster flesh. (Retain the shell to protect the delicate flesh from intense heat.)
3 Barbecue the lobster on a preheated and oiled grill. First, turn the cut side down to seal, just for a few seconds. Then use tongs to turn the pieces over and cook covered for 5 minutes or until the shells turn pink. Serve lobster with lemon wedges, a lemony mayonnaise and a tossed green salad.

Chili Scallop and Shrimp Kebabs

If you are not too sure about your chili tolerance, reduce the chili bean sauce.

PREPARATION TIME:
20 MINUTES + 10 MINUTES MARINATING
COOKING TIME:
8 MINUTES
SERVES 6–8

1 clove garlic, crushed
1 tablespoon grated fresh ginger
2 teaspoons sesame oil
1 tablespoon oriental chili bean sauce (see note)
1 tablespoon soy sauce
2 teaspoons tomato paste
1 tablespoon sugar
1 tablespoon lemon juice
2 lb large uncooked shrimp
8 oz scallops

1 Combine the crushed garlic, ginger, sesame oil, chili bean sauce, soy sauce, tomato paste, sugar and lemon juice.
2 Shell shrimp and devein, leaving tail shells on. Clean the scallops. Add shrimp and scallops to the marinade. Cover and marinate for 10–15 minutes.
3 Skewer shrimp and scallops on flat metal skewers.
4 Cook on a preheated lightly oiled barbecue grill for 4 minutes each side. Baste with the remaining marinade during cooking. Serve with rice.

Note: Chili bean sauce is an oil-based soya bean, garlic and extra hot chili paste. Use with caution. Available from Chinese and Asian food outlets.

Barbecued Lobster (above). Blackened Fish Fillets (right). Chili Scallop and Shrimp Kebabs

Moroccan Fish with Fresh Tomato Sauce

This type of tomato sauce, also called 'salsa', makes a great quick sauce for grilled or fried fish.

PREPARATION TIME: 30 MINUTES + 3 HOURS STANDING
COOKING TIME: 5–10 MINUTES
SERVES 6

1 1/2 lb white fish fillets, skinned
1 medium red onion, peeled and finely chopped
1 clove garlic, crushed
2 tablespoons chopped cilantro
1/3 cup chopped flat-leaved parsley
1/2 teaspoon ground sweet paprika
1/4 teaspoon chili powder
1/3 cup olive oil
2 tablespoons lemon juice

TOMATO SAUCE
4 large, ripe, red tomatoes, peeled, seeded and chopped
2 small fresh red chiles, cut in half, seeded and finely sliced
4 green onions, including some green, finely sliced
1/2 bunch fresh cilantro, chopped finely
1/2 cup extra virgin olive oil
ground pepper
lemon or lime juice (optional)
1 red onion, finely chopped (optional)

1 Cut fish across the grain into 3/4 in squares. Combine onion, garlic, cilantro, parsley, paprika, chili powder, olive oil and lemon juice and spoon over fish cubes. Mix well and allow to marinate for at least 2 hours or overnight.
2 Place fish on metal skewers and barbecue, turning frequently, until lightly browned on all sides.
3 To make Tomato Sauce: Combine tomatoes, chiles, green onions and cilantro in a bowl, add olive oil and pepper to taste.
4 Add lemon or lime juice and chopped onion if using.
5 Allow the Tomato Sauce to stand for at least an hour in the refrigerator before serving with the fish.

Barbecued Scallops

Serve with steamed rice and accompany with a little chili sauce if desired.

REPARATION IME:
5 MINUTES +
5 MINUTES
ARINATING
OOKING TIME:
MINUTES
ERVES 4–6

1 lb scallops
2 tablespoons olive oil
1 clove garlic, crushed
2 green onions, finely shredded
salt and pepper, to taste

1 Rinse the scallops, removing any visible veins or dirt. Mix together the remaining ingredients and stir in the scallops. Marinate for 15 minutes in the refrigerator.

2 Cook on a moderately hot griddle (or in a cast iron skillet on the grill) at the edge of the barbecue where the heat is not too fierce, until they turn white. Do not overcook or they will toughen.

Note: Scallops require a short cooking time. They can easily become tough and rubbery with excess cooking so wait until your guests are ready before you cook them. If you are using scallops which have been frozen, allow them to defrost completely in the refrigerator and drain well before marinating.

Citrus Fish with Avocado Salsa

PREPARATION TIME: 20 MINUTES
COOKING TIME: 10 MINUTES
SERVES 4

1 tablespoon finely grated orange rind
1 tablespoon finely grated lemon rind
1 tablespoon lime juice
2 tablespoons olive oil
4 firm white fish steaks, about 6 oz each

AVOCADO SALSA
$1^1/_2$ teaspoons ground cumin
1 large avocado, finely chopped
1 red onion, very finely chopped
1 small fresh red chile, seeds removed and finely chopped
2 teaspoons lemon juice
2 teaspoons olive oil

1 Combine the orange and lemon rind, lime juice and olive oil and season with freshly ground black pepper. Pour over the fish and set aside to marinate for about 5 minutes.

2 Lightly oil a preheated barbecue grill and cook the fish for 3–5 minutes on each side, or until just tender.

3 To make the Avocado Salsa: Dry-fry the cumin in a skillet on the stove for about 40 seconds, shaking the pan. Mix together the cumin with the avocado, onion, chile, lemon juice and olive oil in a bowl. Serve the fish steaks with the Avocado Salsa and steamed baby potatoes.

Jumbo Shrimp with Noodles and Coconut Dressing

REPARATION IME:
0 MINUTES +
0 MINUTES
ARINATING
OOKING TIME:
2 MINUTES
ERVES 4

24 uncooked jumbo shrimp
1 cup coconut milk
1 tablespoon grated fresh ginger
1 tablespoon sweet chili sauce
1–2 fresh red chiles, finely chopped
1/4 cup chopped fresh basil
5 oz dried soba noodles
fresh basil leaves, to garnish

1 Shell and devein the shrimp, leaving the tail shells intact. Combine the coconut milk, ginger, sweet chili sauce, red chiles and basil in a bowl. Pour the marinade over the shrimp and refrigerate for 20 minutes, then drain the shrimp and reserve the marinade.

2 Place the shrimp in a single layer on a lightly oiled and preheated barbecue grill and cook for 2–3 minutes, turning once, until cooked through. Set aside on a warm plate.

3 Use a saucepan to heat the reserved coconut mixture on the stove or barbecue. Bring to a boil briefly, just enough to heat the mixture through. Do not overheat or the coconut milk will become oily.

4 Meanwhile, cook the soba noodles in a large pan of boiling, salted water, following the manufacturer's instructions. Then add a cup of cold water and drain. Divide the noodles and shrimp among four warm plates and spoon the sauce over. Garnish with the basil leaves.

Sardines with Capers and Baby Garlic Potatoes

PREPARATION TIME:
20 MINUTES +
15 MINUTES
MARINATING
COOKING TIME:
12 MINUTES
SERVES 4

24 fresh sardines, gutted and butterflied
1/4 cup olive oil
2 tablespoons lime juice
2 cloves garlic, crushed
1/2 teaspoon dried oregano leaves
1 tablespoon baby capers, drained
fresh oregano sprigs
2 limes, quartered

BABY GARLIC POTATOES
2 x 16 oz cans baby potatoes or cooked baby new potatoes
2 tablespoons butter
2 cloves garlic, crushed

1 Lay the sardines in a single layer in a non-metallic dish. Combine the olive oil, lime juice, garlic and oregano leaves in a bowl. Pour the marinade over the sardines and refrigerate for 15 minutes. Do not marinate them for any longer or they start to 'cook' and will break up when heated. Drain the sardines, reserving the marinade.

2 To make the Baby Garlic Potatoes: Dry the potatoes well with paper towels. Melt the butter in a heavy-based skillet and add the garlic and potatoes. Shake and turn the potatoes over high heat for about 3–4 minutes, or until golden. Drain on paper towels and keep warm.

3 Lightly brush a preheated barbecue grill with olive oil. Add the sardines in a single layer (it may be necessary to cook them in batches) and cook for about 2 minutes, turning once. Brush several times with the reserved marinade while cooking and take care not to overcook the sardines or they may fall apart.

4 Place the sardines on a warm plate and top with the baby capers, oregano sprigs and some freshly ground black pepper. Serve with the lime wedges and a few of the Baby Garlic Potatoes.

Scallops with Sesame Bok Choy

'REPARATION
IME:
0 MINUTES +
5 MINUTES
'ARINATING
:OOKING TIME:
 MINUTES
:ERVES 4

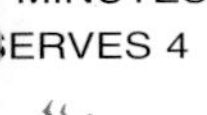

24 large scallops with corals (roe)
2 tablespoons light soy sauce
1 tablespoon Thai fish sauce
1 tablespoon honey
1 tablespoon kecap manis or soy sauce
grated rind and juice of 1 lime
2 teaspoons grated fresh ginger
1 lime, in wedges, to garnish

SESAME BOK CHOY
1 tablespoon sesame oil
1 tablespoon sesame seeds
1 clove garlic, crushed
8 baby bok choy, halved lengthwise

1 Rinse the scallops, remove the dark vein and dry with paper towels. Combine the soy and fish sauces, honey, kecap manis, lime rind and juice and ginger. Pour over the scallops, cover and refrigerate for about 15 minutes. Drain and reserve the marinade.
2 To make the Sesame Bok Choy: Pour the oil onto a preheated barbecue griddle (or in a cast iron skillet on the grill) and add the sesame seeds and garlic. Cook, stirring, for 1 minute, or until the seeds are golden. Arrange the bok choy in a single layer on the griddle and pour the reserved marinade over. Cook for 3–4 minutes, turning once, until tender. Remove and keep warm.
3 Wipe clean the griddle, brush with some oil and reheat. Add the scallops and cook, turning, for about 2 minutes, or until they become opaque. Place the scallops on top of the Sesame Bok Choy and serve with the lime wedges.

Swordfish Kebabs with Roast Potatoes

PREPARATION TIME:
40 MINUTES
COOKING TIME:
1 HOUR
SERVES 4

1 1/4 lb potatoes, cut in half
2 cloves garlic, crushed
1 red onion, cut into 8 wedges
1 red sweet bell pepper, cut into cubes
2 zucchini, cut into pieces
2 lb swordfish, cut into cubes
bay leaves, torn in half
olive oil
1 tablespoon lemon juice

1 Preheat the oven to 375°F. Brush the potatoes with olive oil and place cut-side up in a baking dish. Bake for 40 minutes, or until crisp.

2 Preheat a lightly oiled barbecue griddle (or a cast iron skillet on the grill). Add the garlic, onion and red pepper and cook, stirring, for 5 minutes. Toss in the zucchini and cook for another 5 minutes, or until the vegetables are tender. Remove from the heat and season to taste.

3 Thread the swordfish cubes onto eight metal skewers, interspersed with the bay leaves. Lightly coat with olive oil and the lemon juice.

4 Lightly oil the hot grill and cook the kebabs for about 4 minutes, turning frequently. Arrange the vegetables on four warm plates, top with the kebabs and serve the potatoes on the side.

Garlic Calamari with Parmesan

PREPARATION TIME:
0 MINUTES +
0 MINUTES
MARINATING
COOKING TIME:
MINUTES
SERVES 2–4

12 oz fresh calamari (or squid) tubes, cleaned
4 cloves garlic, chopped
2 tablespoons olive oil
2 tablespoons finely chopped fresh parsley
1 large tomato, peeled, seeded and finely chopped
1/4 cup grated Parmesan

1 Cut the calamari tubes in half lengthwise, wash and pat dry. Lay them flat, with the soft, fleshy side facing upwards, and cut into rectangular pieces, about 2 1/2 x 1 in. Finely honeycomb by scoring the fleshy side with diagonal strips, one way and then the other, to create a diamond pattern.

2 Mix the garlic, oil, half the parsley, salt and pepper in a bowl. Add the calamari and refrigerate for at least 10 minutes.

3 Heat a lightly oiled barbecue griddle (or a cast iron skillet on the grill) until very hot. Cook the calamari in 2 batches, tossing regularly, until they turn white. Add the chopped tomato and toss through to just heat.

4 Arrange the calamari on a plate and scatter the Parmesan and remaining parsley over.

Tuna Steaks with Tapenade

PREPARATION TIME:
15 MINUTES +
10 MINUTES
MARINATING
COOKING TIME:
6 MINUTES
SERVES 4

2 tablespoons tapenade (olive paste)
2 tablespoons olive oil
2 cloves garlic, finely chopped
2 teaspoons finely grated lemon rind
4 tuna steaks
chopped green onion, to garnish

1 Combine the olive paste, oil, garlic, lemon rind and some black pepper. Spread over both sides of the tuna and refrigerate for 10 minutes.

2 Place the tuna steaks on a lightly oiled and preheated barbecue grill and cook, turning once, for about 3 minutes each side. When cooked, the steak should still be pink in the center. Sprinkle with the green onion.

Shrimp with Mango Salsa

REPARATION IME:
5 MINUTES +
HOUR
ARINATING
OOKING TIME:
0 MINUTES
ERVES 4–6

2 lb uncooked large shrimp
1/3 cup lemon juice
1/3 cup olive oil
1/4 cup chopped fresh dill
1 lb mango (fresh or canned), cubed
1 onion, finely diced
1 fresh red chile, seeded and finely chopped
1 tablespoon grated lemon rind
5 oz (5 cups) arugula leaves

1 Shell and devein the shrimp, keeping the tail shells intact.

2 Combine the lemon juice, olive oil, dill and a teaspoon of salt in a bowl, add the shrimp and toss well. Cover and refrigerate for 1 hour.

3 Preheat a deep-sided cast iron skillet on the grill until very hot. Drain the shrimp, reserving the marinade, and cook for 3 minutes, or until they change color. Remove the shrimp. Add the reserved marinade to the pan, boil for 5 minutes and mix in to the shrimp. Cool the mixture slightly.

4 In a bowl, combine the mango, onion, chile, lemon rind and some salt and pepper. Add the shrimp to the salsa and serve on a bed of arugula.

Salmon with Gremolata and Griddle Cakes

PREPARATION TIME:
25 MINUTES
COOKING TIME:
20 MINUTES
SERVES 4

GREMOLATA
1/3 cup finely chopped fresh parsley
grated rind of 1 lemon
grated rind of 1 orange
2 cloves garlic, crushed

POTATO GRIDDLE CAKES
8 oz potatoes
8 oz sweet potatoes, peeled
1/3 cup chopped fresh chives
2 tablespoons all-purpose flour
1 egg, lightly beaten
4 salmon fillet portions, about 6 oz each
2–3 teaspoons baby capers

1 To make the Gremolata: Combine the parsley, lemon and orange rind and garlic.

2 To make the Potato Griddle Cakes: Coarsely shred the peeled potatoes and sweet potatoes and squeeze handfuls of the mixture to remove any excess moisture. Mix with the chives, flour, egg and salt and pepper. Preheat a barbecue griddle (or a cast iron skillet on the grill) and drizzle with some olive oil. Use a heaped tablespoon of the mixture to make each cake. Add this to the griddle and flatten slightly. You may need to cook the cakes in two batches. Cook, turning once, for about 5 minutes, or until golden.

3 Drizzle some oil over the griddle and add the salmon portions. Cook for 2–3 minutes each side, or until just tender.

4 Place the salmon on warmed plates and top with the Gremolata and the drained capers. Serve immediately with the Potato Griddle Cakes.

Scallops with Green Peppercorns

PREPARATION TIME:
20 MINUTES + 20 MINUTES MARINATING
COOKING TIME:
5 MINUTES
SERVES 4

1/4 cup olive oil
2 teaspoons pickled green peppercorns, drained and chopped
2 teaspoons finely grated lime rind
1 teaspoon finely grated fresh ginger
1 lb scallops with corals (roe), deveined
salad leaves
strips of pickled ginger

1 Combine the oil, peppercorns, rind and fresh ginger. Add the scallops and refrigerate for 20 minutes.
2 Heat a barbecue griddle (or a cast iron skillet on the grill) until very hot. Cook the scallops in batches, stirring gently for about 2 minutes, or until they become golden brown.
3 Place the scallops on the salad leaves and top with the ginger strips.

Tuna Steaks with Rosemary Potatoes

PREPARATION TIME:
20 MINUTES
COOKING TIME:
40 MINUTES
SERVES 4

ROSEMARY POTATOES
1¼ lb new potatoes, unpeeled
2 tablespoons butter
¼ cup olive oil
2 cloves garlic, crushed
1 tablespoon chopped fresh rosemary

4 thick tuna steaks, about 6 oz each
rind and juice of 1 lemon or lime
1 tablespoon finely chopped fresh parsley

1 To make the Rosemary Potatoes: Wash the potatoes, pat dry with paper towels and cut into halves.
2 Heat the butter and olive oil on a barbecue griddle, add the potatoes and season with freshly ground black pepper. Cook over medium heat, tossing regularly to make sure that the potatoes are evenly colored, for about 30 minutes, or until they are tender, crisp and golden.
3 Stir in the garlic, rosemary and some salt and toss to coat for a few minutes. Remove and keep warm.
4 Add the tuna steaks to the hot grill and cook for 3–4 minutes each side. When cooked, the tuna steaks should still be pink inside. Sprinkle with the lemon or lime rind and juice and the parsley. Serve at once with the Rosemary Potatoes.

Note: You can use another kind of fish to replace the tuna. Try swordfish or salmon.

Jumbo Shrimp with Dill Mayonnaise

PREPARATION TIME:
0 MINUTES +
HOURS
MARINATING
COOKING TIME:
0–15 MINUTES
SERVES 4

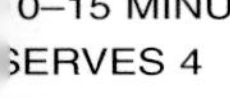

MARINADE

1/2 cup olive oil
1/3 cup lemon juice
2 tablespoons coarse grain mustard
2 tablespoons honey
2 tablespoons chopped fresh dill
16–20 uncooked jumbo shrimp

DILL MAYONNAISE

3/4 cup whole egg mayonnaise
2 tablespoons chopped fresh dill
1 1/2 tablespoons lemon juice
1 gherkin pickle, finely chopped
1 teaspoon chopped capers
1 clove garlic, crushed

1 To make the marinade: Combine the olive oil, lemon juice, mustard, honey and dill in a bowl, pour over the unpeeled shrimp and coat well. Cover and refrigerate shrimp for at least 2 hours, turning occasionally.

2 To make the Dill Mayonnaise: In a small bowl, whisk together the mayonnaise, dill, lemon juice, gherkin, capers and garlic. Cover and refrigerate.

3 Lightly oil a preheated barbecue grill. Add the drained shrimp and cook in batches over high heat for 4 minutes, turning frequently until pink and cooked through. Serve with the Dill Mayonnaise.

Minty Barbecued Fish Cakes

PREPARATION TIME: 15 MINUTES
COOKING TIME: 10 MINUTES
SERVES 6

1 lb firm white fish fillets
1 medium brown onion, chopped
3 macadamia nuts or 6 cashew nuts
1 teaspoon chili powder
1/2 teaspoon turmeric
1 tablespoon finely chopped fresh lemongrass
1 teaspoon finely chopped Vietnamese mint (optional)
1/2 teaspoon ground black pepper
salt, to taste
1 tablespoon sugar
1/2 cup thick coconut milk
1 tablespoon ground roasted dried coriander
pieces of banana leaf or baking (silicone) paper, 6 1/2 in square

1 Remove any small bones from the fish fillets. Cut into large pieces, about 1 1/4 in square. Combine in a food processor with the remaining ingredients, except for the banana leaves, until smooth. Alternatively, finely chop the fish with a cleaver to make a paste and mix in the remaining ingredients.
2 Soften the banana leaves in boiling water for 1–2 minutes. Dry on paper towels. Place 2 tablespoons of the fish mixture onto a piece of banana leaf and fold into a parcel. Fasten with a cocktail pick. Repeat with the

remaining filling. If banana leaves are unavailable, use squares of silicone paper, then wrap the paper in foil the same size.
3 Place fish parcels on a preheated barbecue grill. Cook for 5 minutes each side or until fish is cooked.

Note: Silicone paper is available at good supermarkets and cookware stores.

Chili Crab

Peanut oil is unrefined and has quite a strong peanutty fragrance and flavor. You can simply use a wok on your conventional barbecue if you don't have a wok attachment.

PREPARATION TIME:
20 MINUTES
COOKING TIME:
15 MINUTES
SERVES 2–4 AS AN ENTRÉE

- **3 medium-sized cooked crabs (Dungeness or blue)**
- **1/3 cup peanut oil**
- **3 cloves garlic, crushed**
- **2 fresh red chiles, finely chopped**
- **1 teaspoon grated fresh ginger**
- **1 tablespoon chili paste or sambal oelek**
- **1/3 cup ketchup**
- **2 tablespoons sugar**
- **1 tablespoon soy sauce**
- **1 teaspoon oriental sesame oil**

1 Using a cleaver or heavy-bladed sharp knife, cut the crabs in half. Wash the crabs under cold water, remove fibrous tissues and stomach bag.
2 Heat the wok, add the oil and swirl to heat. Stir-fry crab halves for 5 minutes and remove to a dish.
3 Reduce heat and stir-fry the garlic, chiles and ginger for 3 minutes, then add chili paste, ketchup, sugar, soy sauce and sesame oil. Mix well and bring to a boil.
4 Return the crabs to the wok, stir well and simmer for 5 minutes, adding a little water or broth if the dish is in danger of drying out. Serve immediately.

Minty Barbecued Fish Cakes (left). Chili Crab

Thai Fish Cakes

In Bangkok they serve these spicy morsels as an appetizer. Double the quantities for a main dish.

PREPARATION TIME:
30 MINUTES
COOKING TIME:
8 MINUTES
SERVES 6

10 large spinach leaves
8 oz bream (porgy) fillets
1 tablespoon Thai fish sauce
1/4 cup finely chopped green onions
1 tablespoon finely chopped cilantro leaves, roots and stems
2 teaspoons grated lime rind
1 clove garlic, crushed
1 teaspoon chili sauce
1/4 teaspoon ground pepper
1/4 cup thick coconut milk
1 egg

1 Blanch the spinach leaves in boiling water for 10 seconds and cool them in iced water.
2 Remove skin, any stray bones and cut fish fillets into pieces. Combine in a food processor with the remaining ingredients until the mixture is smooth. Divide the fish mixture between six spinach leaves, placing two leaves together if they are small. Roll the spinach over to enclose the fish filling. Wrap each parcel in foil.
3 Place the cakes on a preheated barbecue grill and cook for 4 minutes each side, turning once. Serve immediately and let each person remove the foil from their portion.

Note: The use of the roots of fresh cilantro in this recipe is not a mistake. It lends a stronger flavor to the dish and is used in most Thai recipes.

Mexican Fish Cakes in Corn Husks

If cooking corn without the husks, wrap in foil or place on the coolest part of the barbecue.

PREPARATION TIME:
30 MINUTES + 10 MINUTES STANDING
COOKING TIME:
20 MINUTES
SERVES 4

4 corn cobs, complete with husks
1 lb firm white fish fillets, diced
2 cloves garlic, crushed
2 teaspoons Mexican chili powder
1/3 cup finely chopped cilantro
1 tablespoon chopped canned jalapeño chiles
1 egg, beaten
1/2 teaspoon ground black pepper
1 tablespoon lemon juice
2 tablespoons chopped green onions
1 teaspoon ground cumin
foil squares, for wrapping

Remove only four husks from each corn cob nd set aside. Turn back the remaining husks (being areful not to detach them) and then remove the hread-like cornsilk. Pull the husks back into position o enclose the corn. Soak the cobs in cold water for 0–15 minutes.

Process fish in a processor until just smooth, and hen combine with remaining ingredients. Divide into ight equal portions.

Wrap each portion in two of the reserved corn usks taken from the corn cobs. Then wrap parcels n squares of foil.

Start grilling the corn cobs on the barbecue for 0 minutes, turning them once or twice.

Place wrapped fish cakes on the medium hot grill uring the last 8 minutes and both should be ready at he same time.

Shrimp with Lemon and Garlic

Sea salt is available from good kitchen shops and leading food outlets.

PREPARATION TIME:
20 MINUTES + 10 MINUTES MARINATING
COOKING TIME:
5 MINUTES
SERVES 4–6

2 lb large uncooked shrimp
1/4 cup olive oil
1 tablespoon lemon juice
2 cloves garlic, crushed
2 green onions, finely chopped
1/2 teaspoon sea salt
ground black pepper, to taste
lemon quarters, to serve

1 Shell and devein shrimp. Mix remaining ingredients in a glass or ceramic bowl and stir in shrimp. Allow to marinate for 10 minutes.

2 On a barbecue griddle (or skillet on the grill) over full heat, toss shrimp until they start to curl up and become opaque. Serve with lemon quarters.

Shrimp Burgers

A delicious burger variation to serve for special occasions.

PREPARATION TIME: 15 MINUTES
COOKING TIME: 4 MINUTES
SERVES 6

1 lb large uncooked shrimp, shelled and deveined
1 egg, lightly beaten
1 tablespoon dry sherry
1 teaspoon grated fresh ginger
1 clove garlic, crushed
2 1/2 tablespoons cornstarch
1/4 cup finely chopped green onions
2 tablespoons finely chopped water chestnuts
1/2 cup cornflake crumbs
salt, to taste
1/4 cup oil

SAUCE
2 teaspoons Worcestershire sauce
1 tablespoon white wine vinegar
2 tablespoons water
2 teaspoons sugar
1 teaspoon grated fresh ginger
Tabasco, to taste
lime wedges, to serve
6 hamburger buns, to serve

Barbecued Spiced Fish (above). Shrimp Burgers

1 Finely chop the shrimp and combine with egg, sherry, ginger, garlic, cornstarch, green onions, water chestnuts and cornflake crumbs. Mix well. Season to taste.
2 To make the sauce: Combine ingredients in a small bowl.
3 Heat the barbecue griddle (or skillet on the grill) to medium-hot and brush with oil. Divide shrimp mixture evenly into six portions and cook in egg rings brushed with oil. Cook for 2 minutes on each side or until set and firm. Do not overcook. Serve Shrimp Burgers with combined sauce ingredients, lime wedges and hamburger buns.

Note: Serve with a crisp salad.

Barbecued Spiced Fish

PREPARATION TIME:
15 MINUTES
COOKING TIME:
20 MINUTES
SERVES 4

4 large, firm white fish fillets
1/4 cup butter, melted

DRY MARINADE
1/2 teaspoon salt
2 teaspoons ground sweet paprika
1/2 teaspoon white pepper
1/2 teaspoon ground cayenne
1/4 teaspoon ground dried oregano
1/4 teaspoon dried basil
1/4 teaspoon dried thyme
1 teaspoon garlic powder
1 teaspoon onion powder

1 Dry fish fillets with paper towels and brush with melted butter, set aside.
2 To make the dry marinade: Combine all the dry spices and sprinkle over the buttered fish fillets.
3 Cook the fillets on a lightly greased grill for 8–10 minutes, turning once during cooking time.

Note: You may find it easier to make a double quantity of this dry marinade and store the remaining mixture for later use. Store in a covered airtight jar in the freezer for best results. It adds flavor to seafood, poultry and beef.

Cilantro Chili Shrimp

It's a nice idea to offer finger bowls to everyone with this dish.

PREPARATION TIME:
20 MINUTES + 1 HOUR MARINATING
COOKING TIME:
10 MINUTES
SERVES 8

48 uncooked jumbo shrimp
1/3 cup finely chopped cilantro
2 tablespoons oil
1/4 cup soy sauce
1/4 cup sweet chili sauce
1 tablespoon kecap manis or soy sauce
2 tablespoons plum sauce
zest of 2 limes
1/4 cup lime juice

1 Using a sharp knife, cut down the back of each shrimp and remove the vein, leaving the shell intact. Discard any shrimp with broken shells.
2 Combine remaining ingredients in large mixing bowl, stir until well combined. Add shrimp, mix well. Cover with plastic wrap, refrigerate 1 hour. Drain and reserve marinade.
3 Place shrimp on lightly oiled barbecue griddle. Cook for 5–10 minutes or until the shrimp are pink and crisp. Baste with marinade while cooking.

Firecracker Shrimp

These shrimp certainly have some fire, but if you really like them spicy, adjust the cayenne pepper according to your taste.

PREPARATION TIME: 15 MINUTES
COOKING TIME: 8 MINUTES
SERVES 6

2 lb large uncooked shrimp
2 tablespoons olive oil

DRY SPICE MIXTURE
2 teaspoons black pepper
1/2 teaspoon salt
1 teaspoon onion powder
1 teaspoon dried chili flakes
1 teaspoon ground sweet paprika
1/2 teaspoon cayenne pepper
1 teaspoon ground dried oregano
1 teaspoon thyme
1 teaspoon garlic powder

1 Shell the shrimp, leaving tail shells on. Skewer six shrimp on each of eight metal skewers. Brush with olive oil.
2 To make the dry spice mixture: Combine ingredients and sprinkle over the shrimp on both sides. Cook on a hot barbecue grill for 4 minutes each side or until shrimp are pink and tender. Serve with Garlic Herb Hollandaise (see page 237).

Firecracker Shrimp (left). Herb-stuffed Bream

Herb-stuffed Bream

Make sure you do not overcook the fish, which would cause the flesh to toughen and dry. When ready, the flesh should be tender and white.

PREPARATION TIME:
15 MINUTES
COOKING TIME:
20 MINUTES
SERVES 4

1 large bream (porgy), gutted and scaled

FILLING
1 cup fresh bread crumbs
2 tablespoons chopped fresh parsley
1 tablespoon chopped fresh thyme
1 lemon
1/2 teaspoon salt
1/2 teaspoon white pepper
1 tablespoon butter, melted
2 tablespoons olive oil
lemon wedges, to serve

1 Clean the inside cavity of the fish with paper towels dipped in coarse salt. Score both sides of the fish at 3/4 in intervals with a sharp knife.

2 To make the filling: Place the bread crumbs, parsley and thyme in a small bowl. Finely grate the rind of the lemon, squeeze and strain juice. Add to the bread crumbs with salt, pepper and melted butter; mix well.

3 Fill the fish cavity with the prepared filling and secure with small metal skewers. Brush the outside with a little olive oil.

4 Place the fish in a fish frame and barbecue on a lightly oiled grill for 15–20 minutes, turning once, or until cooked. Serve with wedges of lemon.

Note: A fisheroo or fish frame is obtained from barbecue or camping accessory outlets. Fish can also be cooked in a well greased foil parcel of double thickness. Thyme can be used fresh or dried, it is a herb that improves with drying.

Dill Fish with Lemon Sauce

PREPARATION TIME:
10 MINUTES +
3 HOURS
MARINATING
COOKING TIME:
10 MINUTES
SERVES 4

4 boneless white fish fillets
2 tablespoons lemon pepper
1–2 tablespoons chopped fresh dill
1/3 cup lemon juice

LEMON SAUCE
2 tablespoons lemon juice
1/2 cup whipping cream
3 tablespoons butter, chopped
2 tablespoons chopped fresh chives

1 Rinse the fish under cold water.

2 Sprinkle pepper all over fillets and place in a shallow non-metal dish. Combine dill and lemon juice. Pour over the fish, cover and refrigerate several hours. Prepare and heat the barbecue 1 hour before cooking.

3 Cook the fish on a hot lightly greased barbecue griddle for 2–3 minutes each side or until the flesh flakes back easily with a fork. Serve with Lemon Sauce, barbecued citrus slices and a green salad.

4 To make the Lemon Sauce: Simmer the lemon juice in a small pan until reduced by half. Add cream and stir until mixed through. Whisk in the butter a little at a time until all the butter has melted; stir in the chives.

Thai Marinated Fish

REPARATION
IME:
0 MINUTES +
HOURS
ARINATING
OOKING TIME:
5 MINUTES
ERVES 4

1 medium-sized white-fleshed fish, cleaned and scaled
3/4 cup cilantro leaves
2 cloves garlic, crushed
1 tablespoon soy sauce
1 tablespoon Thai fish sauce
1 tablespoon sweet chili sauce
2 teaspoons sesame oil
3 green onions, finely chopped

2 teaspoons grated fresh ginger
1 tablespoon lime juice
1 teaspoon soft brown sugar

1 Place the fish in a large, shallow non-metal dish.
2 Fill the fish cavity with cilantro leaves.
3 Combine garlic, soy, fish and chili sauces, oil, green onions, ginger, juice and sugar in a bowl; mix well. Pour marinade over the fish. Cover and refrigerate for 2–3 hours. Prepare and heat the barbecue 1 hour before cooking.
4 Cook fish on a hot lightly greased grill in a fish frame for about 15 minutes, taking care not to burn the skin of the fish. (Move the fish away from the flame and dampen the fire if the fish begins to stick.) Brush it frequently with marinade until flesh flakes back easily with a fork, and has turned opaque. Serve with noodles or rice, and garnish with lightly grilled lemon or lime wedges as desired.

Barbecued Seafood

PREPARATION TIME:
20 MINUTES +
1 HOUR
MARINATING
TIME
COOKING TIME:
5 MINUTES
SERVES 4

8 baby octopus
1/2 cup red wine
1 tablespoon olive oil
2 cloves garlic, crushed
2 tablespoons chopped parsley
12 large uncooked shrimp
8 scallops with roe
freshly ground pepper

1 Remove heads and beaks of octopus and cut the tentacles in halves.

2 Combine the wine, oil, garlic and parsley and marinate octopus for an hour or more in refrigerator.

3 Have barbecue griddle (or skillet on a grill) very hot. Remove octopus from marinade, dry on paper towels and cook for 4–5 minutes.

4 Add shrimp and cook for 3–4 minutes. Add scallops and cook for 1–2 minutes (they toughen if overcooked). Serve seafood immediately with freshly ground pepper.

Salmon Steaks with Fruit Salsa

PREPARATION TIME:
20 MINUTES +
3 HOURS MARINATING
COOKING TIME: 10 MINUTES
SERVES 4

4 salmon steaks
2 tablespoons seasoned pepper
2 tablespoons lemon juice
1/2 cup lime juice
1 tablespoon chopped fresh thyme

FRUIT SALSA
1/2 small papaya, peeled
1/4 small pineapple, peeled
3 green onions, chopped
1 tablespoon chopped cilantro
2 tablespoons lime juice
1 tablespoon superfine sugar
salt, to taste

1 Sprinkle salmon steaks all over with seasoned pepper.

2 Place salmon in a shallow non-metal dish. Combine lemon juice, lime juice and thyme in a small bowl. Pour over salmon steaks. Cover and refrigerate for several hours.

3 Place salmon on hot lightly greased barbecue grill; brush with any remaining marinade. Cook 5–10 minutes each side, turning once, until outside is lightly browned and flesh is just cooked on the inside. Serve with Fruit Salsa.

4 To make Fruit Salsa: Chop papaya and pineapple into 1/2 in cubes. Combine in medium bowl with green onions, cilantro, lime juice, sugar and salt.

Barbecued Salmon with Cucumber Vinaigrette

This recipe is best suited to a Weber barbecue. As an alternative, buy salmon steaks, place a slice of tomato and a slice of lemon on each and wrap well in foil. Cook them on the barbecue for 10–15 minutes.

PREPARATION TIME:
30 MINUTES + SEVERAL HOURS REFRIGERATION
COOKING TIME:
40–50 MINUTES
SERVES 12

1 small (about 7 lb) whole salmon, gutted and scaled
1 large tomato, thickly sliced
1 lemon, thinly sliced
1/4 cup butter, melted
1 clove garlic, crushed
salt, pepper

CUCUMBER VINAIGRETTE
1/2 cup olive oil
2 tablespoons lime juice
1 tablespoon honey
1 clove garlic, crushed
1/2 teaspoon ground coriander
1 tomato, seeded, chopped
1 large cucumber, seeded and chopped

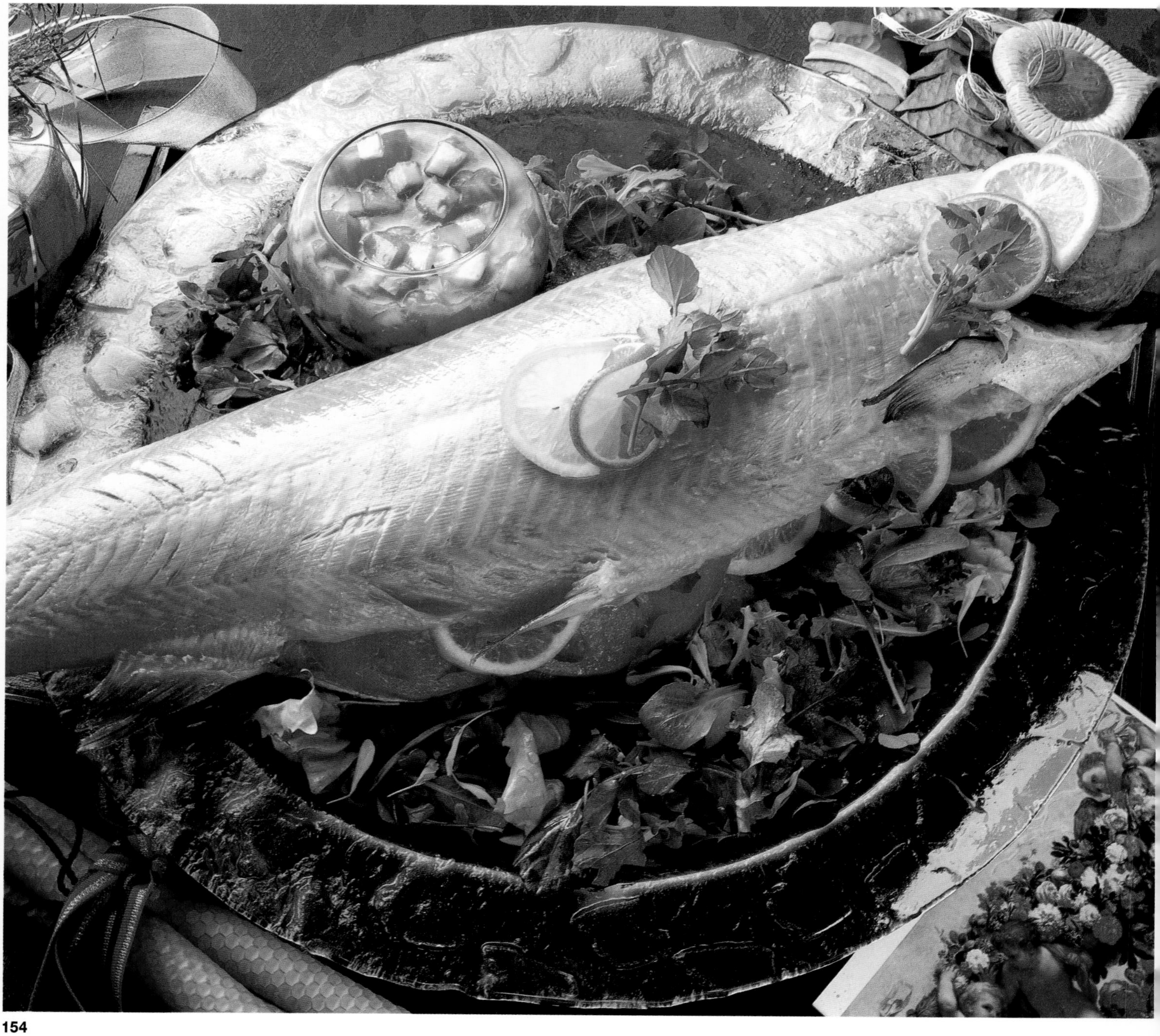

Light the barbecue using about 4 lb charcoal iquettes and about eight solid firestarters. Allow 5–30 minutes for the coals to be fully alight. oals should be arranged either side of the grill, ot directly underneath. Rinse and pat dry salmon, side and out. Trim fins and tail with scissors. Place lmon on a sheet of oiled foil large enough to nclose the whole fish. Arrange tomato and lemon ices inside the fish cavity.

Combine butter, garlic, salt and pepper in small owl. Brush liberally over fish. Pour any remaining ixture inside cavity. Wrap the salmon firmly in foil. Vrap in foil a second time to keep the fish together.

Curl the fish to a size to fit the barbecue and tie ith string at regular intervals to retain its shape. You may wish to make string handles for easier fting once cooked.)

Sit the fish, gut-side down, on the center of the arbecue grill with a drip tray underneath; cover ith lid, leaving vents open throughout cooking. Cook for 40 minutes. Remove from the coals. Let and covered for 10 minutes. Transfer to serving latter. Gently peel back skin to expose cooked esh; discard skin. Accompany with Cucumber Vinaigrette.

To make Cucumber Vinaigrette: Combine all ngredients in a small bowl. Refrigerate for several ours or overnight if possible.

Vhole Fish with Lemon Herb Butter

Although this recipe is ideal for a kettle arbecue, it can also be cooked on an pen grill with double-thickness foil.

REPARATION IME:
5 MINUTES
OOKING TIME:
HOUR
ERVES 4

4 lb whole white-fleshed fish
1 small lemon, sliced

HERB BUTTER
1/3 cup butter, softened
1 tablespoon chopped parsley
1 tablespoon thyme leaves
1 tablespoon chopped chives
2 teaspoons grated lemon rind

1 Prepare the Weber (kettle) barbecue for indirect cooking at moderate heat (normal fire).

2 Wash and scale the fish and pat it dry with paper towels. Place fish on a large sheet of oiled aluminum foil.

3 To make Herb Butter: Blend the butter, herbs and lemon rind in a small bowl and beat until smooth. Spread half of the butter mixture inside the cavity of the fish. Transfer the remaining butter mixture to a serving bowl.

4 Lay lemon slices over the fish, enclose fish in foil and place on the barbecue grill. Cover, cook for 1 hour or until the flesh flakes back easily with a fork. Serve with extra Herb Butter.

Sweet and Sour Fish Kebabs

PREPARATION TIME: 20 MINUTES + 3 HOURS MARINATING
COOKING TIME: 10 MINUTES
MAKES 12 SKEWERS

$1^{1}/_{2}$ lb boneless white fish fillets
1 cup canned pineapple pieces
1 large red sweet bell pepper
1 tablespoon soy sauce
2 tablespoons soft brown sugar
2 tablespoons white vinegar
2 tablespoons ketchup
salt, to taste

1 Soak wooden skewers in water for several hours.

2 Cut the fish into 1 in cubes. Drain the pineapple, reserving 2 tablespoons of liquid. Cut the red pepper into 1 in pieces. Thread the pepper, fish and pineapple alternately onto skewers.

3 Place the kebabs in a shallow non-metal dish. Combine the soy sauce, reserved pineapple juice, sugar, vinegar, ketchup and salt in a small bowl and mix well. Pour the marinade over the kebabs. Cover; refrigerate for 2–3 hours. Prepare and heat the barbecue 1 hour before cooking.

4 Barbecue kebabs on a hot lightly greased grill, brushing frequently with marinade, 2–3 minutes each side or until just cooked through. Serve immediately with cooked noodles and a dressed green salad.

Cajun Calamari

REPARATION ME:
5 MINUTES +
HOURS
ARINATING
OOKING TIME:
MINUTES
ERVES 4

$1^1/_4$ lb large calamari (or squid) tubes, cleaned
$^1/_4$ cup lemon juice
2 cloves garlic, crushed
2 teaspoons tomato paste
1 teaspoon garam masala
2 teaspoons ground coriander
2 teaspoons paprika
2 teaspoons seasoned pepper
2 teaspoons superfine sugar
1 tablespoon grated fresh ginger
1 tablespoon olive oil
$^1/_4$ teaspoon ground nutmeg
pinch chili powder

1 Wash calamari thoroughly, removing any membrane. Pat dry with paper towels.

2 Using a sharp knife, cut through one side of each tube, and open out to give a large, flat piece of flesh. With inside facing up, score flesh diagonally, in a criss-cross pattern, taking care not to cut all the way through. Against the grain of those cuts, slice flesh into long strips about $^3/_4$ in thick.

3 Combine juice, garlic, tomato paste, spices, sugar, ginger, oil, nutmeg and chili in a bowl; mix well. Add calamari strips; stir to combine. Cover and refrigerate several hours or overnight. Prepare and heat barbecue 1 hour before cooking.

4 Cook calamari and marinade on a hot lightly greased barbecue grill for 5 minutes or until flesh curls and turns white. Remove from the heat and serve immediately.

Steamed Fish and Vegetable Parcels

PREPARATION TIME:
5 MINUTES
COOKING TIME:
0 MINUTES
SERVES 4

4 thin white-fleshed fish fillets (bream or porgy)
2 tablespoons prepared horseradish cream
1 small tomato, finely chopped
1/2 cup canned corn kernels, drained
2/3 cup shredded cheddar cheese
1 stalk celery, finely chopped
1/2 red sweet bell pepper, finely chopped
3 green onions, chopped
1 1/2 teaspoons dried mixed herbs
salt and pepper, to taste

1 Prepare and heat the barbecue.
2 Grease four large foil sheets, each double thickness.
3 Place a piece of fish in the center of each piece of foil. Spread each fish fillet with a quarter of the horseradish cream.
4 Top each fillet with tomato, corn, cheese, celery, red pepper and green onions. Sprinkle with herbs, salt and pepper. Bring the foil edges together, enclosing the fish in a neat parcel.
5 Cook parcels, fish-side down, on a hot barbecue grill for 5–10 minutes, without turning, until the fish is cooked through. (Check the fish after 5 minutes; cooked fish flakes easily and the flesh turns opaque.) Serve fish and vegetables immediately.

Barbecued Tuna with Onions

PREPARATION TIME:
0 MINUTES +
3 HOURS MARINATING
COOKING TIME:
0 MINUTES
SERVES 4

4 fresh tuna steaks
4 small onions
1 1/2 cups red wine
1/4 cup soft brown sugar
salt and pepper, to taste

Steamed Fish and Vegetable Parcels (above). Barbecued Tuna with Onions

1 Place the tuna in a shallow non-metal dish.
2 Cut the onions in half and slice them finely. Sprinkle them over the fish. Combine the wine, sugar, salt and pepper in a bowl and mix well.
3 Pour the marinade over the fish. Cover and refrigerate for 2–3 hours. Prepare and heat the barbecue 1 hour before cooking.
4 Drain the fish and onion, reserving the marinade.
5 Cook the tuna steaks and onions on a hot lightly greased barbecue griddle (or in a cast iron skillet on the grill) for 8–10 minutes or until lightly browned and just cooked through. Pour the marinade over the tuna and onions, a little at a time, during cooking.

Creole-style Barbecued Shrimp

PREPARATION TIME:
30 MINUTES
COOKING TIME:
8 MINUTES
SERVES 4

1 lb uncooked jumbo shrimp
1/4 cup melted butter
1 teaspoon ground black pepper
1 1/2 teaspoons coarsely cracked black pepper
2 tablespoons Creole Seasoning
2 tablespoons Worcestershire sauce
1 teaspoon crushed garlic
2 tablespoons dry sherry
1/2 cup whipping cream

CREOLE SEASONING
2 tablespoons paprika
1 1/2 tablespoons salt
1 tablespoon onion powder
1 tablespoon garlic powder
2 teaspoons ground black pepper
1 teaspoon cayenne pepper
1 teaspoon ground dried thyme
1 teaspoon ground dried oregano

1 To make Creole Seasoning: Combine all the ingredients thoroughly and store in an airtight container.
2 Remove only the hard portion of the shell covering the shrimp head. Split the shell down the curve of the back with kitchen scissors, but do not

remove it. Lift out the sandy vein. Rinse and dry the shrimp and put them into a bowl.
3 Make a marinade with all the other ingredients except the cream, pour it over the shrimp and mix well. Let stand for at least 10 minutes, or cover and refrigerate until ready to cook and serve.
4 Transfer the shrimp to a preheated lightly greased barbecue grill, reserving the marinade. Cook the shrimp for 5–8 minutes or until they turn pink.
5 Heat the marinade in a small saucepan, add the cream and stir until the sauce bubbles. Pour over the shrimp. Serve with crusty bread. This is finger food, so supply bowls of warm water with a wedge of lemon for freshening up afterwards.

Honeyed Shrimp and Scallop Skewers

PREPARATION TIME:
15 MINUTES + 3 HOURS MARINATING
COOKING TIME:
5 MINUTES
MAKES
8 SKEWERS

1 lb medium uncooked shrimp
8 oz fresh scallops with corals (roe) intact
1/4 cup honey
2 tablespoons soy sauce
1/4 cup bottled barbecue sauce
2 tablespoons sweet sherry

1 Soak eight wooden skewers in water.
2 Remove heads from shrimp. Shell and devein shrimp, keeping the tail shells intact. Clean scallops, removing brown vein.
3 Thread shrimp and scallops alternately onto eight skewers (about three of each per skewer). Place in the base of shallow non-metal dish. Combine honey, sauces and sherry in a bowl and pour over skewers. Cover and refrigerate several hours or overnight. Prepare and heat barbecue 1 hour before cooking.
4 Cook skewers on a hot lightly greased barbecue grill for 5 minutes or until cooked through. Brush frequently with marinade while cooking.

Fish Patties

PREPARATION TIME:
25 MINUTES
COOKING TIME:
10 MINUTES
MAKES
8–10 PATTIES

1 1/2 lb boneless white fish fillets, cut into cubes
1 cup stale white bread crumbs
3 green onions, chopped
1/4 cup lemon juice
2 teaspoons seasoned pepper
1 tablespoon chopped fresh dill
2 tablespoons chopped fresh parsley
3/4 cup shredded cheddar cheese
1 egg
1/2 cup all-purpose flour, for dusting

HERBED MAYONNAISE
1/2 cup mayonnaise
1 tablespoon chopped fresh parsley
1 tablespoon chopped fresh chives
2 teaspoons chopped capers

1 Prepare and heat barbecue. Place fish in food processor bowl. Process for 20–30 seconds until smooth.
2 Place ground fish in a large bowl. Add bread crumbs, green onions, juice, pepper, herbs, cheese and egg. Mix well. Divide into eight to ten portions. Shape into round patties. Place on tray and refrigerate 15 minutes or until firm.
3 Toss patties in flour, shake off excess. Cook on a hot well-greased barbecue grill for 2–3 minutes each side until browned and cooked through. Serve with Herbed Mayonnaise and a green salad.
4 To make Herbed Mayonnaise: Combine mayonnaise, herbs and capers in a small bowl.

Honeyed Shrimp and Scallop Skewers (above). Fish Patties

Seafood and Vegetable Parcels

These tasty parcels are almost a meal on their own. Serve them with steamed rice or tossed salad.

PREPARATION TIME: 15 MINUTES
COOKING TIME: 15 MINUTES
SERVES 4

4 small bream (porgy) fillets
12 large uncooked shrimp, shelled and deveined
8 scallops, cleaned
1 red sweet bell pepper, cut in strips
2 small carrots, cut in strips
2 small zucchini, cut in strips

MARINADE
1/2 cup chopped cilantro leaves
2 tablespoons finely chopped green onions
1/2 teaspoon grated fresh ginger
2 tablespoons white wine
1 tablespoon olive oil
1 teaspoon lemon pepper
2 tablespoons water
2 teaspoons chicken bouillon granules

1 Prepare four sheets of double foil about 12 in square. Top each square of foil with a piece of baking (silicone) paper about the same size. Place a fish fillet on each square. Place three shrimp and two scallops on each fish fillet.
2 Blanch the vegetables for 1 minute in boiling water. Drain and divide evenly between the parcels.
3 To make the marinade: Combine all the ingredients and spoon over the seafood and vegetables. Bring the paper over the top of the seafood and fold tightly to make an enclosed parcel. Wrap the foil over the paper to enclose and strengthen the parcel. Place on a baking sheet.
4 Cook on a preheated moderately hot barbecue grill for approximately 15 minutes.

Note: Be careful not to overcook, as the seafood will become tough very quickly.

Chili Garlic Shrimp

PREPARATION TIME:
5 MINUTES
COOKING TIME:
MINUTES
SERVES 6

2 lb uncooked jumbo shrimp

CHILI-GARLIC OIL
2/3 cup olive oil
1/3 cup butter, melted
4 cloves garlic, crushed
2 teaspoons finely chopped fresh red chiles
1/2 teaspoon ground black pepper
salt, to taste

Shell and devein the shrimp, slit them through he back to butterfly. Heat six cast iron pots on preheated barbecue grill.
To make Chili-Garlic Oil: Combine the emaining ingredients and heat until bubbling hot n a heavy skillet. Add the shrimp and toss until hey are coated with the mixture.
Divide the garlic mixture between the pots and ook until the shrimp curl and turn pink, about or 3 minutes.
Serve immediately with crusty bread.

eafood and Vegetable Parcels (left). Chili Garlic Shrimp

Grilled Baby Octopus

PREPARATION TIME:
15 MINUTES + 3 HOURS MARINATING
COOKING TIME:
5 MINUTES
SERVES 4

2 lb baby octopus
3/4 cup red wine
2 tablespoons balsamic vinegar
2 tablespoons soy sauce
2 tablespoons hoisin sauce
1 clove garlic, crushed

1 Wash octopus thoroughly and wipe dry with paper towels.
2 Use a small sharp knife to slit open the head; remove the gut. Grasp the body firmly and push the beak out with your finger. Remove and discard beak. If octopus are large, cut tentacles in half.
3 Place octopus in a large bowl. Combine wine, vinegar, sauces and garlic in a bowl; add octopus and stir to coat completely. Cover and refrigerate several hours or overnight. Prepare and heat barbecue 1 hour before cooking.
4 Drain octopus; reserve marinade. Cook octopus on a hot, lightly greased barbecue griddle (or in a cast iron skillet on the grill) for 3–5 minutes until octopus flesh turns white. Pour the reserved marinade over while cooking. Serve warm or cold.

Vegetables, salads and breads

Fortunately we have a fantastic variety of salad greens and vegetables to choose from nowadays, and the recipes in this chapter reflect this. Many of the vegetable dishes in this section can be cooked on the barbecue as you are cooking other dishes. During the cooler seasons, when salad ingredients are less abundant, try some of the following vegetable recipes to complement your barbecue menu. Some of these are meals on their own — there is plenty to choose here for vegetarians — barbecues aren't just for the carnivores!

Always be sure to buy good quality salad ingredients and store them in the refrigerator as soon as possible. Wash them well and allow to dry before storing them in large airtight containers if you have them. Otherwise, use plastic bags and close them securely.

Serve salads with a selection of dressings, making use of some of the wonderful flavored vinegars and oils available. Salads should either complement or contrast the meal, and they are also an excellent source of vitamins and minerals. Make use of fresh herbs from the garden to add fragrance and flavor to your vegetable and salad dishes.

Bread is another essential addition to any barbecue, whether as an appetizer or to accompany the main meal. Bread is easy to prepare and some, like Australian damper, herb or garlic bread, can be cooked directly on the barbecue. If you don't have time to make any of the recipes here, buy a selection of rolls and loaves and serve them with an assortment of flavored butters that can be prepared in advance and frozen.

Grilled Potatoes with Pistachio Salsa

PREPARATION TIME:
25 MINUTES
COOKING TIME:
20 MINUTES
SERVES 4

PISTACHIO SALSA
2 ripe tomatoes, chopped
2 cloves garlic, finely chopped
1 small fresh red chile, finely chopped
1 cup shelled pistachio nuts, toasted and chopped
2 tablespoons chopped fresh parsley
1 tablespoon chopped fresh mint
1 teaspoon finely grated lemon rind

1 lb potatoes
1/4 cup all-purpose flour
2 tablespoons olive oil
sour cream, to serve

1 To make the Pistachio Salsa: Combine the tomatoes with the garlic, chile, nuts, herbs, lemon rind and salt and pepper.
2 Peel the potatoes and cut into large wedges. Place in a pan and cover with water, bring to a boil and cook for 5 minutes. Transfer to a colander and rinse under running water to stop the cooking. Pat the wedges dry with paper towels.
3 Sprinkle the flour over the potatoes in a bowl and toss to lightly coat. Place the potato wedges in a single layer on a lightly oiled preheated barbecue grill. Cook for 5–10 minutes, or until golden brown and tender, drizzling with the olive oil and turning the potatoes regularly while cooking. Serve the potato wedges with the Pistachio Salsa and a bowl of sour cream.

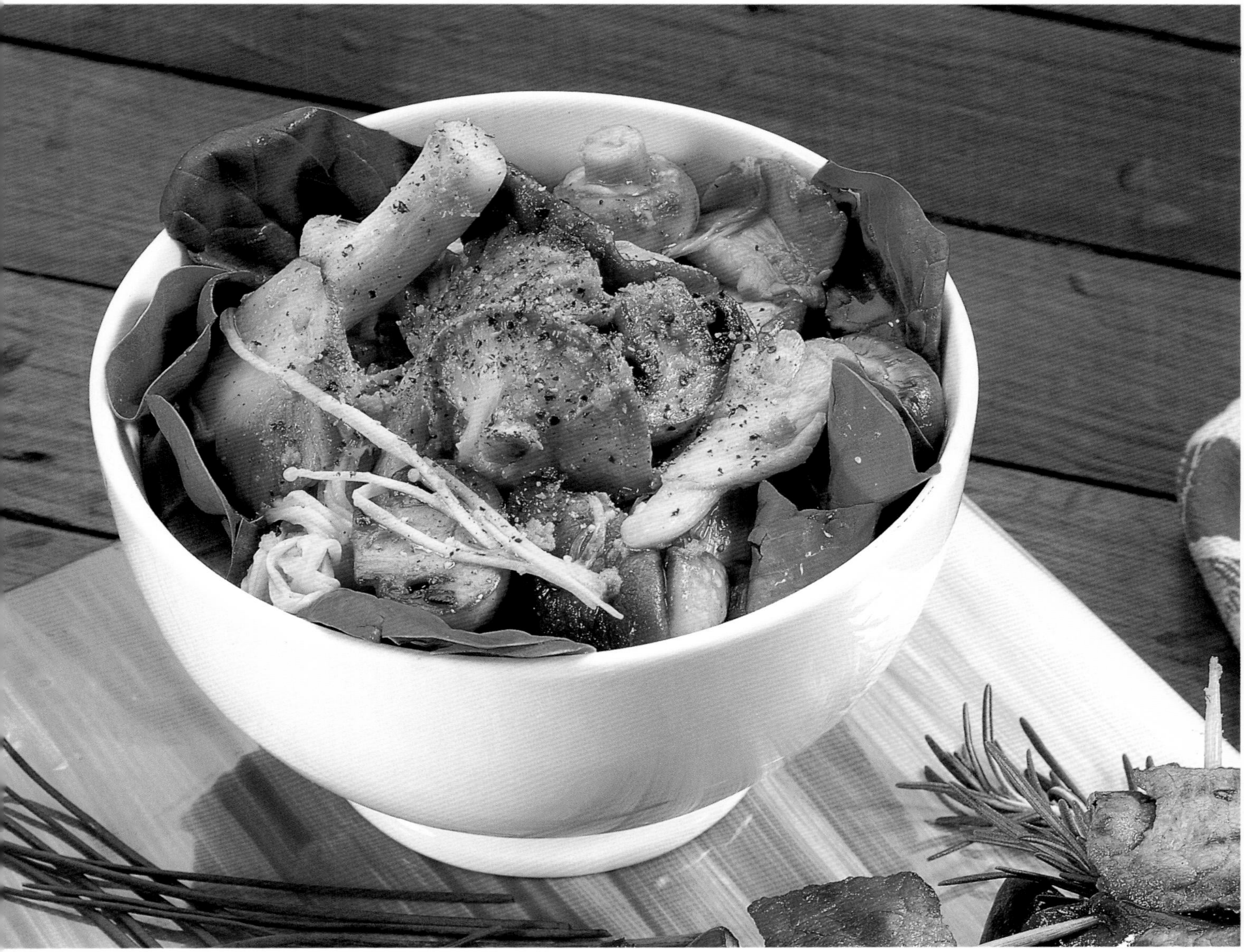

Warm Marinated Mushroom Salad

PREPARATION TIME:
25 MINUTES +
20 MINUTES
MARINATING
COOKING TIME:
5 MINUTES
SERVES 4

$1\frac{1}{2}$ lb mixed mushrooms (such as baby button, oyster, cèpe, shiitake and enoki)
2 cloves garlic, finely chopped
$\frac{1}{2}$ teaspoon green peppercorns, crushed
$\frac{1}{4}$ cup olive oil
$\frac{1}{4}$ cup orange juice
8 oz (about 6 cups) assorted salad leaves, watercress or baby spinach leaves
1 teaspoon finely grated orange rind

1 Trim the mushroom stems and wipe the mushrooms with a damp paper towel. Cut any large mushrooms in half. Mix together the garlic, peppercorns, olive oil and orange juice. Pour over the mushrooms and marinate for about 20 minutes.

2 Arrange the salad leaves in a serving dish.

3 Drain the mushrooms, reserving the marinade. Lightly oil a preheated barbecue grill and cook the flat and button mushrooms for about 2 minutes. Add the softer mushrooms and cook for 1 minute, or until they just soften.

4 Scatter the mushrooms over the salad leaves and drizzle with the marinade. Sprinkle with orange rind and season well with salt and pepper.

Antipasto and Polenta Cakes

PREPARATION TIME:
15 MINUTES +
2 HOURS
REFRIGERATION
COOKING TIME:
35 MINUTES
SERVES 6

3/4 cup polenta (cornmeal)
1 cup shredded cheddar
1/2 cup shredded mozzarella
2 tablespoons chopped fresh parsley
2 teaspoons chopped fresh thyme
1 teaspoon finely chopped fresh rosemary
1/4 cup all-purpose flour
1/4 cup olive oil
10 oz marinated antipasto vegetables

1 Bring 3 cups water to a boil. Gradually add the polenta and stir constantly over medium heat until the mixture comes back to a boil and thickens. Reduce the heat to low and cook, stirring, for about 20 minutes, until the polenta comes away from the side of the pan. Stir in the cheddar and mozzarella, parsley, thyme and rosemary.

2 Lightly brush a 12 x 7 in baking dish with oil, line the base with baking (silicone) paper, spoon in the polenta and smooth the surface. Chill for about 2 hours, or until set.

3 Turn out the solid polenta block and cut out 6 rounds using a 3 in biscuit or cookie cutter. Coat lightly with the flour.

4 Brush a preheated barbecue grill with a little of the olive oil. Cook the polenta cakes, drizzling with the remaining oil, for about 4 minutes on each side, or until they are golden brown. Be careful when handling so the cakes do not break up. Serve with the antipasto vegetables.

Grilled Asparagus

PREPARATION TIME:
5 MINUTES
COOKING TIME:
3 MINUTES
SERVES 4

1 lb asparagus
2 oz piece Parmesan

DRESSING
2 cloves garlic, crushed
2 tablespoons balsamic vinegar
2 tablespoons olive oil

1 Break off any woody ends from the asparagus. Brush with some olive oil and cook on a preheated barbecue grill for about 3 minutes, or until the asparagus is bright green and tender.

2 Using a vegetable peeler, cut shavings from the piece of Parmesan.

3 To make the dressing: Whisk together the garlic, vinegar and olive oil in a bowl.

4 Pour the dressing over the warm asparagus, and top with the Parmesan shavings and lots of freshly ground black pepper.

Barbecued Vegetable Platter

PREPARATION TIME: 25 MINUTES
COOKING TIME: 1 HOUR
SERVES 8

HERB VINAIGRETTE
1/2 cup olive oil
2 tablespoons balsamic vinegar
2 cloves garlic, crushed
2 tablespoons fresh lime juice
1/3 cup chopped fresh mint, basil and cilantro, combined

4 potatoes, unpeeled and halved
12 oz butternut squash, unpeeled and cut into large pieces
10 oz sweet potatoes, unpeeled and cut into large pieces
4 slender eggplants, halved
2 red onions, cut into wedges
1 yellow sweet bell pepper, seeded and quartered
1 red sweet bell pepper, seeded and quartered
1 green sweet bell pepper, seeded and quartered
8 large flat mushrooms, stems trimmed

BASIL MAYONNAISE
4 egg yolks
2 teaspoons mustard
1/4 cup fresh lemon juice
1 2/3 cups olive oil
1/3 cup fresh basil leaves

1 To make the Herb Vinaigrette: Whisk together the ingredients.
2 Preheat the barbecue to high. Brush the potatoes, squash and sweet potatoes with vinaigrette, wrap in foil and cook on the barbecue for 40–50 minutes, or until tender but not so soft they fall apart.
3 Brush the eggplants, onions, peppers and mushrooms with the vinaigrette. Cook vegetables on the barbecue for 10 minutes, or until golden.
4 To make the Basil Mayonnaise: Place the egg yolks, mustard and lemon juice in a food processor and process for 1 minute, or until the mixture is pale and creamy. Slowly add the olive oil while the motor is running. When the mixture is thick, add the basil, salt and pepper and process for 20 seconds.
5 Serve the vegetables drizzled with the remaining vinaigrette and accompanied by the Basil Mayonnaise.

Grilled Kasseri Cheese

PREPARATION TIME:
0 MINUTES
COOKING TIME:
0 MINUTES
SERVES 4

6 oz kasseri cheese, cut into thick slices
2 tablespoons flour
2 teaspoons chopped fresh oregano
2 teaspoons chopped fresh sage or parsley
1 tablespoon chopped fresh chives
1 red sweet bell pepper, seeded and cut into thick strips
4 plum tomatoes, halved
1 zucchini, cut into thick strips
1 teaspoon superfine sugar

1 Coat the cheese slices lightly in the flour. Heat a barbecue griddle (or cast iron skillet on the grill) until moderately hot and add a little olive oil. Cook the cheese for about 3 minutes each side, or until golden brown all over, sprinkling on the chopped herbs. Remove, cover and keep warm.

2 Wipe clean the hot plate and lightly brush with some olive oil. Add the red pepper, tomatoes and zucchini pieces. Sprinkle on the sugar and cook, turning frequently, for 5 minutes, or until softened.

3 Place the vegetables on a plate, top with the cheese and serve with toasted French bread or focaccia.

Note: Kasseri cheese can be substituted with Provolone, Fontina and mozzarella cheeses, if desired.

Lentil and Chickpea Burger with Cilantro Garlic Cream

Cilantro Garlic Cream is delicious with chicken or fish burgers.

PREPARATION TIME: 30 MINUTES
COOKING TIME: 20 MINUTES
MAKES 10 BURGERS

1 cup red lentils
1 tablespoon oil
2 onions, sliced
1 tablespoon tandoori mix powder
16 oz can chickpeas, drained
1 tablespoon grated fresh ginger
1 egg
1/4 cup chopped fresh parsley
2 tablespoons chopped cilantro
2 1/4 cups stale bread crumbs
flour, for dusting

CILANTRO GARLIC CREAM
1/2 cup sour cream
1/2 cup whipping cream, softly whipped
1 clove garlic, crushed
2 tablespoons chopped cilantro
2 tablespoons chopped fresh parsley

1 Prepare and heat the barbecue.
2 Bring a large pan of water to a boil. Add the lentils to boiling water and simmer uncovered for 8 minutes or until tender. Drain well.
3 Heat oil in pan and cook the onions until tender. Add the tandoori mix; stir until fragrant; cool the mixture slightly.
4 Place the chickpeas, half the lentils, ginger, egg and onion mixture in a food processor bowl. Process for 20 seconds or until smooth. Transfer to a bowl. Stir in the remaining lentils, parsley, cilantro and bread crumbs and combine well.
5 Divide the mixture into ten portions. Shape the portions into round patties using your hands. (If the mixture is too soft, refrigerate for 15 minutes or until firm.) Coat the patties in flour. Shake off excess.
6 Place the patties on a hot lightly greased barbecue grill. Cook for 3–4 minutes each side or until browned, turning once. Serve with Cilantro Garlic Cream.
7 To make Cilantro Garlic Cream: Combine the sour cream, cream, garlic and herbs in a bowl and mix well.

Spiced Sweet Potatoes

PREPARATION TIME:
20 MINUTES
COOKING TIME:
25 MINUTES
SERVES 4–6

1 lb sweet potatoes
1/4 cup demerara sugar
3/4 teaspoon mixed spice
2 tablespoons butter, chopped
1/3 cup orange juice

1 Prepare the Weber (kettle) barbecue for indirect cooking at moderate heat (normal fire). Peel the sweet potatoes and cut into thick slices.
2 Arrange the slices in layers in a shallow greased baking pan. Sprinkle the combined sugar and mixed spice over and dot with butter. Sprinkle with the orange juice.
3 Cover the pan with foil, place on the grill of the barbecue, replace the lid and cook for 20 minutes. Remove the foil and test with a sharp knife; cook for a few more minutes, if necessary. Sprinkle with a little more orange juice if the potatoes begin to dry out.

Stuffed Golden Nugget Squash

Prepare these stuffed squash up to the final stages of cooking, set aside and finish the cooking just prior to serving.

PREPARATION TIME:
10 MINUTES
COOKING TIME:
10 MINUTES
SERVES 6–8

2 golden nugget or acorn squash

FILLING

- **4 green onions, chopped**
- **10 green beans, chopped**
- **1/2 red sweet bell pepper, chopped**
- **1 small seedless cucumber, halved and chopped**
- **1 clove garlic, crushed**
- **1 tablespoon beef bouillon granules**
- **1 teaspoon turmeric**
- **1/2 teaspoon ground pepper**
- **1/2 cup pecan pieces**
- **1/2 cup fresh bread crumbs**
- **2 teaspoons Worcestershire sauce**
- **1/4 cup olive oil**

1 Remove tops from the squash. Remove seeds with a spoon and discard. Cover with plastic wrap; microwave on High (100%) for 3 minutes. Or blanch squash in boiling water until barely tender, drain and cool under running water. Let stand while you prepare the filling.
2 Blend the green onions, beans, red pepper and cucumber in a food processor until finely chopped. Add the remaining ingredients and mix well. Spoon the mixture into the squash.
3 Barbecue over a high heat for 10 minutes.
4 Cut each squash into three slices or quarters to serve.

Note: If preferred, substitute 12 medium mushroom caps for the squash. Cook directly on the barbecue for 4–5 minutes. Serve immediately. Squash can also be cooked in a 350°F oven for 15–20 minutes or until tender. Larger zucchini may also be used for this recipe. Slice in half lengthwise and remove the center with a small teaspoon. Place the stuffing inside the hollow and barbecue over a low heat for 8 minutes.

Barbecued Vegetable Kebabs

For extra flavor, serve with Herb Butter (see page 239).

PREPARATION TIME:
20 MINUTES
COOKING TIME:
15 MINUTES
SERVES 6

- **6 small onions**
- **12 button mushrooms**
- **2 small zucchini**
- **1 red sweet bell pepper**
- **12 large cherry tomatoes**

MARINADE

- **1/2 cup olive oil**
- **2 tablespoons lemon juice**
- **1 teaspoon lemon pepper**
- **2 teaspoons chopped fresh thyme or 1/2 teaspoon dried thyme**

1 Peel the onions and blanch in boiling water for 5 minutes or until barely tender. Drain, cool in iced water and set aside.
2 Trim the mushrooms, slice the zucchini and cut the red pepper into large pieces. Thread all the vegetables and tomatoes alternately onto skewers and place in a shallow dish.
3 To make the marinade: Combine all the ingredients and pour over the vegetables. Allow to marinate for 30 minutes, turning occasionally.
4 Cook the kebabs on a preheated barbecue for 8 minutes or until vegetables are tender, turning after 4 minutes and basting from time to time with the remaining marinade.

Note: When buying cherry tomatoes for kebabs, choose those which are hard and firm so they will remain on the skewers when barbecued. Use any fresh seasonal vegetables for this recipe. When purchasing vegetables, always select items free from blemishes and decay. Vegetables that have been grown locally and purchased in season are less costly than those imported when they otherwise would not be available.

Stuffed Golden Nugget Squash (above). Barbecued Vegetable Kebabs. Australian Damper (page 207)

Barbecued Portobellos

Any type of fresh mushroom with a large, flat cap can be used in this recipe.

PREPARATION TIME: 10 MINUTES
COOKING TIME: 5 MINUTES
SERVES 6

6 Portobello mushrooms
1/4 cup butter, melted
2 cloves garlic, crushed
2 tablespoons finely chopped fresh chives
1 tablespoon fresh thyme leaves
1/2 cup grated Parmesan

1 Prepare and heat the barbecue. Carefully peel the skin from the mushroom caps. Remove the stalks.
2 Combine the butter and garlic in a small bowl. Brush the tops of mushrooms with garlic butter, place top-side down on hot barbecue and cook over the hottest part of the fire for 2 minutes or until the tops have browned. Turn the mushrooms over. Brush with garlic butter; cook for 2 minutes.
3 Sprinkle with combined chives and thyme, then the cheese and cook another 3 minutes, until the cheese begins to melt. Serve immediately.

Barbecued Portobellos (above). Chinese Vegetable Stir-fry

Chinese Vegetable Stir-fry

REPARATION
IME:
0 MINUTES
OOKING TIME:
MINUTES
ERVES 4–6

1 medium red sweet bell pepper
3 oz oyster mushrooms
16 oz can baby corn
1 lb Chinese cabbage
1 tablespoon olive oil
8 oz fresh bean sprouts
5 green onions, cut into $1^1/_4$ in pieces
2 cloves garlic, crushed
1 tablespoon olive oil
2 teaspoons sesame oil
2 tablespoons teriyaki marinade
$^1/_2$ teaspoon sugar
sweet chili sauce, to taste

Prepare and heat the barbecue. Cut the red epper in half and remove the seeds and membrane. Cut into thin strips.

Slice the mushrooms in half. Cut any large baby orn in half. Cut the cabbage into thick slices, then rosswise into squares.

Brush the barbecue griddle (or a wok on the rill) with oil. Stir-fry the red pepper, mushrooms, orn, cabbage, sprouts, green onions and garlic for minutes, tossing and stirring to prevent burning r sticking.

Pour the combined olive oil, sesame oil, teriyaki arinade and sugar over and stir thoroughly to coat. Cook for 1 minute longer. Serve immediately. Drizzle with sweet chili sauce.

Marinated Grilled Vegetables

REPARATION
IME:
0 MINUTES +
HOUR
IARINATING
OOKING TIME:
MINUTES
ERVES 6

3 small slender eggplants
2 small red sweet bell peppers
3 medium zucchini
6 medium mushrooms

MARINADE
$^1/_4$ cup olive oil
$^1/_4$ cup lemon juice
$^1/_4$ cup shredded basil leaves
1 clove garlic, crushed

1 Cut the eggplants into diagonal slices. Place on paper towels in a single layer; sprinkle with salt and let them stand for 15 minutes. Rinse thoroughly and pat dry with more paper towels.

2 Trim the red peppers, removing the seeds and membrane, and cut into long, wide pieces. Cut the zucchini into diagonal slices. Trim each mushroom stalk so that it is level with the cap. Place all the vegetables in a large, shallow non-metal dish.

3 To make the marinade: Place the oil, juice, basil and garlic in a small screw-top jar. Shake vigorously to combine. Pour over the vegetables and combine well. Store, covered with plastic wrap, in the refrigerator for 1 hour, stirring occasionally. Prepare and heat the barbecue.

4 Place the vegetables on a hot, lightly greased barbecue grill. Cook each vegetable piece over the hottest part of the fire for 2 minutes each side. Transfer to a serving dish once browned. Brush the vegetables frequently with any remaining marinade while cooking.

Corn on the Cob with Tomato Relish

PREPARATION TIME:
15 MINUTES
COOKING TIME:
1 HOUR
SERVES 6

TOMATO RELISH
16 oz can peeled tomatoes
2/3 cup white vinegar
1/2 cup sugar
1 clove garlic, finely chopped
2 green onions, finely chopped
4 sun-dried tomatoes, finely chopped
1 small fresh red chile, finely chopped
1/2 teaspoon salt
1/2 teaspoon cracked black pepper

6 large cobs fresh corn
1–2 tablespoons olive or vegetable oil
1/4 cup butter, to serve
salt to taste

1 To make the Tomato Relish: Coarsely chop the tomatoes or process them briefly in a food processor.

2 Combine the vinegar and sugar in a medium pan. Stir over a medium heat until the sugar dissolves. Bring to a boil. Reduce the heat and simmer for 2 minutes.

3 Add the tomatoes, garlic, green onions, sun-dried tomatoes and chile. Bring to a boil, reduce heat and simmer for 35 minutes, stirring frequently. Add salt and pepper and continue to cook until the relish has thickened. Remove from the heat and allow to cool.

4 Prepare and heat the barbecue. Brush the corn with oil and cook on the hot lightly greased barbecue grill for 5 minutes each side, until the corn is soft and flecked with brown in places. Using tongs, lift the corn onto a serving platter and moisten each with a square of butter. Sprinkle with salt. Serve at once with Tomato Relish.

Baked Vegetables

If barbecuing a chicken or leg of lamb, cook the vegetables simultaneously, timing them to be ready with the meat.

PREPARATION TIME:
20 MINUTES
COOKING TIME:
1 HOUR
15 MINUTES
SERVES 6

6 medium potatoes
1/4 cup butter, melted
1/4 teaspoon paprika
1 1/2 lb butternut squash
6 small onions
5 oz green beans
5 oz broccoli
1 tablespoon butter, chopped, extra

1 Prepare the Weber (kettle) barbecue for indirect cooking at moderate heat (normal fire). Peel the potatoes and cut in half.

2 Using a small, sharp knife, make deep, fine cuts into the potatoes, taking care not to cut all the way through. Take two large sheets of aluminum foil, fold them in half and brush liberally with some melted butter. Place the potatoes unscored-side down on the foil and fold up the edges of foil to create a tray. Brush potatoes generously with melted butter and sprinkle with paprika.

3 Cut the squash into three wedges and cut each wedge in half. Peel the onions and trim the bases slightly, so they will sit flat on the grill. Brush the squash and onions with melted butter. Place the foil tray of potatoes, squash pieces and onions on the barbecue grill. Put the lid on the barbecue and cook for 1 hour.

4 Trim the beans; cut the broccoli into florets. Place them on a sheet of foil brushed with melted butter. Dot with extra butter and enclose completely in foil. Add the 'parcel' to the other vegetables on the grill and cook another 15 minutes. (See photograph page 50.)

Red Potato Salad

PREPARATION TIME:
20 MINUTES
COOKING TIME:
10 MINUTES
SERVES 6

2 1/2 lb red-skinned potatoes
1 medium red onion
2 teaspoons oil
3 slices bacon, finely chopped
3/4 cup whole egg mayonnaise
3/4 cup plain yogurt
3 green onions, finely chopped

1 Scrub the potatoes thoroughly and cut into 1 1/4 in pieces. Cook potatoes in a large pan of boiling water for 5 minutes or until just tender. Drain and cool completely.

2 Cut the onion in half and slice finely. Heat the oil in a skillet. Cook the bacon for 5 minutes or until well browned and crisp. Drain on paper towels.

3 Place potatoes, bacon and onion in a large mixing bowl. Combine the mayonnaise, yogurt and green onions in a small mixing bowl and pour over the potato mixture.

4 Fold in gently, taking care not to break up the potatoes. Transfer to a large serving bowl and serve at room temperature.

Beets with Mustard Cream Dressing

PREPARATION TIME: 10 MINUTES
COOKING TIME: APPROXIMATELY 1 HOUR 15 MINUTES
SERVES 6–8

2 slices bacon, finely chopped
1 bunch fresh beets

MUSTARD CREAM DRESSING
1 cup sour cream
1 tablespoon prepared horseradish cream
1 tablespoon grainy mustard
1/2 teaspoon hot mustard powder (optional)
salt and pepper, to taste
3–4 fresh chives

1 Cook the bacon in a skillet for 5–10 minutes until crisp. Drain on paper towels and set aside.
2 Trim the beets by removing the stems and leaves. Place in a pan and cover with cold water. Bring to a boil, reduce the heat and simmer gently for 1 hour or until the beets are tender.
3 Drain the beets and set aside until cool. Peel and cut them into wedges. (Leave any small beets whole.) Arrange in a serving bowl.
4 To make Mustard Cream Dressing: Combine the sour cream, horseradish and mustard and beat until smooth. Add the hot mustard and season with salt and pepper. Pour the dressing over the beets and top with fried bacon and snipped chives.

Rosemary Sautéed Potatoes

PREPARATION TIME:
10 MINUTES
COOKING TIME:
25 MINUTES
SERVES 6

4–5 large potatoes
$^1/_3$ cup olive oil
1 tablespoon chopped fresh rosemary
1 clove garlic, crushed
salt and black pepper, to taste

1 Peel the potatoes and cut them into $^3/_4$ in cubes. Rinse the potatoes in cold water, drain well and dry thoroughly on a clean tea towel.

2 Heat the oil in a large heavy-based skillet. Add the potatoes and cook slowly, shaking the pan occasionally, for 20 minutes or until tender. Turn the potatoes frequently to prevent sticking. Partially cover the pan halfway through the cooking. The steam will help to cook the potatoes through.

3 Add the rosemary and garlic, with salt and pepper to taste, in the last few minutes of cooking. Increase the heat to crisp the potatoes, if required.

Stuffed Squash with Cheesy Sauce

These stuffed squash are a meal in one. Make them in advance and set aside. Do the final stages of cooking when ready to serve. Two medium butternut squash can be used.

PREPARATION TIME:
35 MINUTES
COOKING TIME:
35 MINUTES
SERVES 8

8 golden nugget or acorn squash
3 small carrots, peeled
3 small zucchini
3 oz mushrooms
1 large potato, peeled
3 oz green beans
1/4 cup olive oil
2 onions, finely chopped
1 clove garlic, crushed

SAUCE
2 tablespoons butter
1/4 cup all-purpose flour
3/4 cup whipping cream
3/4 cup milk
1 cup shredded cheddar
2 tablespoons chopped chives
salt and pepper, to taste

1 Remove the tops from the squash and scoop out the seeds with a spoon. Place the squash and tops in a large baking pan with 1/4 cup water. Cover with foil and bake in a preheated 400°F oven for 20 minutes or until tender. Allow to cool.
2 Slice the carrots, zucchini and mushrooms and dice the potato. Trim the beans and cut them into bite-size pieces.
3 Heat the olive oil in a large pan and cook the onions and garlic until soft and golden. Add the carrots and potatoes. Stir to coat with the oil, cover and cook the vegetables over a low heat for 5 minutes. Add the remaining vegetables and cook covered until tender, adding a little water from time to time to prevent them sticking.

Marinated Barbecued Mushrooms (above). Stuffed Squash with Cheesy Sauce

4 To make the sauce: In a separate pan, melt the butter and add the flour. Stir over a moderate heat for 1–2 minutes. Remove the pan from the heat and add the cream and milk. Continue to cook, stirring, until the sauce simmers and thickens. Add half the shredded cheese, chives, salt and pepper to taste.
5 Add the sauce to the vegetables and mix well. Spoon the prepared vegetables into the squash shells. Sprinkle with a little extra cheese and replace the tops. Place in a shallow baking pan, with a little water to prevent burning. Cover with foil and then set aside.
6 Place onto a preheated barbecue grill and cook for 10–15 minutes or until the cheese melts and squash are heated through. Serve immediately.

Marinated Barbecued Mushrooms

For best results, use white button mushrooms, fully closed; the firmer, the better.

PREPARATION TIME:
10 MINUTES
COOKING TIME:
2–5 MINUTES
SERVES 4–6

1 lb firm button mushrooms
$^{1}/_{4}$ cup olive oil
1 clove garlic, crushed
2 tablespoons lime juice
salt and pepper, to taste

1 Wipe any dirt from the mushrooms with damp paper towels. Trim the ends off the stems and discard. Slice the mushrooms, not too thinly.
2 In a bowl, combine the oil, garlic, lime juice, salt and pepper. Toss the sliced mushrooms in this dressing and allow to stand for about half an hour before cooking.
3 Cook the mushrooms over a high heat on the barbecue griddle (or in a cast iron skillet on the grill). Toss the mushroom slices constantly until starting to brown. Serve as a side dish to meat or chicken.

Ratatouille

A flavorsome combination of vegetables. Make it in advance and warm in a large pan on the edge of the barbecue. This is also a perfect vegetarian meal for four people when served with crusty bread rolls.

PREPARATION TIME:
25 MINUTES
COOKING TIME:
40 MINUTES
SERVES
8 AS AN ACCOMPANIMENT

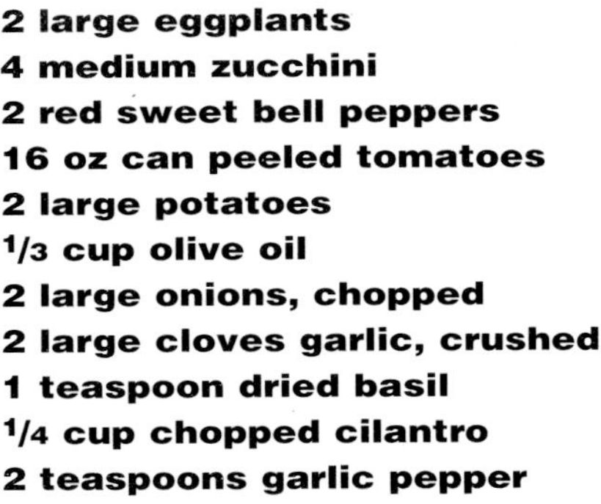

2 large eggplants
4 medium zucchini
2 red sweet bell peppers
16 oz can peeled tomatoes
2 large potatoes
1/3 cup olive oil
2 large onions, chopped
2 large cloves garlic, crushed
1 teaspoon dried basil
1/4 cup chopped cilantro
2 teaspoons garlic pepper seasoning

1 Wash the eggplants, zucchini and red peppers. Cut the eggplants into large pieces and thickly slice zucchini. Remove the seeds from the peppers and cut them into large pieces. Drain the tomatoes, reserving the liquid, and coarsely chop. Peel the potatoes and cut into large cubes.
2 Heat the olive oil in a large pan or wok, and cook the onions and garlic until the onions are tender. Add the prepared eggplants, zucchini and peppers. Cook for 1–2 minutes. Add the tomatoes and reserved juice with the potatoes, basil, cilantro and garlic pepper seasoning. Cover and cook, adding a little water to prevent sticking if necessary, for 30 minutes or until the vegetables are tender.
3 Serve hot immediately or keep warm on the edge of the barbecue, stirring occasionally until served.

Note: If you enjoy a more fiery dish, try adding 2 teaspoons of sambal oelek or chili paste with the peeled tomatoes. Sambal oelek is a prepared chili relish of Indonesian origin, containing chile, garlic and salt. It is used as a flavor enhancer, making the dish hotter and more appetizing. Sambal oelek is available from most supermarkets and Asian food stores.

Broccoli and Cauliflower with Sesame Soy Dressing

If your barbecue set-up does not include a wok, this can easily be prepared back in the kitchen. Simply steam the broccoli and cauliflower over a little boiling water or microwave until tender. Prepare the sauce in a small pan and spoon over the vegetables when ready to serve.

PREPARATION TIME:
10 MINUTES
COOKING TIME:
4 MINUTES
SERVES 6

4 cups water
4 cups broccoli florets
4 cups cauliflower florets

SAUCE
1/4 cup dry sherry
2 tablespoons water
1/4 cup dark soy sauce (see note)
2 teaspoons grated fresh green ginger
2 teaspoons sugar
1/2 cup toasted sesame seeds, crushed
2 teaspoons cornstarch
1/4 cup water

1 Bring water to a boil in a wok or large pan. Drop in the broccoli and cauliflower and boil, covered, for 4 minutes. Drain; place on a serving dish.
2 To make the sauce: Place the sherry, water, soy sauce, ginger, sugar and crushed sesame seeds in the wok. Bring to a boil. Meanwhile, combine the cornstarch and water, and add to the simmering mixture. Stir until thickened and pour over the broccoli and cauliflower. Serve with barbecued fish.

Note: Dark soy sauce is less salty and more caramelized than the lighter styles of soy sauces available.

Ratatouille (above). Broccoli and Cauliflower with Sesame Soy Dressing

Hot Mushrooms and Tomatoes

When making foil parcels for the barbecue, use a double thickness of foil.

PREPARATION TIME:
10 MINUTES
COOKING TIME:
10 MINUTES
SERVES 6

12 oz button mushrooms
3 tomatoes, finely diced
6 green onions, finely chopped
2 teaspoons herb pepper seasoning
1/4 cup butter
Tabasco sauce, to taste

1 Wipe the mushrooms and place evenly into the base of six small foil pot pie dishes. Alternatively, prepare six squares of heavy-duty or industrial-strength foil.

2 Put the diced tomatoes and chopped green onions into the pie dishes or on the foil squares. Sprinkle each parcel with herb pepper seasoning to taste. Dot the tops of each parcel with a little butter and Tabasco sauce. Cover the foil dishes with foil or enclose the ingredients in the prepared foil squares.

3 Place on the outer edge of a preheated barbecue grill and cook for 10 minutes or until heated through. Serve immediately as a side dish to meat and poultry.

Spicy Mint Potatoes

This subtle combination of sharp cheese and spicy curry powder helps lift the humble potato to new heights of flavor.

PREPARATION TIME:
25 MINUTES
COOKING TIME:
30 MINUTES
SERVES 6

6 medium potatoes
2 tablespoons butter
1/4 cup lemon juice
1 tablespoon chicken bouillon granules
2 tablespoons hot milk
1/2 cup finely chopped fresh mint
2 green onions, finely chopped
1/2 cup shredded cheddar
1 teaspoon mild curry powder

1 Wash the potatoes and pierce with a fork or skewer. Place evenly around the turntable of the microwave. Cook the potatoes on High (100%) for 12 minutes and allow to stand for 10 minutes. Or cook the potatoes on a rack in a preheated 350°F oven for about 30 minutes or until just tender. Cut the potatoes in half and scoop out the centers. Place the shells in a shallow baking pan and the potato flesh into a bowl.

2 Mash the potato flesh and add the butter, lemon juice, chicken bouillon and milk. Mix until smooth. Add the chopped mint and green onions. Spoon the mixture into the potato shells.

3 Combine cheese with curry powder and sprinkle on top of the potatoes. Cover the tray with foil.

4 Place the tray on a preheated barbecue and cook over a moderate heat for about 15 minutes or until the potatoes are hot and the cheese is bubbly.

Jacket Potatoes

Jacket potatoes always go down well at a barbecue. Cook them alongside the other food or in the oven, and try them with one of the following toppings.

PREPARATION TIME:
10 MINUTES
COOKING TIME:
30–60 MINUTES
SERVES 4

4 large baking potatoes

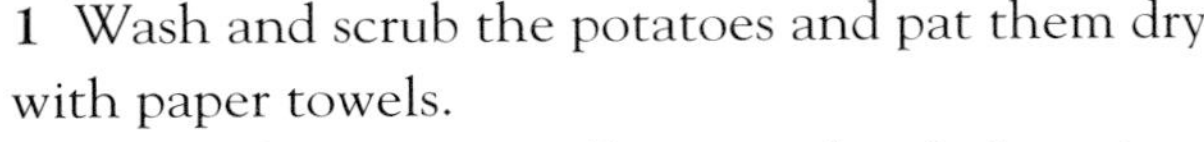

1 Wash and scrub the potatoes and pat them dry with paper towels.
2 Pierce the potatoes all over with a fork or skewer and wrap them individually with foil.
3 Place the wrapped potatoes around the hot coals of the barbecue or on the top grill of a preheated kettle barbecue. Cook for 30–60 minutes (depending on the size of the potatoes). Insert a sharp knife or skewer in the center to test if potatoes are cooked.
4 When cooked, remove the foil from the potatoes and cut a large cross in the top of each. Squeeze to open and soften the potato flesh by mashing it gently with a fork. Mix a flavored butter (see page 239) into the flesh and top with the topping of your choice. Serve hot.

Herbed Sour Cream Topping

PREPARATION TIME:
5 MINUTES
COOKING TIME:
NONE
SERVES 2–4

1 cup sour cream
1 tablespoon chopped chives
1 tablespoon chopped oregano
1 tablespoon chopped parsley
2 teaspoons chopped mint
salt and pepper, to taste
1 clove garlic, crushed (optional)

1 Combine all the ingredients in a bowl and mix well. Spoon over hot jacket potato and serve.

Jacket Potatoes with: Herbed Sour Cream Topping (above); Sweet Chili Vegetable Topping (center); Mushroom and Bacon Topping

Sweet Chili Vegetable Topping

REPARATION
IME:
0 MINUTES
OOKING TIME:
–4 MINUTES
ERVES 1–2

1 tablespoon sesame oil
1 clove garlic, crushed
1 tablespoon soy sauce
2–3 teaspoons sweet chili sauce
1 tablespoon plum sauce
1 small carrot, thinly sliced
1/2 red sweet bell pepper, thinly sliced
3/4 cup small broccoli florets
1 small zucchini, thinly sliced
2 green onions, sliced
salt and pepper, to taste

Heat the sesame oil in a wok or large skillet and dd the garlic, soy sauce, chili sauce, plum sauce, arrot, red pepper, broccoli and zucchini. Cook for –3 minutes.

Add the green onions and season with pepper and alt. Spoon over the hot jacket potatoes and serve.

Mushroom and Bacon Topping

REPARATION
IME:
MINUTES
OOKING TIME:
–6 MINUTES
ERVES 2–4

2 tablespoons butter
1 clove garlic, crushed
2 slices bacon, thinly sliced
10 large mushrooms, sliced
1/4 cup whipping cream
1 tablespoon chopped chives
salt and pepper, to taste
shaved Parmesan, to serve

Heat the butter in a skillet and add the garlic nd bacon. Cook for 1 minute.

Stir in the sliced mushrooms and cook another –4 minutes until the mushrooms are soft.

Stir in the cream and chives, season with salt nd pepper and cook for 1 minute.

Spoon the mixture over hot jacket potatoes nd serve sprinkled with shaved Parmesan.

Baby Barbecued Potatoes

PREPARATION
TIME:
20 MINUTES +
1 HOUR STANDING
COOKING TIME:
20 MINUTES
SERVES 6

1 1/2 lb baby potatoes
2 tablespoons olive oil
2 tablespoons fresh thyme leaves
2 teaspoons crushed sea salt

1 Wash potatoes under cold water. Cut any large potatoes in half so they are uniform for even cooking.
2 Boil, steam or microwave the potatoes until just tender. (Potatoes should remain whole and intact.) Drain and lightly dry with paper towels.
3 Place the potatoes in a large mixing bowl; add oil and thyme. Toss gently to coat potatoes and let stand for 1 hour. Prepare and heat the barbecue.
4 Place potatoes on a hot, lightly greased barbecue griddle (or a cast iron skillet on the grill). Cook for 15 minutes, turning frequently and brushing with remaining oil and thyme mixture, until golden brown. Place in a serving bowl and sprinkle with salt and extra thyme sprigs, if desired.

Avocado, Mango and Walnut Salad

PREPARATION TIME: 15 MINUTES
COOKING TIME: 5 MINUTES
SERVES 6

3 slices bacon
1 butter lettuce (Boston or Bibb)
2 mangoes
2 avocados
1/2 cup walnut halves

DRESSING
1/4 cup olive oil
2 tablespoons lemon juice
1 teaspoon French mustard
1 tablespoon whipping cream

1 Coarsely chop the bacon. Cook the bacon in a lightly oiled pan until crisp. Allow to cool on paper towels.
2 Wash the lettuce, separate the leaves, dry gently and place in a serving bowl.
3 A short time before required, peel and slice the mangoes and avocados. Arrange them over the lettuce and sprinkle with chopped bacon and walnut halves. Cover with plastic wrap but do not chill as the flavors are best at room temperature.
4 To make the dressing: Place the ingredients in a small bowl and whisk until well combined. Drizzle over the Avocado, Mango and Walnut Salad when ready to serve.

Avocado, Mango and Walnut Salad, (above). Tomato and Mozzarella Salad (right). Five Bean Salad

Five Bean Salad

PREPARATION TIME:
10 MINUTES
COOKING TIME:
NONE
SERVES 8–10

1/3 cup mayonnaise
1 small red onion or 2 green onions, chopped
ground pepper, to taste
8 oz fresh mung bean sprouts
24 oz (about 3 cups) canned mixed beans, drained
16 oz can corn kernels, drained
1/4 cup dried currants
2 tablespoons golden raisins
1 red sweet bell pepper, diced
1/4 cup pecan pieces, toasted

1 In a large bowl, mix together the mayonnaise, onion and pepper. Add all the other ingredients, except pecans, and mix well. Cover with plastic wrap. Chill.
2 Toss the salad just before serving. Sprinkle the top with pecans to garnish.

Note: Red or Italian onions are milder than their brown or white cousins, and ideal in salads.

Tomato and Mozzarella Salad

PREPARATION TIME:
10 MINUTES
COOKING TIME:
NONE
SERVES 8

6 firm, ripe tomatoes
8 oz mozzarella, thinly sliced
1 small red onion, finely chopped
20 fresh basil leaves, finely chopped
1 tablespoon capers

DRESSING
1/4 cup extra virgin olive oil
1 tablespoon lemon juice
salt and pepper, to taste

1 Slice the tomatoes 1/8 in thick, and alternate with slices of cheese in a large serving dish. Sprinkle with chopped onion, basil and capers.
2 To make the dressing: Combine all the ingredients in a small bowl. Drizzle the dressing over the salad when ready to serve.

Rice Salad with Lime

PREPARATION TIME:
10 MINUTES
COOKING TIME:
NONE
SERVES 6

4 cups cold cooked rice
2 seedless cucumbers, diced
1 red sweet bell pepper, finely diced
1 cup finely chopped cilantro

DRESSING
1/4 cup olive oil
2 tablespoons lime juice
2 teaspoons grated lime rind
1 teaspoon ground sweet paprika
1/2 teaspoon salt
1 clove garlic, crushed

1 Place the rice in a bowl, add cucumbers, red pepper and cilantro. Mix well.
2 To make the dressing: Combine all the ingredients and pour over the rice mixture. Toss lightly together and serve the rice salad immediately.

Note: Lime juice adds a particular flavor to this salad. As a second choice, lemon juice can be used if limes are not available.

Mixed Herb Tabbouleh

PREPARATION TIME:
20 MINUTES
COOKING TIME:
NONE
SERVES 8

3/4 cup bulghur (cracked wheat)
3/4 cup hot water
2 bunches fresh parsley
1 bunch chives
1 1/2 cups fresh basil leaves
1/2 cup fresh mint leaves
4 green onions, finely chopped
3 medium tomatoes, chopped
1/3 cup lemon juice
1/4 cup olive oil

1 Combine the bulghur and hot water in a medium bowl and stand for 15 minutes or until all the water has been absorbed.
2 Remove the large stalks from the parsley and discard. Wash and dry the other herbs thoroughly. Chop well with a large, sharp knife or in a food processor. (If using a food processor, take care not to over-process.)
3 Place the bulghur, parsley, chives, basil, mint, green onions, tomatoes, juice and oil in a serving bowl; toss to combine. Refrigerate until required.

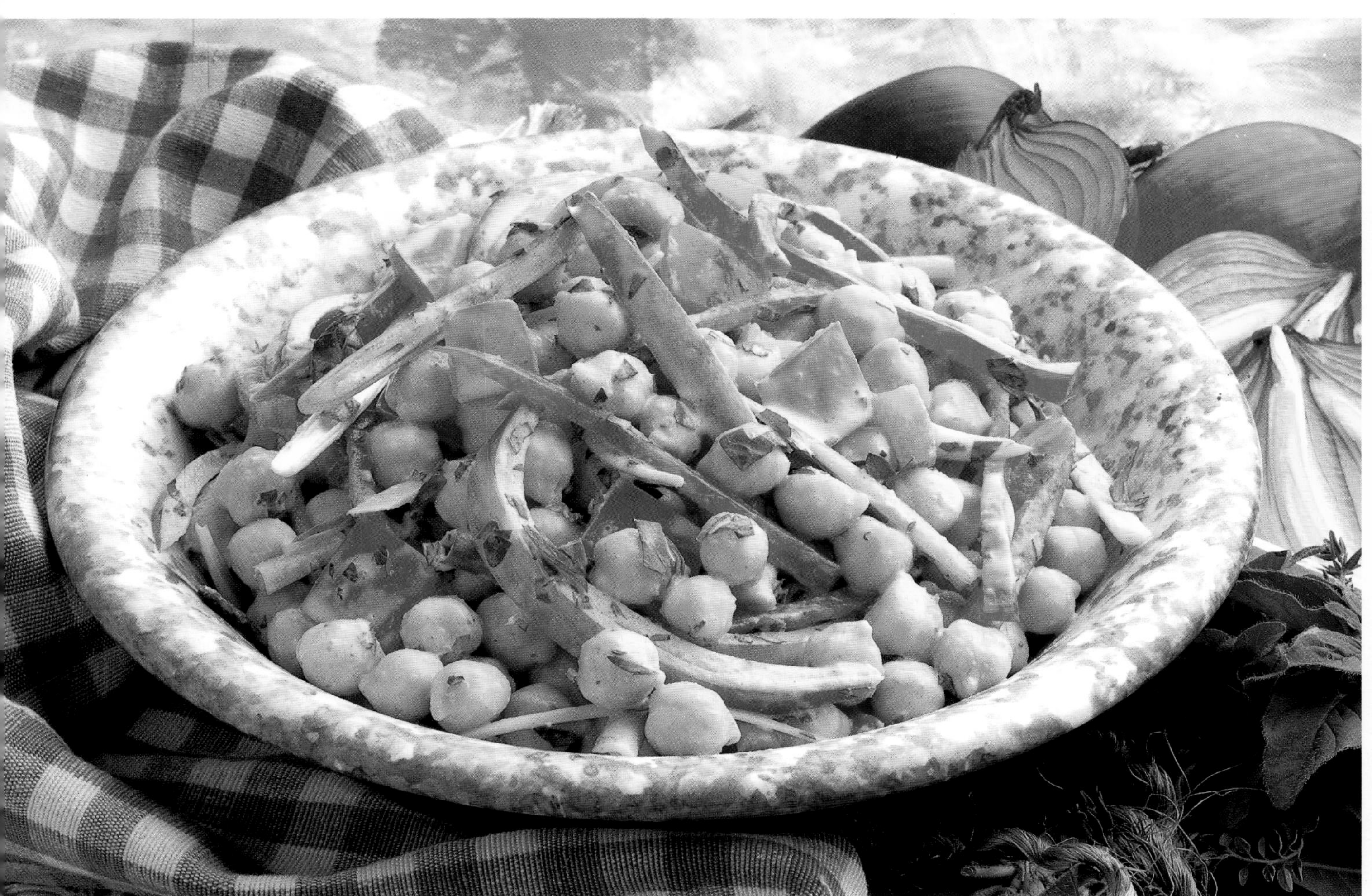

Chickpea Salad

REPARATION
IME:
0 MINUTES
OOKING TIME:
ONE OR
HOURS
0 MINUTES (IF
SING DRIED
EAS)
ERVES 6–8

1 3/4 cups dried chickpeas, or 2 large cans chickpeas
7 cups water
1/4 cup olive oil
1 medium red onion
3 medium tomatoes
1 small red sweet bell pepper
4 green onions
1 cup chopped fresh parsley
2–3 tablespoons chopped fresh mint leaves

DRESSING
2 tablespoons tahini (sesame paste)
2 tablespoons fresh lemon juice
2 tablespoons water
1/4 cup olive oil
2 cloves garlic, crushed
1/2 teaspoon ground cumin
salt and pepper, to taste

1 If using dried chickpeas, place in a medium pan. Cover with water and oil; bring to a boil. Partially cover and cook on a medium heat for 2fi hours or until tender. (Chickpeas will cook in about 30 minutes in a pressure cooker.)
2 Pour the chickpeas into a colander. Rinse them thoroughly with cold water and set aside to drain. If using canned chickpeas, drain well, rinse and drain again.
3 Peel the onion and slice it thinly. Cut the tomatoes in half and remove the seeds with a spoon. Cut the tomato flesh into small pieces. Slice the red pepper and green onions into long thin strips.
4 Combine the onion, tomatoes, red pepper and green onions in a bowl. Add the cooled chickpeas, parsley and mint.
5 To make the dressing: Combine the tahini, juice, water, oil, garlic, cumin, salt and pepper in a screw-top jar and shake vigorously to make a creamy liquid. Pour over the salad and mix well.

Greek Village Salad

PREPARATION TIME:
20 MINUTES
COOKING TIME:
NONE
SERVES 6–8

6 tomatoes, cut into thin wedges
1 red onion, cut into thin rings
2 small, narrow cucumbers, sliced
1 cup Kalamata olives
6 oz feta cheese
1/2 cup extra virgin olive oil
dried oregano, to sprinkle

1 Combine the tomato wedges with the onion rings, sliced cucumber and Kalamata olives in a large bowl. Season to taste with salt and freshly ground black pepper.

2 Break up the feta into large pieces with your fingers and scatter over the top of the salad. Drizzle with the olive oil and sprinkle with some oregano.

Caesar Salad

PREPARATION TIME:
5 MINUTES
COOKING TIME:
0 MINUTES
SERVES 4

4 slices white bread, crusts removed, cubed
3 slices bacon, chopped
1 Romaine lettuce
1/2 cup Parmesan shavings, plus extra to serve

DRESSING
2–4 canned anchovies
1 egg
2 tablespoons lemon juice
1 clove garlic, crushed
1/2 cup olive oil

1 Preheat the oven to 375°F. Spread the bread cubes on a baking sheet and bake for 15 minutes, or until golden.

2 Cook the bacon over medium heat until it is crisp. Drain on paper towels.

3 Tear the lettuce leaves into pieces and put in a serving bowl with the bread cubes, bacon and Parmesan.

4 To make the dressing: Process the anchovies, egg, lemon juice and garlic in a food processor for 20 seconds, or until smooth. With the motor running, add the oil in a thin stream until the dressing is thick and creamy. Drizzle over the salad, sprinkle with the extra Parmesan and serve immediately.

Gado Gado

PREPARATION TIME:
30 MINUTES
COOKING TIME:
35 MINUTES
SERVES 4

6 new potatoes
2 carrots
8 oz Chinese yard-long beans
2 tablespoons peanut oil
8 oz firm tofu, chopped
2 cups baby spinach leaves
2 short, narrow cucumbers, cut into thick strips
1 large red sweet bell pepper, cut into thick strips
1 cup fresh bean sprouts
5 hard-cooked eggs

PEANUT SAUCE
1 tablespoon peanut oil
1 onion, finely chopped
2/3 cup peanut butter
1/4 cup kecap manis (Indonesian sweet soy sauce) or soy sauce
2 tablespoons ground coriander
2 teaspoons chili sauce
3/4 cup canned coconut cream
1 teaspoon grated palm sugar or soft brown sugar
1 tablespoon lemon juice

1 Cook the potatoes in boiling water until tender. Drain and cool slightly. Cut into quarters. Cut the carrots into thick strips and the beans into 4 in lengths. Cook the carrots and beans separately in pans of boiling water until just tender. Plunge into iced water, then drain.
2 Heat the oil in a non-stick skillet and cook the tofu in batches until crisp. Drain on paper towels.
3 To make the Peanut Sauce: Heat the oil in a pan over low heat and cook the onion for 5 minutes, or until golden. Add the peanut butter, kecap manis, coriander, chili sauce and coconut cream. Bring to a boil, then reduce heat and simmer for 5 minutes. Stir in the sugar and lemon juice until dissolved.
4 Arrange the vegetables and tofu on a plate. Halve the eggs and place in the center. Serve with the sauce.

Lemon, Fennel and Arugula Salad

PREPARATION TIME:
5 MINUTES
COOKING TIME:
MINUTES
SERVES 4

2 lemons
2 oranges
1 large fennel bulb or 2 baby fennel
2–3 cups arugula leaves
3/4 cup pecans, chopped
1/2 cup stuffed green olives, halved lengthwise

TOASTED SESAME DRESSING
1 tablespoon sesame oil
1 tablespoon sesame seeds
1/4 cup olive oil
2 tablespoons white wine vinegar
1 teaspoon French mustard

1 Peel the lemons and oranges, removing all the white pith. Cut into thin slices and remove any seeds. Thinly slice the fennel. Wash and dry the arugula and tear into pieces. Chill while making the dressing.

2 To make the dressing, heat the oil in a small pan over moderate heat. Add the sesame seeds and fry, stirring constantly, until light golden. Remove from the heat and cool. Pour into a small bowl, whisk in the remaining ingredients and season with salt and ground black pepper.

3 Combine the fruit, fennel, arugula, pecans and olives in a shallow serving bowl. Drizzle with the dressing before serving.

Note: Blood oranges have a lovely tart flavor and, when in season, are delicious in this recipe.

Summer Bread Salad

PREPARATION TIME:
20 MINUTES
COOKING TIME:
15 MINUTES
SERVES 6–8

2 red sweet bell peppers
2 yellow sweet bell peppers
6 plum tomatoes, cut into large chunks
1/3 cup capers, drained
3 oz canned anchovy fillets, drained and halved
3/4 cup black olives
5 oz bocconcini (fresh mozzarella), halved
1 Italian wood-fired loaf
2 cups basil leaves

DRESSING
4 cloves garlic, finely chopped
1/4 cup red wine vinegar
1/2 cup extra virgin olive oil

1 Cut the red and yellow peppers into large pieces, removing the seeds and white membrane. Place, skin-side up, under a hot broiler, until the skin blackens and blisters. Cool peppers in a plastic bag or under a tea towel, then peel away the skin and cut into thick strips.
2 Put the peppers, tomatoes, capers, anchovies, olives and bocconcini in a bowl and toss to combine.
3 To make the dressing: Put the ingredients in a screw-top jar and shake to combine.
4 Cut the bread into large pieces and place in a serving bowl. Drizzle with the dressing and mix until the bread is coated. Add the tomato mixture and basil leaves, and toss gently.

Note: This recipe is based on a Tuscan favorite which uses leftover crusty bread to make a salad.

Crunchy Cheese Salad

PREPARATION TIME: 30 MINUTES + 2 HOURS MARINATING
COOKING TIME: 20 MINUTES
SERVES 6–8

2 red sweet bell peppers
10 oz provolone, kasseri or mozzarella cheese
2 cloves garlic, crushed
1/4 teaspoon chili flakes
1/4 cup olive oil
2 teaspoons chopped marjoram
1 small loaf fig and walnut bread or fruit bread, thickly sliced
8 oz watercress, trimmed
8 oz yellow pear tomatoes, halved
2 avocados, sliced
12 oz canned tuna chunks in brine, drained

DRESSING
2 tablespoons red wine vinegar
2 cloves garlic, crushed
1 teaspoon honey
1 tablespoon walnut oil
1/4 cup olive oil

1 Cut the red peppers into large pieces, removing the seeds and membrane. Place, skin-side up, under a hot broiler until the skin blackens and blisters. Cool under a tea towel or in a plastic bag, then peel away the skin and slice into thick strips.

2 Cut the cheese into thick slices and place in a shallow dish. Combine the garlic, chili flakes, olive oil and marjoram, and pour the mixture over the cheese. Cover the dish and refrigerate for 2 hours. Drain, reserving the marinade.

3 Toast one side of the fig and walnut bread slices until golden brown. Turn over and place a slice of the marinated cheese on the untoasted side. Broil under high heat until the cheese is golden brown. Arrange the watercress on individual serving plates or a large platter, and top with tomatoes, avocado, peppers and tuna. Cut the cheese toasts in half and arrange around the edge of the salad.

4 To make the dressing: Put the reserved marinade, red wine vinegar, crushed garlic, honey, walnut oil and olive oil in a bowl and whisk to combine. Drizzle over the salad and serve immediately.

Papaya and Gorgonzola Salad

PREPARATION TIME:
20 MINUTES
COOKING TIME:
20 MINUTES
SERVES 4

1 cup orange juice
1 tablespoon oil
1 tablespoon soft brown sugar
1 fennel bulb, sliced
2 heads Belgian endive, quartered
8 oz watercress, ends trimmed
1 papaya, sliced
6 oz Gorgonzola cheese, crumbled
1/2 cup hazelnuts, coarsely chopped

DRESSING
1 cup loosely packed basil leaves
1/2 cup olive oil

1 Put the orange juice in a skillet and cook over high heat until reduced by a third.
2 Stir the oil and brown sugar in a separate skillet over low heat until the sugar dissolves. Add the fennel, endive and orange juice, cover and cook for 15 minutes, or until the vegetables have caramelized. Check a couple of times during cooking; if it is looking too dry, add a little water.
3 Divide the watercress among four serving plates, top with the papaya, caramelized vegetables, Gorgonzola and hazelnuts.
4 To make the dressing, process the basil and oil in a food processor until combined, then strain and drizzle over the salad.

Note: Gorgonzola is a blue-veined cheese with a strong, sharp flavor. It is named after the Italian town where it originated, and is made from pressed cows milk. If Gorgonzola cheese is not available, you can use Roquefort or a creamy Danish blue cheese.

Coconut and Chickpea Salad

REPARATION
IME:
5 MINUTES
OOKING TIME:
ONE
ERVES 6–8

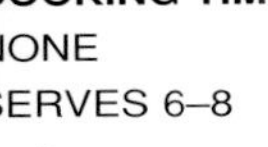

1 green mango, sliced
1 fresh green chile, finely chopped
2 x 14 oz cans chickpeas, rinsed and drained
1/4 cup unsweetened dry grated coconut
1/4 cup coarsely chopped cilantro

DRESSING
1 clove garlic, crushed
1/4 cup coconut milk
1 tablespoon Thai fish sauce
2 tablespoons lime juice
1 teaspoon grated fresh ginger
1 teaspoon sugar

1 Combine the mango with the chile, chickpeas, coconut and cilantro.
2 To make the dressing, shake the ingredients together in a screw-top jar to combine.
3 Pour the dressing over the salad, cover and refrigerate for up to 3 hours to allow the flavors to develop.

Note: If green mango is not available, use a firm, underripe mango.

Snow Pea Salad

Sesame oil is a very strongly flavored oil used in many Asian dishes. It should be used sparingly as its flavor tends to dominate.

PREPARATION TIME: 10 MINUTES
COOKING TIME: NONE
SERVES 6–8

5 oz fresh snow peas
1 bunch fresh asparagus
2 medium carrots, peeled
16 oz can (about 2 1/2 cups) baby corn, drained
8 oz can (about 1 cup) bamboo shoots, drained

DRESSING
1/4 cup vegetable oil
1 tablespoon sesame oil
1 tablespoon soy sauce

1 Trim the snow peas and cut in half. Remove the woody ends from the asparagus and cut them into 2 in lengths. Cut carrots into matchsticks.
2 Place the snow peas and asparagus in a heatproof bowl and cover with boiling water. Let stand for 1 minute, drain and plunge into iced water. Drain and dry thoroughly on paper towels.
3 Combine the snow peas, asparagus, carrots, corn and bamboo shoots in a serving bowl.
4 To make dressing: Place the oils and sauce in a small screw-top jar; shake well to combine. Pour over the vegetables and combine well.

Fabulous Mixed Leaf Salad

Any variety of lettuce can be used in this salad.

PREPARATION TIME:
20 MINUTES
COOKING TIME:
NONE
SERVES 8

6 oz (about 2 cups) fresh snow peas, sliced diagonally
1 large red sweet bell pepper, sliced
4 leaves leaf lettuce
5 leaves escarole
12–15 cherry tomatoes
$1\frac{1}{2}$ cups watercress sprigs
Parmesan shavings, to serve

GARLIC CROUTONS
3 slices white bread
$\frac{1}{4}$ cup olive oil
1 clove garlic, crushed

DRESSING
2 tablespoons olive oil
1 tablespoon mayonnaise
1 tablespoon sour cream
2 tablespoons lemon juice
1 teaspoon brown sugar
cracked pepper to taste

1 Slice the snow peas, and wash the lettuce leaves and the tomatoes.
2 Combine the snow peas, red pepper, watercress, lettuce and tomatoes in a large mixing bowl.
3 To make Garlic Croutons: Remove the crusts from the bread slices. Cut the bread into $\frac{1}{2}$ in squares. Heat the oil in a small, heavy-based skillet and add garlic. Stir in the bread and cook until golden and crisp. Remove from the heat and drain on paper towels.
4 To make the dressing: Whisk all the ingredients in a small mixing bowl for 2 minutes or until well combined. Just before serving, pour the dressing over salad. Stir to combine. Top with Garlic Croutons and shavings of Parmesan.

Apple and Pear Waldorf

Golden raisins, chopped pitted dates and even diced dried figs are delicious additions to this salad. Their sweetness complements the tartness of the apples.

PREPARATION TIME:
20 MINUTES
COOKING TIME:
NONE
SERVES 8–10

2 crisp red apples
2 pears
1/4 cup lemon juice
1 stalk celery, sliced
1/2 cup walnut or pecan pieces
1/2 cup mayonnaise
1 tablespoon shredded pickled ginger (optional)
1/2 teaspoon white pepper
1 tablespoon toasted sesame seeds (optional)

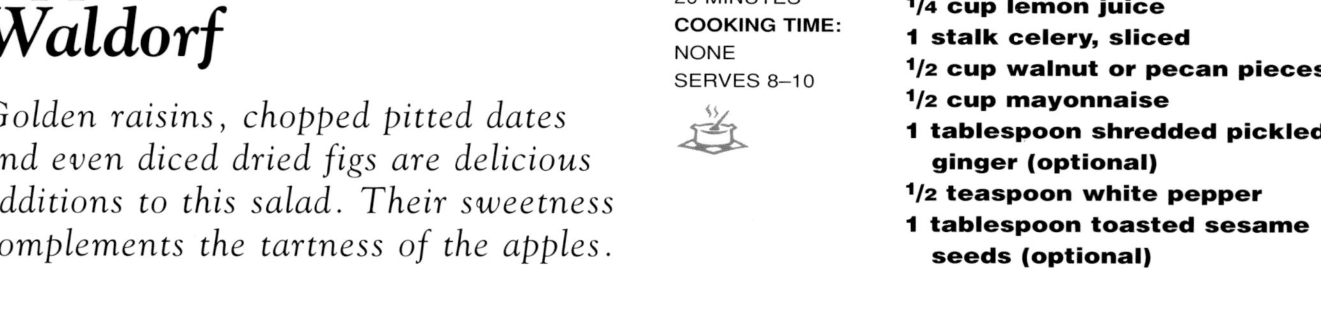

1 Core and dice the apples and pears. Toss in lemon juice to prevent the fruit from discoloring.
2 Reserving a teaspoon each of sesame seeds and ginger for the garnish, combine the remaining ingredients, mixing well. Add the fruit, stirring to coat the apples and pears with dressing. Sprinkle with sesame seeds and then sprinkle with ginger.

Note: Shredded pickled ginger has a distinctive pink color and sweet-salty flavor. It is available in Asian food stores.

Two Potato Salad

If you're using a store-bought mayonnaise, be sure to choose a sharp tasting one for the best result.

PREPARATION TIME:
20 MINUTES
COOKING TIME:
0 MINUTES
SERVES 8–10

8 medium potatoes, scrubbed well or peeled
2 medium sweet potatoes
1/2 cup mayonnaise
3/4 cup sour cream
ground pepper, to taste
1 red onion, finely chopped
1 red sweet bell pepper, diced
1 yellow or green sweet bell pepper, diced
8 oz (about 1 1/4 cups) cooked leg ham, cut into slivers

1 Peel and cut the potatoes and sweet potatoes into small cubes. Cook separately in boiling water for 5 minutes, or until tender but not mushy. Drain.
2 In a large bowl, mix the mayonnaise, sour cream, pepper and onion together. Add the cooked, drained potatoes while hot.
3 Gently stir in the sweet peppers and ham until just combined. Serve while warm or cover, refrigerate overnight and serve chilled.

Note: It is important to cut the potatoes into equal sizes for even cooking. This method of preparing the potatoes shortens the cooking time and makes sure that the potatoes are not starchy in the middle, which sometimes happens when they are cooked whole.

Apple and Pear Waldorf (above). Two Potato Salad

Wild and Brown Rice Salad

PREPARATION TIME:
10 MINUTES
COOKING TIME:
1 HOUR
15 MINUTES
SERVES 6–8

1 cup brown rice
1/2 cup wild rice
1 medium red onion
1 small red sweet bell pepper
2 stalks celery
2 tablespoons chopped parsley
1/3 cup chopped pecans

DRESSING
1/4 cup orange juice
1/4 cup lemon juice
1 teaspoon grated orange rind
1 teaspoon grated lemon rind
1/3 cup olive oil

1 Cook the brown rice in a pan of boiling water for 25–30 minutes until just tender. Drain well and cool completely. Boil the wild rice for 30–40 minutes; drain well and cool.
2 Chop the onion and red pepper finely. Cut the celery into thin slices. Combine in a bowl with the parsley and the cooked brown and wild rice.
3 Place the pecans in a dry skillet and stir over a medium heat for 2–3 minutes until lightly toasted. Transfer to a plate to cool.
4 To make the dressing: Place the juices, rinds and oil in a small screw-top jar and shake well.
5 Pour the dressing over the salad and fold in. Add pecans and lightly mix.

Red Cabbage Salad

PREPARATION TIME: 20 MINUTES
COOKING TIME: NONE
SERVES 8–10

1/2 small red cabbage, shredded
3 medium carrots, shredded
1 medium raw beet, peeled and shredded
1 red sweet bell pepper, seeded and finely sliced
3 green onions, chopped
1 orange, peeled and diced
16 oz can unsweetened pineapple pieces in natural juice

DRESSING
1 egg, room temperature
1 teaspoon dry mustard
salt and pepper, to taste
1 tablespoon honey
1 tablespoon cider vinegar
1 tablespoon raspberry or white wine vinegar
1/4 cup vegetable oil

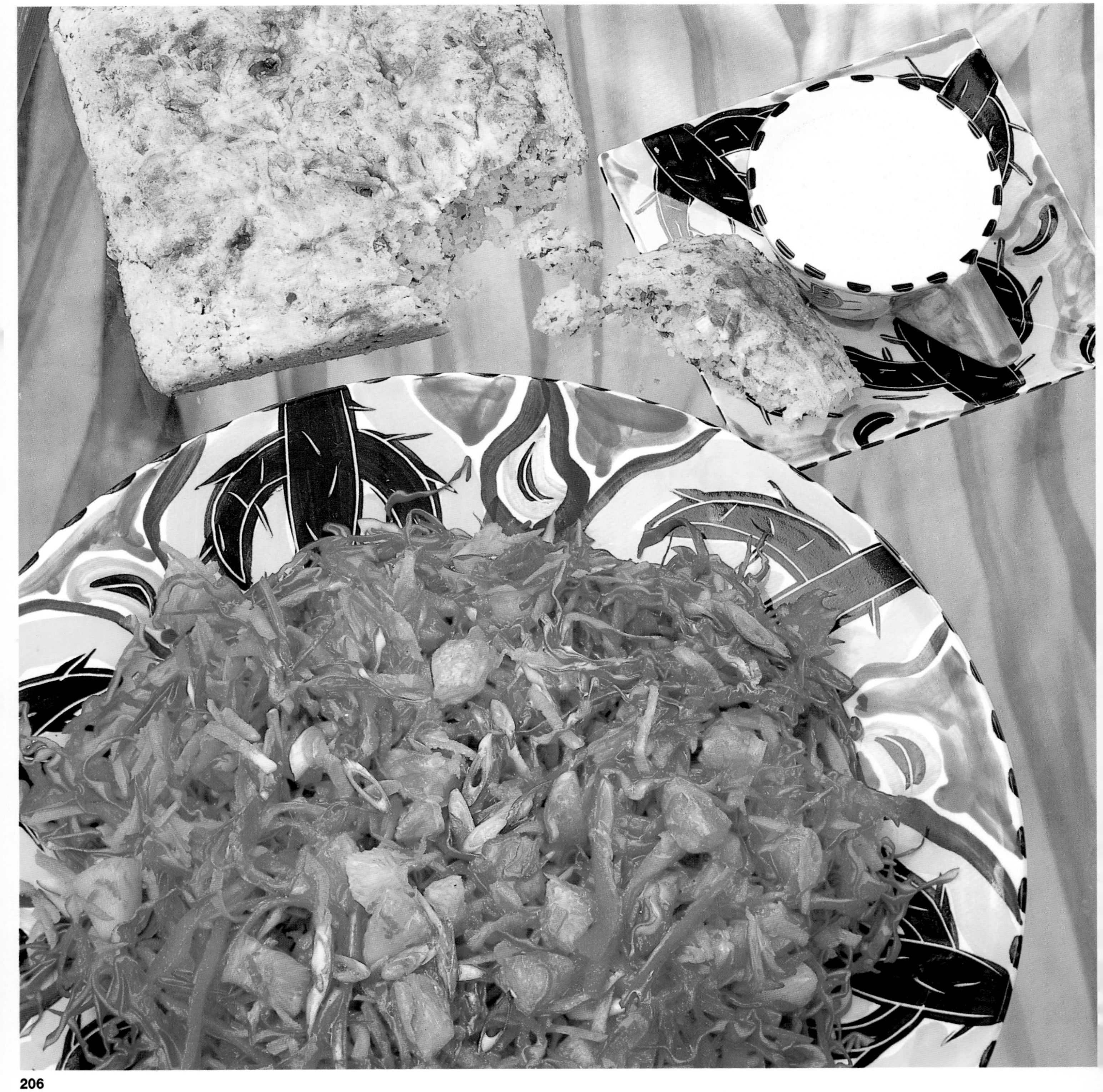

In a large bowl, combine the cabbage, carrots, eet, red pepper, green onions and orange. Drain he pineapple pieces and add to the salad. Toss well.
. To make the dressing: Place the egg, dry mustard, alt and pepper, honey and vinegars in a blender nd process until smooth.
With the motor still running, gradually add he oil to the egg mixture. Blend until the oil is ncorporated and the mixture is thick and creamy. 'our dressing over the salad, toss well and serve.

Savory Cornbread

Vhether hot off the barbecue or straight 'rom the oven, the aroma alone of this :uperb bread will tempt the fussiest guest.

PREPARATION 'IME:
5 MINUTES
:OOKING TIME:
5 MINUTES
SERVES 8

1/4 cup butter
2 tablespoons olive oil
1/2 cup finely chopped green onions
1 clove garlic, crushed
2 canned jalapeño chiles, chopped
1/2 cup chopped cilantro
1 cup milk
1 egg, lightly beaten
1 cup self-rising flour
1 teaspoon salt
2 teaspoons baking powder
1 cup yellow cornmeal (polenta)
1/2 cup shredded cheddar
1/4 teaspoon ground sweet paprika

. Melt the butter, and add the olive oil, green onions, ;arlic, chiles, cilantro, milk and egg. Mix well.
: Sift the self-rising flour, salt, baking powder and :ornmeal into a bowl. Add the mixed ingredients nd beat to a smooth batter.
3 Pour the mixture into a lightly greased and lined) in square baking pan. Sprinkle with shredded cheese nd paprika. Bake in a preheated 375°F oven for 0 minutes or until cornbread is golden brown.
4 To barbecue: Preheat kettle barbecue to medium iigh, then lower the heat. Place the cornbread on a 2 in high rack which has been covered with a double layer of foil. Cook using indirect heat, hood down, for 35 minutes or until the cornbread pulls away from the sides of the pan. Cut the Savory Cornbread into squares to serve.

:ed Cabbage Salad. Savory Cornbread (above)

Australian Damper

Best cooked on a kettle barbecue.

PREPARATION TIME:
15 MINUTES
COOKING TIME:
30–35 MINUTES
SERVES 8

3 cups self-rising flour
1 teaspoon salt
1/3 cup butter, chopped
1 cup milk
1 egg, lightly beaten
1 tablespoon sesame seeds
1/4 teaspoon ground sweet paprika

1 Sift the flour and salt into a large bowl. Cut the butter into the flour until the mixture resembles fine bread crumbs.
2 Make a well in the center and add the combined milk and beaten egg. Mix to a firm dough with a flat-bladed knife, bringing the mixture together with your hands if necessary.
3 Shape the dough into a round and place on a baking sheet lined with a double layer of heavy-duty foil, placed shiny-side down. Pat out to a diameter of 8 in. Brush with a little water, sprinkle with sesame seeds and paprika.
4 Preheat the kettle barbecue to medium high. Cook the damper on indirect heat, hood down, for 25–35 minutes, elevated on a 2 in high rack. The damper should be firm and hollow sounding when tapped. Reduce heat to medium if damper browns too quickly. Alternatively, bake in a preheated 350°F oven for 20 minutes or until the loaf sounds hollow when tapped. Serve the damper immediately with butter (see photograph page 175).

Note: Damper can be made and shaped up to two hours in advance. Cover with plastic wrap and allow to stand at room temperature.

Chili, Corn and Red Pepper Muffins

PREPARATION TIME:
15 MINUTES
COOKING TIME:
25 MINUTES
MAKES 12 MUFFINS

1 cup all-purpose flour
1/4 teaspoon salt
4 teaspoons baking powder
1 cup yellow cornmeal (polenta)
1 tablespoon soft brown sugar
1 egg
1/4 cup corn oil
2/3 cup milk or buttermilk
1 fresh red chile, finely chopped
1 small red sweet bell pepper, finely chopped
2 tablespoons chopped basil leaves
16 oz can corn kernels, drained

1 Grease twelve 1/2-cup capacity muffin cups. Preheat the oven to 400°F. Sift the flour, salt and baking powder into a bowl and mix in the cornmeal and sugar. Beat together the egg, oil and milk and add to the dry ingredients. Stir just until moistened, but do not overmix. Add the chile, red pepper, basil and corn and mix briefly.
2 Spoon the mixture into the muffin cups. Bake for 25 minutes, or until the muffins are well risen. Cool for a few minutes, before turning out onto a wire rack.

Fougasse

PREPARATION TIME:
20 MINUTES
+ 1 HOUR
30 MINUTES
RISING
COOKING TIME:
35 MINUTES
SERVES 4–6

1 envelope active dry yeast
1 teaspoon sugar
3 cups all-purpose flour
1 cup whole-wheat flour
2 teaspoons salt

1 Mix the yeast, sugar and 1/2 cup of warm water in a bowl. Cover and set aside in a warm place for 10 minutes, or until foamy.
2 Sift the flours and salt, return the husks and make a well in the center. Pour in 1 cup of extra warm water and the foamy yeast. Mix to a soft dough and gather into a ball. Turn out onto a floured surface and knead for 10 minutes, or until smooth.
3 Place in a large, lightly oiled bowl, cover loosely with greased plastic wrap and let stand in a warm place for 1 hour, or until doubled in size.
4 Punch down the dough and knead for 1 minute. Press into a large, oval shape 3/4 in thick and make several cuts on either side. Lay on a large, floured baking sheet, cover with greased plastic wrap and allow to rise for 20 minutes. Preheat oven to 425°F.
5 Bake for 35 minutes, or until crisp. After 15 minutes, spray with water to make the crust crispy.

Chili, Corn and Red Pepper Muffins (above). Fougasse

Savory Biscuit Scroll

PREPARATION TIME: 35 MINUTES
COOKING TIME: 35 MINUTES
SERVES 6

1 cup shredded cheddar
1/4 cup grated Parmesan
1 onion, chopped
1 red sweet bell pepper, chopped
2/3 cup chopped pancetta or cooked ham
1/4 cup chopped fresh parsley
3 cups self-rising flour
1 teaspoon salt
1/4 cup butter, cubed
1 1/4 cups buttermilk
2 tablespoons olive oil

1 Lightly grease a baking sheet. Preheat oven to 400°F. To make the filling, combine the cheddar, Parmesan, onion, red pepper, pancetta or ham and parsley. Season well with salt and pepper.

2 Sift the flour and salt into a large bowl. Add the butter and cut in until the mixture is crumbly. Make a well in the center and pour in the buttermilk; mix to a soft dough and gather into a ball. Turn out onto a lightly floured surface and knead until smooth and elastic.

3 Roll out to a 20 x 10 in rectangle. Sprinkle the filling over the top, leaving a 3/4 in border, and press the filling down slightly. Roll up lengthwise, enclosing the filling. Bring the ends together to form a ring and brush the ends with some water. Press to seal.

4 Place on the prepared baking sheet and snip the outside edge of the scroll with scissors at regular intervals, so the filling is exposed. Bake for 15 minutes, then reduce the oven to 350°F and bake for another 20 minutes, or until golden brown. Brush with the olive oil.

Grissini

PREPARATION TIME:
40 MINUTES +
30 MINUTES
RISING
COOKING TIME:
30 MINUTES
MAKES 18

1 envelope active dry yeast
1 tablespoon superfine sugar
2/3 cup milk
3 tablespoons butter
4 cups all-purpose flour
1 teaspoon salt
sea salt flakes, sesame seeds or poppy seeds, to decorate

1 Grease three baking sheets. Mix the yeast, sugar and 1/2 cup of warm water. Cover and set aside for 10 minutes, or until foamy. In a small pan, heat the milk and butter until the butter has melted.

2 Mix 3 1/2 cups of the flour and salt in a bowl. Make a well in the center and pour in the milk mixture and foamy yeast. Add enough of the remaining flour to mix to a soft dough, then turn out onto a lightly floured surface and knead for 10 minutes, or until smooth and elastic. Divide into 18 pieces.

3 Roll each piece to the thickness of a pencil and a length of 12 in. Place the grissini 1 1/4 in apart on the baking sheets. Cover loosely with greased plastic wrap and let stand for 20 minutes.

4 Preheat the oven to 425°F. Brush the grissini with cold water and sprinkle with the sea salt or your choice of sesame or poppy seeds. Bake for 15–20 minutes, or until golden brown. Remove from the oven and cool on a wire rack. Reduce the temperature to 350°F. Return the grissini to the baking sheets, and bake for another 5–10 minutes, or until crisp.

Ricotta and Dill Rolls

PREPARATION TIME: 20 MINUTES + 1 HOUR 40 MINUTES RISING
COOKING TIME: 45 MINUTES
MAKES 8

1 envelope active dry yeast
2 tablespoons superfine sugar
8 oz (1 cup) ricotta cheese
2 tablespoons butter, softened
1/4 small onion, grated
1/4 teaspoon baking soda
1 egg
3 3/4 cups all-purpose flour
2 tablespoons chopped dill

1 Mix together the yeast, sugar and 1/4 cup warm water in a bowl. Cover the bowl and set aside in a warm place for 10 minutes, or until foamy.

2 Put the ricotta, butter, onion, baking soda and egg in a food processor with 1 teaspoon of salt and process until smooth. Add the foamy yeast and 3 cups of the flour. Add the remaining flour and mix to a smooth dough. Turn out the dough onto a floured surface and knead for 6–8 minutes, or until smooth. Add the dill during the last minute of kneading.

3 Put the dough in an oiled bowl, cover loosely with greased plastic wrap and set aside for 1 hour, or until doubled in size. Lightly grease an 8 x 12 in baking sheet.

4 Punch down the dough and divide into 8 pieces. Shape into rounds and lay on the sheet. Make 2 slashes on each roll. Cover with a damp tea towel for 30 minutes, or until well risen.

5 Preheat the oven to 350°F. Bake the rolls for 40–45 minutes, or until golden. Check after 20 minutes and reduce the oven to 325°F if they are too brown.

Caramelized Onion Braids

PREPARATION TIME: 1 HOUR + 1 HOUR 35 MINUTES RISING
COOKING TIME: 1 HOUR 35 MINUTES
SERVES 8–10

2 1/2 cups all-purpose flour
1 cup buckwheat flour
1 teaspoon salt
1/2 oz fresh compressed yeast or 1 envelope active dried yeast
1 1/4 cups warm milk
2 tablespoons butter
1 tablespoon oil
2 lb onions, thinly sliced into rings
1 egg, lightly beaten
2 teaspoons fennel seeds

1 Sift the flours and salt into a large bowl and make a well in the center. Dissolve the yeast in 1/2 cup of the warm milk in a small bowl, then add the remaining warm milk. Pour into the well and mix to a dough. Turn out onto a floured surface and knead for 8 minutes, or until smooth. Place in a large oiled bowl, cover loosely with greased plastic wrap and let stand in a warm place for 45 minutes to 1 hour, or until doubled in size.
2 Melt the butter and oil in a skillet, add the onions and cook over medium-low heat for 40–50 minutes, or until golden.
3 Punch down the dough, turn out onto a lightly floured surface and knead for 10 minutes, or until smooth and elastic.
4 Lightly grease two baking sheets. Divide the dough in half. Working with one piece at a time, divide it into three pieces. Roll each piece out to a 12 x 4 in rectangle. Divide the onion mixture into six portions and spread a portion along the middle of each rectangle, leaving a 3/4 in border. Brush the edge with some of the beaten egg and roll up lengthwise to enclose the filling.
5 Braid the three pieces together and place seam-side down on a baking sheet. Pinch the ends together. Repeat with the remaining dough and caramelized onions. Cover with a clean damp towel and let stand in a warm place for 45 minutes, or until well risen.
6 Preheat the oven to 350°F. Brush the tops with the beaten egg and sprinkle with the fennel seeds. Bake for 35–45 minutes, or until well browned. Transfer to a wire rack to cool.

Bacon, Cheese and Onion Quick Bread

PREPARATION TIME: 25 MINUTES
COOKING TIME: 1 HOUR 5 MINUTES
SERVES 6–8

1 tablespoon oil
3 onions, thinly sliced into rings
2 teaspoons soft brown sugar
4 slices bacon, trimmed of excess fat and finely chopped
3 cups self-rising flour
1/3 cup butter, chilled
3/4 cup shredded cheddar
1/2 cup milk

1 Heat half of the oil in a large, heavy-based skillet. Add the onions and cook over medium heat for 10 minutes, stirring occasionally. Add the brown sugar and continue to cook for 10–15 minutes more, or until the onions are golden brown. Set aside and allow to cool. Heat the remaining oil in a small skillet, add the bacon and cook over moderately high heat until the bacon is crisp. Drain the bacon on paper towels and add to the onion mixture.

2 Lightly grease a baking sheet. Sift the flour into a large bowl, cut the butter into small cubes and rub into the flour with your fingertips until the mixture resembles bread crumbs.

3 Add three-quarters of the onion mixture and 1/2 cup of the cheddar to the flour mixture and mix well. Make a well in the center and add the milk with about 1/2 cup of water (add enough water to bring the dough together). Using a flat-bladed knife, mix to a soft dough. Gently knead together to form a ball. Preheat the oven to 425°F.

4 Lay the dough on the sheet and press out to form a 9 in circle. Using a sharp knife, mark the dough into quarters, cutting two-thirds of the way through. Sprinkle with the rest of the onion mixture and the remaining cheddar. Bake for 15 minutes, then reduce the oven to 350°F. Cover the top loosely with foil if it starts getting too brown. Bake for another 20–25 minutes, or until the base sounds hollow when tapped.

Mini Bagels

PREPARATION TIME:
50 MINUTES + 1 HOUR 25 MINUTES RISING
COOKING TIME:
30 MINUTES
MAKES 22

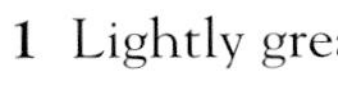

1/2 oz fresh compressed yeast or 1 envelope active dry yeast
1 tablespoon sugar
2/3 cup warm milk
4 cups all-purpose flour
1 teaspoon salt
2 tablespoons butter, melted
1 egg, lightly beaten
1 tablespoon poppy seeds

1 Lightly grease three baking sheets. Combine the yeast, sugar and milk in a bowl. Cover and set aside in a warm place for 10 minutes, or until foamy. Sift the flour and salt into a large bowl. Make a well in the center and add the butter, foamy yeast and 2/3 cup of warm water. Mix to a soft dough and gather into a ball. Knead for 10 minutes, or until elastic. Place in a lightly oiled bowl, cover loosely with greased plastic wrap and let stand for 1 hour, or until doubled in size.

2 Punch down the dough, and then knead on a well-floured surface until smooth. Divide into 22 pieces. Working with one piece at a time (keeping the others covered with a clean damp towel), roll into tight balls. Push a finger through the center and gently enlarge the hole until it forms a doughnut. Lay on the baking sheets, cover with the towel and let stand for 10–15 minutes, or until risen.

3 Bring a large skillet of water to a boil. Add three to four bagels at a time and cook for 1 minute. Remove with a slotted spoon and lay on the sheets. They will be deflated at this stage.

4 Preheat the oven to 400°F. Brush the bagels with the egg and sprinkle with the poppy seeds. Bake for 25 minutes, or until browned.

Pesto Rolls

PREPARATION TIME:
10 MINUTES
COOKING TIME:
5–10 MINUTES
SERVES 6

6 small dinner rolls
1/4 cup toasted pine nuts
2–3 tablespoons freshly grated Parmesan cheese
1–2 cloves garlic, peeled
2 tablespoons olive oil
1/4 cup butter, chopped
3–4 teaspoons lemon juice
1 cup fresh basil leaves
salt and pepper, to taste
Parmesan shavings, to serve

1 Cut each dinner roll in half vertically.
2 Combine the rest of the ingredients in a food processor and process for 20–30 seconds or until smooth. (Add a little more butter or oil if pesto is dry.)
3 Spread each half roll with the pesto and toast under a preheated broiler for 5–10 minutes or until they have heated through. Serve with Parmesan shavings. Alternatively, place the roll halves together and wrap them in foil. Place them on a hot barbecue grill, turning occasionally to make sure they cook evenly.

Savory Bread

PREPARATION TIME:
10 MINUTES
COOKING TIME:
10–15 MINUTES
SERVES 6–8

1 Vienna loaf
1/2 cup shredded cheddar
2 tablespoons grated Parmesan cheese
1 green onion, finely sliced
2 slices bacon, finely chopped
pepper, to taste

1 Across the top of the Vienna loaf, at 3/4 in intervals, cut diagonal slits 1/2 in deep in one direction. Make similar slits in the other direction to make a diamond pattern. Place the bread on a foil-lined baking sheet.
2 Combine the rest of the ingredients in a small bowl. Sprinkle the mixture over the top of the loaf.
3 Bake the loaf in a preheated 350°F oven for 10–15 minutes or until the cheese has melted and the bacon is crisp.

Garlic Bread

PREPARATION TIME:
10 MINUTES
COOKING TIME:
10–15 MINUTES
SERVES 6–8

1 French loaf
1/2 cup softened butter
2–3 cloves garlic, crushed
1 tablespoon finely chopped parsley
pepper, to taste

1 Cut the French loaf into thick diagonal slices three-quarters of the way through.
2 Combine the other ingredients in a small bowl and beat them together until smooth.
3 Spread the garlic mixture between each slice of bread, then wrap the loaf in foil and place it on a baking sheet.
4 Bake the loaf in a preheated 350°F oven for 10–15 minutes or until the butter has melted and the bread is hot. Or place the wrapped bread on a hot barbecue grill, turning occasionally to make sure it heats evenly.

Olive Bread

PREPARATION TIME:
10 MINUTES
COOKING TIME:
10–15 MINUTES
SERVES 6–8

1 French loaf
green or black olive paste (tapenade), to spread
2 tomatoes
thin slices mozzarella or bocconcini (fresh mozzarella)
2–3 tablespoons finely shredded basil leaves
pepper, to taste

1 Cut the French loaf into 3/4 in slices and spread each slice with a small amount of olive paste.
2 Thinly slice the tomatoes and place one or two slices on each slice of bread.
3 Top with mozzarella or bocconcini and sprinkle with basil and pepper.
4 Place the bread slices on a foil-lined baking sheet and bake in a preheated 350°C oven for 10–15 minutes or until the cheese has melted and the bread has heated through. Serve warm.

Savory Bread (above left). Garlic Bread. Olive Bread. Pesto Rolls

Cheese Bread

Be creative with this recipe by using other combinations of cheese for variety. Best cooked on a kettle barbecue.

PREPARATION TIME:
15 MINUTES
COOKING TIME:
8 MINUTES
SERVES 8

1 crusty French loaf
1/3 cup olive oil
1/2 cup butter, softened
1 clove garlic, crushed
2 tablespoons French mustard
1 cup shredded cheddar
1 cup shredded mozzarella
1/4 cup sesame seeds

1 Slice the French loaf diagonally about 3/4 in apart and three-quarters of the way through. Whip together the olive oil, softened butter, crushed garlic and mustard until creamy.
2 Spread the bread slices with the whipped mixture and place on a baking sheet. Combine the cheeses, sprinkle the mixture between the bread slices and top with sesame seeds.
3 Wrap the bread in a heavy-duty or industrial-strength foil. Place on a baking sheet or in a cake pan on the grill of a hot kettle barbecue. Cover and cook for 8 minutes or until the cheese bubbles. Alternatively, bake the bread in a 350°F oven for about 10 minutes. Do not overcook.

Honey Garlic Dressing

Pour over a tossed green salad.

PREPARATION TIME: 5 MINUTES
COOKING TIME: NONE
MAKES 1 CUP

1/4 cup peanut oil
2 tablespoons lemon or lime juice
1 teaspoon grated lemon rind
2 tablespoons honey
1–2 cloves garlic, crushed
1 tablespoon chopped fresh chives
salt and pepper, to taste

1 Combine all the ingredients in a screw-top jar and shake until well combined.

Orange and Sesame Dressing

Delicious with an arugula and watercress salad.

PREPARATION TIME: 5 MINUTES
COOKING TIME: NONE
MAKES fi CUP

1 tablespoon sesame oil
2 tablespoons orange juice
2 teaspoons toasted sesame seeds
1 teaspoon grated orange rind
1–2 teaspoons soy sauce
3/4 teaspoon grated fresh ginger
salt and pepper, to taste

1 Combine all the ingredients in a screw-top jar and shake until well combined.

Vinaigrette Dressing

This classic dressing goes well with a fresh garden salad.

PREPARATION TIME: 5 MINUTES
COOKING TIME: NONE
MAKES fi CUP

1/4 cup white wine vinegar
1/4 cup oil
salt and pepper, to taste
1–2 tablespoons freshly chopped herbs (optional)

1 Combine all the ingredients in a screw-top jar and shake until well combined.

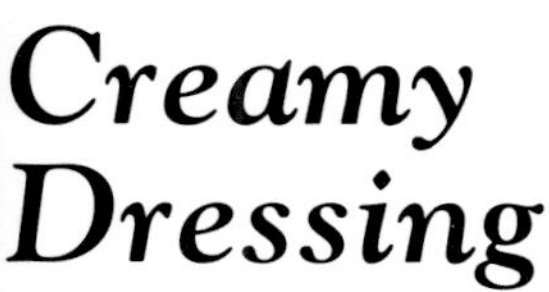

Creamy Dressing

This dressing goes well with a Caesar salad.

PREPARATION TIME: 5 MINUTES
COOKING TIME: NONE
MAKES fi CUP

2 tablespoons olive oil
1 tablespoon mayonnaise
1 tablespoon sour cream
2 tablespoons lemon juice
1 teaspoon soft brown sugar
salt and cracked black pepper, to taste
1 clove garlic, crushed (optional)
1 tablespoon chopped fresh chives (optional)

1 Combine all the ingredients in a screw-top jar and shake until well combined.

Honey Garlic Dressing

Creamy Dressing

Vinaigrette Dressing

Orange and Sesame Dressing

Salsas and dips

Once you have the main elements of the meal organised, it's time to think about the finishing touches. Dips served with fresh vegetables, breads and crackers can stave off any early pangs of hunger at the beginning of the barbecue, while refreshing salsas elevate the flavor of barbecued meats and seafood to new heights. All of the delicious recipes in this chapter are simple to make and, best of all, can be prepared ahead of time, leaving you free to enjoy the company of your friends.

Part of the charm of a barbecue is the casual and informal feeling it evokes. While the meat's on the grill and your guests are relaxing with a cool drink, tempt them with some homemade dips, accompanied by chopped fresh vegetables, crackers and fresh crusty bread. If you have time, you could make up some crunchy dippers of your own. Crisp up thin slices of Lebanese bread, potato skins are always popular, or try making bagel chips with a little Parmesan and pesto sprinkled over the top. Just make sure your guests don't eat too much or they won't have room for all the other treats you have in store!

Salsas are a must at any barbecue. They are delicious (and decidedly more-ish) served as a dip with corn chips or toasted flat bread. When accompanying the main meal, salsas can transform an ordinary piece of barbecued meat or fish into an extraordinary taste sensation. Refreshing and light, they give a lift to the rich flavor of meat and chicken, and complement the subtlety of all types of seafood.

The secret to a good salsa or dip is to buy only the freshest ingredients. To enhance the refreshing quality of salsas, serve them chilled. Dips made with dairy products should also be kept refrigerated before use.

Peach, Red Pepper and Ginger Salsa

Shown here with grilled chicken breast. Good with seafood and barbecued meats.

PREPARATION TIME:
20 MINUTES
COOKING TIME:
NONE
SERVES 4

- **1/4 cup white wine vinegar**
- **2 tablespoons superfine sugar**
- **2 teaspoons grated fresh ginger**
- **1 clove garlic, crushed**
- **1/2 teaspoon ground cumin**
- **1/4 cup chopped cilantro**
- **1/4 cup chopped mint**
- **1 red sweet bell pepper, diced**
- **1 small red onion, finely diced**
- **1 small fresh red chile, finely chopped**
- **3 canned or fresh peaches, diced**

1 Combine the vinegar, sugar, ginger, garlic, cumin, cilantro and mint.
2 Put the red pepper, onion, chile and peaches in a large bowl. Gently stir in the vinegar herb mixture and serve at once.

Bocconcini, Tomato and Sun-dried Pepper Salsa

Shown here with grilled beef steak. Try it with barbecued chicken or tuna steaks.

PREPARATION TIME:
20 MINUTES
COOKING TIME:
NONE
SERVES 6

- **6 oz bocconcini (fresh mozzarella), diced**
- **2 tomatoes, diced**
- **1/3 cup drained sun-dried red peppers in oil, chopped**
- **1 green onion, thinly sliced**
- **1 tablespoon extra virgin olive oil**
- **2 teaspoons red wine vinegar**
- **1 tablespoon shredded basil leaves**
- **1 tablespoon chopped flat-leaf parsley**

1 Mix together the bocconcini, tomatoes, sun-dried red peppers and sliced green onion in a large bowl.
2 Whisk together the oil and vinegar until thoroughly blended. Stir in the basil and parsley.
3 Toss the dressing with the bocconcini and tomato mixture and season to taste with salt and black pepper. Serve at room temperature.

Roasted Red Pepper, Tomato, Lime and Chile Salsa

Shown here with grilled lamb steaks. Also good with veal, beef, chicken, fish and seafood.

REPARATION IME: 5 MINUTES
OOKING TIME: 5 MINUTES
ERVES 6

2 red sweet bell peppers
2 tomatoes
1/2 small red onion
1–2 small fresh red chiles
2 limes
2 tablespoons olive oil
1 teaspoon sugar

1 Preheat the oven to 350°F. Cut the red peppers into quarters and discard the membrane and seeds. Place peppers in an oiled baking dish and bake for 30 minutes, turning regularly. If the peppers begin to burn, add 2 tablespoons of water to the baking dish. Allow to cool and then chop into small cubes.

2 Score a cross in the base of each tomato. Place in a bowl of boiling water for 10 seconds, then plunge into cold water and peel the skin away from the cross. Cut the tomatoes in half and scoop out the seeds with a teaspoon. Cut the tomato flesh into thin strips.

3 Finely chop the onion and chiles. Peel the limes, then cut off the pith and carefully cut the flesh into fine segments.

4 Mix together the red peppers, tomatoes, onion, chiles, lime segments, olive oil and sugar in a bowl. Season well with salt and freshly ground black pepper. Cover and allow to stand for at least 15 minutes for the flavors to blend, before serving.

Chili Avocado Salsa

Shown here with lamb chops. Also good with corn chips, pita bread, grilled meats and any Mexican food.

PREPARATION TIME:
30 MINUTES
+ 3 HOURS REFRIGERATION
COOKING TIME:
NONE
SERVES 6

3 tomatoes, seeded and diced
1 small red onion, finely chopped
1–2 jalapeño chiles, seeded and very finely chopped
1/3 cup flat-leaf parsley, chopped
1–2 cloves garlic, crushed
1/4 cup light olive oil
1 ripe avocado
2 limes, to garnish

1 Mix together the tomatoes, onion, chiles, parsley, garlic and olive oil. Season to taste, cover and refrigerate for 3 hours.

2 Just before serving, halve the avocado, remove the stone and gently mash the flesh with a fork while it is still in the skin. Scoop out the avocado and stir into the salsa. Serve with lime wedges.

Papaya and Black Bean Salsa

Shown here with grilled white fish steaks. Also good with salmon or tuna steaks, chicken, beef and lamb.

PREPARATION TIME:
25 MINUTES
COOKING TIME:
NONE
SERVES 4

1 small red onion, finely chopped
1 papaya (about 1 lb), peeled, seeded and cubed
1 fresh birds-eye chile, seeded and finely chopped
1 tablespoon canned salted black beans, rinsed and drained
2 teaspoons peanut oil
1 teaspoon sesame oil
2 teaspoons Thai fish sauce
1 tablespoon lime juice
1 tablespoon chopped cilantro
2 teaspoons shredded mint

1 In a bowl, gently toss together the onion, papaya, chile and black beans with your hands.

2 Just before serving, whisk together the peanut oil, sesame oil, fish sauce and lime juice. Pour over the salsa and gently toss. Add the cilantro and mint and serve immediately, at room temperature.

Mexican Layered Dip

PREPARATION TIME: 50 MINUTES
COOKING TIME: NONE
SERVES 12

16 oz can refried beans
1 packet of taco seasoning mix
1¼ cups sour cream
¾ cup ready-made salsa sauce
½ cup shredded cheddar
2 tablespoons chopped pitted black olives
corn chips
1 tablespoon chopped cilantro

GUACAMOLE
3 ripe avocados
1 tomato
1–2 fresh red chiles, finely chopped
1 small red onion, finely chopped
1 tablespoon chopped cilantro
1 tablespoon lime or lemon juice
2 tablespoons sour cream
1–2 drops habanero sauce or Tabasco sauce

1 Using a fork, mix the refried beans and taco seasoning together in a small bowl.

2 To make Guacamole: cut the avocados in half, peel and discard skin and stone (chop into the stone with a sharp knife and lift it out). Coarsely chop avocados, place in a bowl, then mash lightly with a fork. Cut the tomato in half horizontally, scoop out seeds with a teaspoon and discard. Finely dice the flesh and add to the avocado. Stir in the chiles, onion, cilantro, lime or lemon juice, sour cream and habanero or Tabasco sauce. Season with freshly cracked black pepper.

3 To assemble, spread the bean mixture in the middle of a large serving platter (e.g. 12 x 14 in dish), leaving a clear border for corn chips. Spoon sour cream on top, leaving a small border of bean mixture showing. Repeat with guacamole and salsa sauce so that you can see each layer. Sprinkle with cheese and olives.

4 Arrange the corn chips around the edge of the platter just before serving and garnish with cilantro.

Note: Habanero sauce is a very hot condiment sauce made from habanero chiles. Use sparingly to add extra zing to the dip. It is available from delicatessens and speciality stores.

Hint: Always try to wear rubber gloves when you are chopping fresh chiles. If this isn't possible, remember to scrub your hands thoroughly with warm soapy water after chopping. Be careful not to touch your eyes or any other delicate skin or you will cause burning and skin irritation. The dip can be made 1–2 hours in advance and refrigerated, covered with plastic wrap.

Taramasalata

PREPARATION TIME:
25 MINUTES
COOKING TIME:
NONE
SERVES 8

4 slices white bread, crusts removed
1/4 cup milk
3 oz (about 1/3 cup) smoked cod's roe (tarama)
1 egg yolk
1 clove garlic, crushed
1 tablespoon grated onion
1/4 cup olive oil
1/3 cup lemon juice

1 Soak the bread slices in the milk for 5 minutes, then remove and squeeze out the excess liquid.
2 Process the cod's roe and egg yolk in a food processor for 10 seconds. Add the bread, garlic and onion and process for 20 seconds, or until the mixture is well combined and smooth.
3 With the motor running, gradually add the olive oil in a thin stream. Process until all the oil is absorbed.
4 Add the lemon juice in small amounts, to taste. Transfer to a bowl and serve with bread and black olives. Store in the refrigerater in an airtight container, for up to 1 week. Bring to room temperature before serving.

Asparagus, Apple and Avocado Dip

PREPARATION TIME:
40 MINUTES
+ 2 HOURS REFRIGERATION
COOKING TIME:
5 MINUTES
SERVES 10–12

2 bunches asparagus
3 green apples
2 tablespoons lemon juice
3 ripe avocados
1 1/4 cups sour cream
4 drops Tabasco sauce

1 Wash and trim the woody ends from the asparagus. Steam or microwave until just cooked, then plunge into iced water and drain. Chop off the tips and set aside, to serve. Finely chop the remaining asparagus stems.
2 Peel and shred the apples and sprinkle with 1 tablespoon lemon juice to prevent browning. Add the asparagus and mix together. In a separate dish, mash the avocado flesh. Mix in the remaining lemon juice and stir into the apple and asparagus. Add the sour cream and mix well. Add the Tabasco, cover with plastic wrap and refrigerate for 2 hours. Serve with the asparagus tips for dipping.

Moroccan Sweet Carrot and Honey Dip

REPARATION IME:
0 MINUTES + OAKING VERNIGHT
OOKING TIME:
HOUR
ERVES 6

2/3 cup dried chickpeas
1/4 cup butter
1/2 teaspoon ground cumin
1/2 teaspoon ground coriander
1/2 teaspoon ground cinnamon
1/4 teaspoon chili powder
1 1/4 cups chopped carrots
1 tablespoon honey
1/3 cup thick natural yogurt
2 tablespoons chopped parsley
2 tablespoons olive oil
1 tablespoon olive oil, extra

1 Place the chickpeas in a bowl, cover with water and soak overnight. Drain and rinse well, then place in a saucepan and cover with cold water. Bring to a boil, reduce the heat and simmer for 45 minutes or until tender. Skim off any scum that rises to the surface. Drain, rinse and mash well.

2 Melt the butter in a heavy-based skillet; add the cumin, coriander, cinnamon, chili and carrots. Cook, covered, over low heat for 5 minutes, turning the carrots to coat them in the spices. Drizzle with honey. If the carrots start to stick, add 1 tablespoon water. Cover and cook for 20 minutes until the carrots are very tender and a caramel brown color. Cool slightly and mash in the skillet to include all the bits on the base of the pan.

3 Combine the mashed chickpeas and carrots with the yogurt, parsley and olive oil, and season well with salt and pepper. Spoon into a serving bowl and drizzle with extra oil. Serve with celery sticks or blanched green beans.

Hummus

PREPARATION TIME:
15 MINUTES
COOKING TIME:
NONE
SERVES 4–6

16 oz can chickpeas
2–3 tablespoons lemon juice
2 tablespoons olive oil
2 cloves garlic, crushed
1/4 cup tahini (sesame paste)

1 Place the drained chickpeas, lemon juice, olive oil and garlic in a food processor. Season with salt and pepper. Process for 20–30 seconds, or until smooth. Add the tahini and process for another 10 seconds. Delicious served with flat bread or toasted pita bread.

Shrimp, Corn and Sweet Chili Dip

PREPARATION TIME:
1 HOUR
+ 2 HOURS REFRIGERATION
COOKING TIME:
3 MINUTES
SERVES 8

2 lb cooked shrimp (in the shell)
juice and grated rind of 3 limes
2/3 cup frozen corn kernels
8 oz soft cream cheese
1/4 cup finely chopped chives
1 tablespoon sweet chili sauce
4 cooked jumbo shrimp, to garnish

1 Shell, devein and rinse the shrimp; pat them dry and place in a bowl. Add the lime juice to the shrimp, cover and refrigerate for 10 minutes.
2 Cook the frozen corn kernels in boiling water for 2–3 minutes, or until tender. Drain and plunge the kernels into iced water to prevent further cooking, then drain and pat dry with paper towels.
3 Place the shrimp and lime juice in a food processor and process in short bursts for 2–3 seconds until the shrimp are chopped into small pieces but not ground.
4 Transfer the chopped shrimp to a bowl and mix in the cream cheese, corn kernels, lime rind and chives. Add the chili sauce and mix well. Cover the dip with plastic wrap and refrigerate for at least 2 hours. Just before serving, shell and devein the jumbo shrimp, leaving the tail shells intact. Transfer the dip to a serving bowl and garnish with the shelled shrimp. Serve with melba toasts, for dipping.

Guacamole

PREPARATION TIME:
30 MINUTES
COOKING TIME:
NONE
SERVES 6

3 ripe avocados
1 tablespoon lime or lemon juice
1 tomato
1–2 fresh red chiles, finely chopped
1 small red onion, finely chopped
1 tablespoon finely chopped cilantro leaves
2 tablespoons sour cream
1–2 drops Tabasco or habanero sauce

1 Coarsely chop the avocado flesh and place in a bowl. Mash lightly with a fork and sprinkle with the lime or lemon juice to prevent the avocado from discoloring.

2 Cut the tomato in half horizontally and use a teaspoon to scoop out the seeds. Finely dice the flesh and add to the avocado.

3 Stir in the chiles, onion, cilantro, sour cream and Tabasco or habanero sauce. Season with freshly cracked black pepper.

4 Serve immediately or cover the surface with plastic wrap and refrigerate for 1–2 hours. If refrigerated, let stand at room temperature for 15 minutes before serving.

Hint: You will need one to two limes to produce 1 tablespoon of juice, depending on the type of lime. A heavier lime will probably be more juicy. To get more juice from a citrus fruit, pierce it all over with a fork and then heat on High (100%) in the microwave for 1 minute. Don't forget to pierce it or the fruit may burst.

Marinated Roasted Vegetable Dip

PREPARATION TIME:
55 MINUTES
+ 4 HOURS MARINATING
COOKING TIME:
50 MINUTES
SERVES 8

1 small eggplant, sliced
2 zucchini, sliced
3 red sweet bell peppers
1/2 cup extra virgin olive oil
2 cloves garlic, sliced
2 plum tomatoes
7 oz (about 1 cup) canned, drained artichoke hearts
1/4 cup fresh oregano leaves
1 cup ricotta cheese
1/4 cup sliced black olives

1 Place the eggplant and zucchini in a colander over a bowl and sprinkle with the salt, then let stand for 15–20 minutes. Cut the red peppers into large flat pieces, removing the seeds and membrane. Brush with a little olive oil and place, skin-side up, under a hot broiler until the skin blackens and blisters. Cool in a plastic bag, then peel away the skin. Reserve about a quarter of the peppers to garnish and place the rest in a large non-metallic bowl.

2 Place half of the olive oil in a bowl, add one of the garlic cloves and a pinch of salt and mix together well. Rinse the eggplant and zucchini and pat dry with paper towels. Place the eggplant on a non-stick or foil-lined baking sheet and brush with the garlic oil. Cook under a very hot broiler for 4–6 minutes each side, or until golden brown, brushing both sides with the oil during broiling. The eggplant will burn easily, so keep a close watch. Allow to cool while broiling the zucchini in the same way. Add the eggplant and zucchini to the peppers in the bowl.

3 Slice tomatoes lengthwise, place on a non-stick or foil-lined baking sheet and brush with the garlic oil. Reduce the temperature slightly and broil for 10–15 minutes, or until soft. Add to the bowl with the other vegetables.

4 Cut the artichokes into quarters and add to the bowl. Mix in any remaining garlic oil along with the remaining olive oil. Stir in the fresh oregano and remaining garlic. Cover with a tight-fitting lid or plastic wrap and refrigerate for at least 2 hours.

5 Drain vegetables; place in a food processor. Add ricotta and process for 20 seconds, or until smooth. Reserve 1 tablespoon olives to garnish and add remainder to food processor. Mix together in a few short bursts, transfer to a non-metallic bowl and cover with plastic wrap. Chill for at least 2 hours.

6 Slice the reserved roasted red peppers into thin strips and arrange over the top of the dip with the reserved olives.

Baba Ghanoush (Eggplant Dip)

PREPARATION TIME:
15 MINUTES
+ 20 MINUTES STANDING
COOKING TIME:
35 MINUTES
SERVES 6–8

2 medium eggplants
3–4 cloves garlic, crushed
2 tablespoons lemon juice
2 tablespoons tahini (sesame paste)
1 tablespoon olive oil
sprinkle of paprika, to garnish

1 Halve the eggplants lengthwise, sprinkle with salt and leave for 15–20 minutes. Rinse and pat dry with paper towels. Preheat the oven to 350°F.
2 Bake the eggplants for 35 minutes, or until soft. Peel away the skin and discard. Place the flesh in a food processor with the garlic, lemon juice, tahini and olive oil and season to taste with salt and pepper. Process for 20–30 seconds. Sprinkle with paprika and serve with flat bread.

Note: We sprinkle eggplants with salt and allow to stand before using because they can have a bitter taste. The salt draws the bitter liquid from the eggplant. Slender eggplants do not need to be treated before use.

Chili Crab and Tomato Dip

PREPARATION TIME:
25 MINUTES
COOKING TIME:
NONE
SERVES 6

2 x 6 oz cans crabmeat, drained
3/4 cup neufchatel or cream cheese (see note)
2 tablespoons chili sauce
2 teaspoons tomato paste
1 teaspoon grated lemon rind
2 teaspoons lemon juice
1 small onion, finely grated
3 green onions, finely sliced
1 tomato, seeded and finely chopped

1 Squeeze any remaining liquid from the crabmeat. Beat cheese until smooth, then add the crabmeat, chili sauce, tomato paste, lemon rind, lemon juice and onion. Season well with salt and pepper. Mix together well and then spoon into a serving bowl.
2 Scatter the green onions and chopped tomato over the top and chill before serving.

Note: Neufchatel is a lower-fat version of smooth, mild, good-quality cream cheese and is available from delicatessens and supermarkets.

Marinades, sauces and butters

Transform the most ordinary meal into something different and delicious with marinades. They not only add flavor to the dish, but also help to tenderize your meat. Because food is cooked quickly on the barbecue, marinating it beforehand gives it a head start.

Acidic-based marinades containing vinegar, citrus juice or wine break down and tenderize meat fibers and are particularly good for tougher meats. Oil-based marinades will moisturize the meat and are suitable for chicken and pork, which have a tendency to dry out when cooked. Try a yogurt-based marinade for chicken or lamb. The marinade will form a delicious crust over the meat when it is cooked. Dry marinades are usually a combination of salt and ground spices or dried herbs. Pastes are made by adding a little oil to the dry mixture to allow it to adhere more easily to the meat.

If you barbecue regularly, it's a good idea to have a few of your favorite marinades made and stored in the refrigerator. Remember also to use any leftover marinade to baste the food occasionally while you are cooking; but don't use a plastic or nylon bristled brush as it may melt onto the food. Any marinade that contains sugar or honey (or hidden sugar like ketchup) should only be brushed over almost at the end of cooking, or the sugar will caramelize and become very dark and bitter.

Ideally, large cuts of meat and whole chickens should be marinated for some hours in the refrigerator, turning occasionally to allow for as much penetration of flavor as possible. Cubed meats and small portions require less marinating time. Don't marinate seafood for longer than one hour, particularly when using an acidic ingredient in the marinade.

Fresh relishes or a delicious sauce can really dress up simple meat or seafood dishes. Some of those featured here also make good dipping sauces for finger food like barbecued jumbo shrimp or satays.

If you do not have time to prepare a sauce, you could always make a selection of flavored butters and store them in the freezer. Use them to enliven barbecue vegetables or a steak, or use them to flavor bread rolls or jacket potatoes. They are all simple to prepare and make a real difference to the look and flavor of your meal.

Lemon and Wine Marinade

Use to marinate lamb or chicken.

PREPARATION TIME: 5 MINUTES
COOKING TIME: NONE
MAKES 1 CUP

2 tablespoons lemon juice
2 teaspoons grated lemon rind
1 clove garlic, crushed
1/4 cup olive oil
2 tablespoons soft brown sugar
1 tablespoon chopped fresh rosemary
1 tablespoon lemon thyme

Combine all the ingredients in a bowl and mix well.

Teriyaki Marinade

Use to marinate lamb or beef.

PREPARATION TIME: 5 MINUTES
COOKING TIME: NONE
MAKES fi CUP

1/4 cup soy sauce
2 tablespoons teriyaki sauce
1 tablespoon grated fresh ginger
1–2 cloves garlic, crushed
2 tablespoons soft brown sugar
1/4 cup chicken or beef bouillon
1/4 cup sweet sherry

Combine all the ingredients in a bowl and mix well.

Spiced Yogurt Marinade

Use to marinate lamb or beef.

PREPARATION TIME: 5 MINUTES
COOKING TIME: NONE
MAKES 1 CUP

1 cup plain yogurt
1 onion, finely chopped
3/4 teaspoon ground coriander
3/4 teaspoon ground cumin
3/4 teaspoon garam masala
3/4 teaspoon ground cinnamon
1/2 teaspoon ground ginger
1 teaspoon sugar
1 clove garlic, crushed
salt and pepper, to taste
pinch cardamom

Combine all the ingredients in a bowl and mix well.

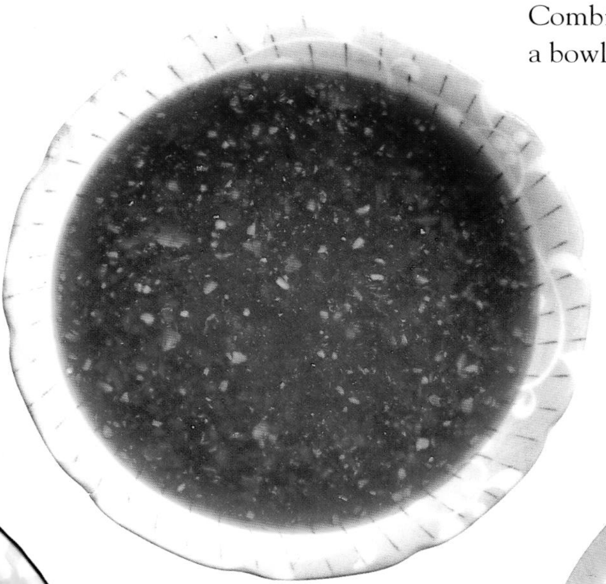

Apricot and Onion Marinade

Use to marinate pork or chicken.

PREPARATION TIME: 5 MINUTES
COOKING TIME: NONE
MAKES 1 CUP

1/3 cup apricot nectar
1 teaspoon Worcestershire sauce
1 tablespoon oil
1 tablespoon cider vinegar
1–2 tablespoons French onion soup mix
2–3 green onions, thinly sliced
1/4 cup red or white wine (optional)

Combine all the ingredients in a bowl and mix well.

Mustard and Herb Marinade

Use to marinate beef or lamb.

PREPARATION TIME: 5 MINUTES
COOKING TIME: NONE
MAKES fi CUP

1/4 cup olive oil
2 tablespoons balsamic vinegar
2 teaspoons soft brown sugar
2–3 teaspoons Dijon, German or coarse grain mustard
1–2 teaspoons mixed dried herbs
1 tablespoon chopped fresh parsley
salt and pepper, to taste

Combine all the ingredients in a bowl and mix well.

Horseradish Cream Sauce

Serve this sauce with fish or beef.

PREPARATION TIME: 10 MINUTES
COOKING TIME: NONE
MAKES 1 CUP

1/2 cup (4 oz) cream cheese
1 tablespoon mayonnaise
1 tablespoon sour cream
1–2 teaspoons prepared horseradish
1 tablespoon chopped chives, lemon thyme or parsley

1 Using an electric mixer, beat the cream cheese until soft and creamy.
2 Add the rest of the ingredients and beat until well combined.

Tartare Sauce

Serve this sauce with seafood.

PREPARATION TIME: 5 MINUTES
COOKING TIME: NONE
MAKES 1 CUP

- **1/2 cup whole egg mayonnaise**
- **1 tablespoon sour cream**
- **1–2 tablespoons halved capers**
- **1 tablespoon finely chopped gherkin pickle**
- **1 tablespoon chopped fresh dill (optional)**

Combine all the ingredients in a small bowl and mix well.

Chili Barbecue Sauce

Serve this sauce with lamb or beef.

PREPARATION TIME: 5 MINUTES
COOKING TIME: NONE
MAKES fi CUP

- **1 tablespoon butter**
- **1 teaspoon ground cumin**
- **1/2 teaspoon ground coriander**
- **1/2 teaspoon ground paprika**
- **1 tablespoon sweet chili sauce**
- **1/3 cup bottled barbecue sauce**
- **2 teaspoons Worcestershire sauce**

1 Heat the butter in a small pan. Add the cumin, coriander and paprika and cook for 30 seconds.
2 Stir in the sweet chili sauce, barbecue sauce and Worcestershire sauce and mix well.

Creamy Mustard Sauce

Serve this sauce with beef or chicken.

PREPARATION TIME: 5 MINUTES
COOKING TIME: NONE
MAKES fi CUP

- **2 tablespoons whole egg mayonnaise**
- **1/3 cup sour cream**
- **2–3 tablespoons Dijon or coarse grain mustard**
- **1 tablespoon of your favorite chopped fresh herbs (optional)**
- **salt and pepper, to taste**

Combine all the ingredients in a small bowl and mix well. If the sauce is too thick, add a little cream to achieve the required consistency.

Cilantro Mayonnaise

Serve this sauce with chicken, seafood or veal.

PREPARATION TIME: 15 MINUTES
COOKING TIME: NONE
MAKES 1 CUP

3 egg yolks
3/4 cup light olive oil
2 tablespoons lemon juice
1–2 tablespoons chopped cilantro
salt and pepper, to taste
1 clove garlic, crushed (optional)

1 Place the egg yolks in a food processor bowl or blender. With the motor constantly running, add the olive oil in a thin stream and process until thick and creamy.

2 Add the lemon juice and cilantro and process until combined. Season the mixture with salt and pepper and the garlic, if using.

Tomato Sauce

Serve this sauce warm or cold with burgers, sausages, steak or fish.

PREPARATION TIME: 10 MINUTES
COOKING TIME: 10 MINUTES
MAKES 1 CUP

1 tablespoon olive oil
1 tablespoon butter
1 small onion, finely chopped
1 clove garlic, crushed
1–2 teaspoons Italian mixed dried herbs
2 large tomatoes, peeled and chopped
1/2 cup tomato purée
2 teaspoons balsamic vinegar
salt and pepper, to taste

1 Heat the olive oil and butter in a small pan and add the onion, garlic and herbs. Cook for 2–3 minutes or until the onion is soft.

2 Stir in the tomatoes, tomato purée and vinegar and cook for 3–4 minutes. Remove from the heat.

3 Place the mixture in a food processor and process until smooth, seasoning with salt and pepper.

Garlic Herb Hollandaise

Serve this sauce with seafood, chicken or beef.

PREPARATION TIME: 15 MINUTES
COOKING TIME: NONE
MAKES 1 CUP

2 egg yolks
2/3 cup melted butter
2–3 tablespoons lemon juice or white wine vinegar
1 tablespoon chopped chives
1 tablespoon chopped basil
1 tablespoon chopped oregano
1 clove garlic, crushed
salt and pepper, to taste

1 Place the egg yolks in a food processor bowl or blender. With the motor constantly running, add the melted butter in a thin stream. Process until thick and creamy.

2 Add the lemon juice or vinegar, chives, basil, oregano and garlic and season with salt and pepper. Process for 10 seconds to combine.

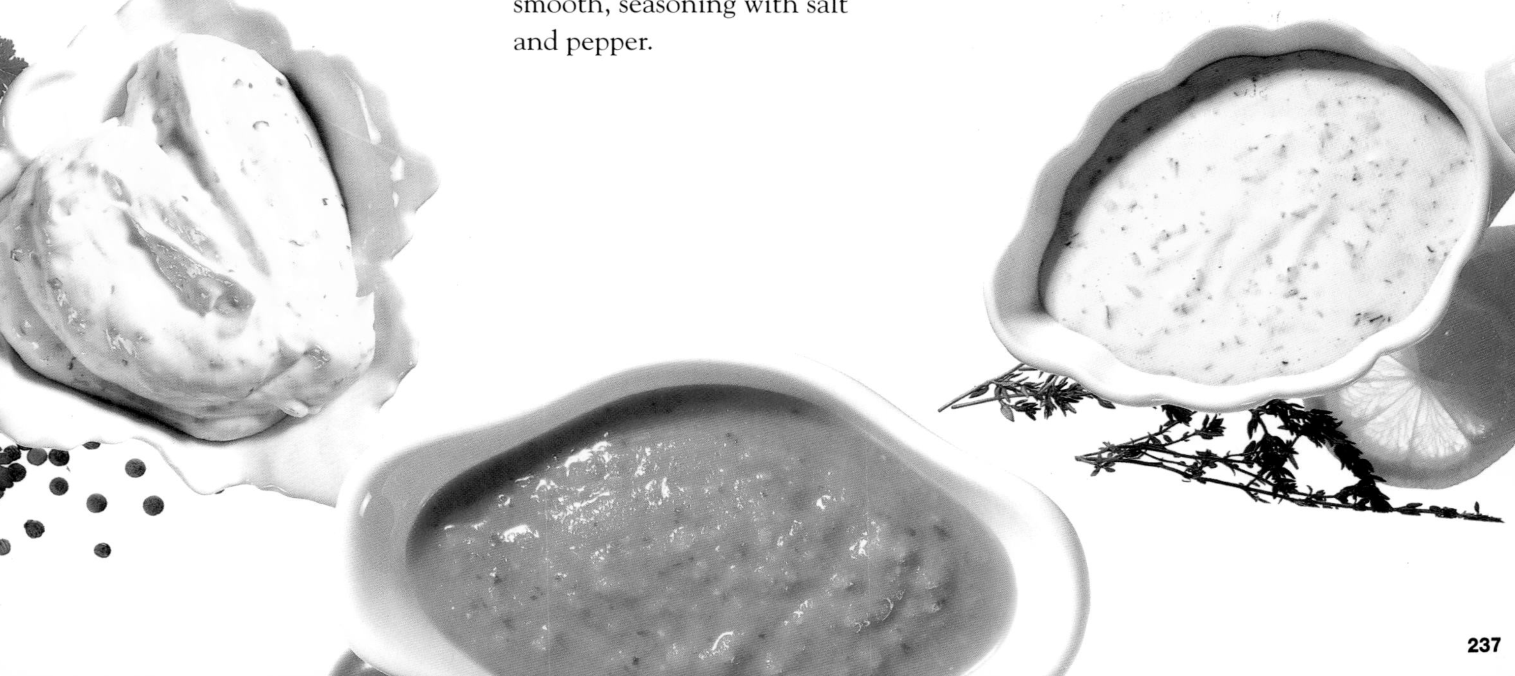

Smoky Cajun Barbecue Sauce

Use this as a dipping sauce or accompaniment to beef, pork or chicken.

PREPARATION TIME: 10 MINUTES
COOKING TIME: 15 MINUTES
MAKES 1fi CUPS

1 medium onion, grated
1 cup ketchup
1/3 cup sweet chili sauce
1 tablespoon cider vinegar
1/3 cup brown sugar
5 cloves garlic, crushed
3/4 teaspoon ground pepper
1 tablespoon liquid hickory smoke (optional)

1 Place all the ingredients except liquid smoke in an enamel-lined or flameproof glass pan.
2 Stir over a low heat until the sugar dissolves, then simmer for 12 minutes, stirring occasionally. Remove from the heat, allow to cool and add the liquid smoke, if using.
3 Stir well and store in a glass jar in the refrigerator.

Note: If using liquid smoke, add one teaspoon at a time at the end of cooking, so you can adjust the quantity to suit your particular taste.

Tomato and Cilantro Relish

Serve this relish with satays, kebabs, vegetable dishes, breads and seafood.

PREPARATION TIME: 10 MINUTES
COOKING TIME: NONE
MAKES ABOUT 3 CUPS

3 firm ripe tomatoes, chopped
2 cups cilantro, chopped
juice of half a lime
1 teaspoon salt
1 teaspoon chili powder (optional)
1 medium onion, finely chopped

Combine all the ingredients in a bowl and mix thoroughly.

Note: This makes an appealing salad combination as well. Slice tomatoes and onions and arrange on a platter, sprinkle with the salt, chili powder and cilantro. Combine lime juice with a little olive oil and drizzle over the salad to serve.

Sweet and Sour Sauce

Use as a dipping sauce or accompaniment to seafood or chicken.

PREPARATION TIME: 5 MINUTES
COOKING TIME: 5 MINUTES
MAKES 1fi CUPS

1/2 cup water
1/2 cup pineapple juice
1/4 cup white vinegar
1 tablespoon brown vinegar
1/4 cup ketchup
1 tablespoon cornstarch
1 tablespoon cold water

1 Place the water, pineapple, vinegar, brown sugar and ketchup in a small pan.
2 Mix the cornstarch and water to a smooth paste. Add to the pan, stirring constantly over a medium heat until the sauce boils and thickens. Cool slightly before serving.

Rosemary Butter

Use with lamb and other meats.

PREPARATION TIME: 10 MINUTES
COOKING TIME: NONE
MAKES fi CUP

1/2 cup butter, softened
2 tablespoons chopped fresh rosemary
squeeze lime juice
1/4 teaspoon ground pepper

Combine the butter with the other ingredients and beat until smooth. Place in a butter container or, using plastic wrap, shape into a log and refrigerate. Slice into 1/2 in thick rounds to serve.

Herb Butter

Use with steaks, chicken, seafood, vegetables and hot breads or rolls.

PREPARATION TIME: 10 MINUTES
COOKING TIME: NONE
MAKES fl CUP

1/2 cup butter, softened
1 tablespoon finely chopped green onion
2 tablespoons chopped fresh parsley
1 tablespoon snipped fresh chives or 2 teaspoons dried mixed herbs
1/4 teaspoon white pepper

Combine the butter with the other ingredients and beat until smooth. Place in a butter container or, using plastic wrap, shape into a log and refrigerate. Slice into 1/2 in thick rounds to serve.

Lime and Chili Butter

Serve with chicken or seafood.

PREPARATION TIME: 10 MINUTES
COOKING TIME: NONE
MAKES 1 CUP

1/2 cup butter
1 tablespoon lime juice
1 teaspoon grated lime rind
1 teaspoon chopped fresh chile
2 teaspoons chopped cilantro

Beat the butter until it is light and creamy. Add the rest of the ingredients and beat again until smooth. Place in a butter container or, using plastic wrap, shape into a log and refrigerate. Slice into 1/2 in thick rounds to serve.

Savory Anchovy Butter

Serve with beef.

PREPARATION TIME: 10 MINUTES
COOKING TIME: NONE
MAKES 1 CUP

3/4 cup butter
4 canned anchovy fillets, drained
2 green onions, chopped
1 clove garlic, peeled
1 tablespoon grated lemon rind

1 Place all the ingredients in a food processor bowl and process for 20–30 seconds or until the mixture forms a smooth paste.
2 Transfer the mixture to small serving pots and refrigerate.

Make interesting shapes with different nozzles

Serving pots can be stored in the refrigerator for several weeks

Shape flavored butter into a log. Freeze and slice rounds as required

Desserts

No matter how much your guests have enjoyed their main meal, they can usually be persuaded to squeeze in a little dessert. Served with coffee, liqueur coffee or perhaps a dessert wine, a sweet offering, whether it be light and refreshing or sinfully rich, is the perfect end to a successful barbecue.

There's no better way to finish a meal than with something sweet. But it's not much fun for you to have to disappear into the kitchen to slave over dessert while everyone else relaxes outside. Fortunately, all the recipes in this chapter can be prepared ahead of time, so that you can have them on the table in minutes.

When entertaining, you need to feel confident that what you are serving will look and taste as good as the recipe suggests, so here are a few tips to help achieve sweet perfection. If you are making the Fresh Fruit Pavlova or Berry Nests, for example, you will want the meringue to be perfect. There are several methods for making meringue, but you must start with a clean, dry mixing bowl. It's best to have your egg whites at room temperature and, if possible, use superfine sugar because it dissolves faster than any of the larger crystal sugars. Beat the egg whites to soft, firm or stiff peaks, as the recipe requires — the aim is to reach maximum volume without overbeating. When you think the meringue is ready, take a little mixture and rub it between your thumb and forefinger. It should feel smooth and slightly gritty; if it's too gritty, it will need extra beating.

Cheesecakes can also be an uncertain entity, and it's often difficult to tell whether they are cooked through. A simple test is to gently wobble the cheesecake with the oven door slightly ajar, leaving the cheesecake in the oven. It should have a slight wobble. If you remove the cheesecake from the oven before it is properly cooked, it will sink. Allow to cool completely before refrigerating overnight for a firm, rich and creamy texture.

Fresh Fruit Pavlova

PREPARATION TIME:
30 MINUTES
COOKING TIME:
40–45 MINUTES
SERVES 6–8

4 egg whites
1 cup superfine sugar
1 1/2 cups whipping cream, whipped
1 banana, sliced
8 oz strawberries (about 1 2/3 cups), sliced
2 kiwi fruit, sliced
pulp from 2 passion fruit (also known as granadilla or lilikoi)

1 Preheat oven to 300°F. Line a large baking sheet with non-stick baking (silicone) paper; draw an 8 in circle on the paper. Beat egg whites with an electric mixer in a large dry bowl until soft peaks form. Add sugar gradually, beating well after each addition. Beat for 5–10 minutes until all sugar has fully dissolved.
2 Spread meringue mixture onto the tray inside the marked circle. Shape the meringue evenly, running the flat side of a flexible metal spatula along the edge and over the top.
3 Run the spatula up the edge of meringue mixture, all the way round, making furrows. This strengthens the pavlova, stops the edge crumbling and gives it a good, decorative finish.
4 Bake 30 minutes, or until pale and crisp. Reduce heat to 250°F and bake another 10–15 minutes. Turn off oven and leave pavlova inside to cool, using a wooden spoon to keep door ajar. Top with whipped cream and fruit. Drizzle with passion fruit pulp.

Note: Fresh passion fruit can be found in Latin markets and supermarkets during its season.

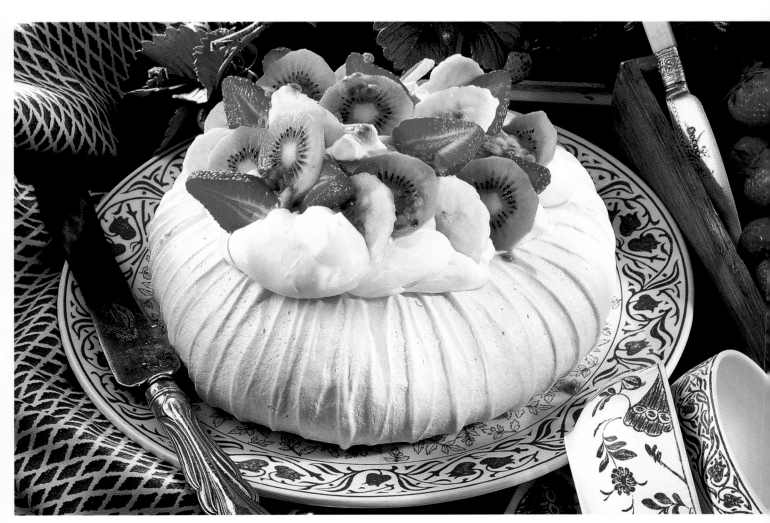

Coconut Cake with Lemon Syrup

PREPARATION TIME:
10 MINUTES
COOKING TIME:
1 HOUR
45 MINUTES
SERVES 8–10

1 cup butter
1 3/4 cups superfine sugar
7 eggs, lightly beaten
1 2/3 cups all-purpose flour
2 1/4 teaspoons baking powder
4 cups unsweetened grated dry coconut

SYRUP
2 cups superfine sugar
1/2 cup lemon juice
1/2 cup water
2 teaspoons finely grated lemon rind
1 small lemon, finely sliced
confectioner's sugar, for dusting

1 Preheat the oven to 325°F. Brush a 10 in springform pan with melted butter or oil, and line the base with baking (silicone) paper. Place the butter and sugar in a large bowl and beat on high speed until light and fluffy. Add the eggs gradually, beating well after each addition.

2 Gently fold the sifted flour and baking powder and the coconut into the egg mixture. Pour into the prepared pan and bake for 1 1/2 hours, or until just firm. (The cake may dip slightly in the center.)

3 Combine the sugar, lemon juice, water and lemon rind in a heavy-based pan. Cook syrup over low heat, stirring constantly until the sugar dissolves. Boil the syrup without stirring for 12 minutes, or until slightly thickened.

4 Remove the cake from the oven, pour hot syrup evenly over hot cake, reserving about 1/2 cup of syrup. Cool completely in the pan. Add the sliced lemon to the remaining syrup and cook over low heat for 5 minutes. Decorate the cake with the glazed lemon slices. Dust with confectioner's sugar before serving.

Cassata

PREPARATION TIME: 50 MINUTES + 2 HOURS + OVERNIGHT FREEZING
COOKING TIME: NONE
SERVES 20

FIRST LAYER
2 eggs, separated
1/3 cup confectioner's sugar
3/4 cup whipping cream
1/2 cup flaked almonds, toasted
almond extract

SECOND LAYER
1 cup chopped semisweet chocolate
1 tablespoon Dutch cocoa
2 eggs, separated
1/3 cup confectioner's sugar
3/4 cup whipping cream

THIRD LAYER
2 eggs, separated
1/4 cup confectioner's sugar
1 cup whipping cream
1/3 cup glacé cherries, halved
2 tablespoons chopped preserved ginger in syrup
1 cup candied fruit (pineapple, apricot, fig and peach), finely chopped
1 teaspoon vanilla extract

1 Line the base and sides of a 3 in deep, 8 in square cake pan with foil.

2 To make the first layer: Beat the egg whites with an electric mixer until soft peaks form. Add the confectioner's sugar gradually, beating well after each addition. In a separate bowl, beat the cream until firm peaks form. Fold the yolks and beaten egg whites into the cream. Add the almonds and a few drops of extract. Stir until combined. Spoon into the pan and smooth the surface. Tap the pan gently on the counter top to level the surface of the mixture. Freeze for 30–60 minutes, or until firm.

3 To make the second layer: Place chocolate in a heatproof bowl over a pan of simmering water, and stir until melted. Add the cocoa, and stir until smooth. Remove from heat, and cool slightly. Proceed as for step 2, beating the egg whites, confectioner's sugar and then the cream. Fold the chocolate into the cream. Fold in the yolks and beaten egg whites, and stir until smooth. Spoon over the frozen first layer. Tap the pan on the counter top to level the surface. Freeze for 30–60 minutes, or until firm.

4 To make the third layer: Proceed as for step 2, beating egg whites, confectioner's sugar and then cream. Fold the yolks and egg white into the cream, then stir in fruit and vanilla extract. Spoon over the chocolate layer in the pan. Freeze overnight. Slice and serve. Wrap the remainder in foil and return to the freezer.

Berry Nests

PREPARATION TIME:
30 MINUTES + COOLING
COOKING TIME:
1 HOUR 15 MINUTES
MAKES 12

4 egg whites
small pinch cream of tartar
1 cup superfine sugar
1 1/4 cups whipping cream
2 teaspoons confectioner's sugar
1 tablespoon brandy
fresh mixed berries

1 Line a large baking sheet with non-stick baking (silicone) paper and preheat the oven to 300°F. Beat the egg whites and cream of tartar until soft peaks form then gradually add the sugar. Beat until stiff and glossy.

2 Fit a pastry bag with a medium-sized star nozzle and use to pipe tightly coiled spirals of meringue (about 3 in across) onto the prepared sheet. Pipe rings on the top edges of the rounds to shape nests.

3 Bake for 30 minutes. Reduce the oven to 250°F and bake for another 45 minutes. Turn the oven off and allow the nests to cool in the oven with the door ajar. Whip the cream with the confectioner's sugar and brandy. Pile into the nests and top with mixed berries of your choice.

Note: The cream of tartar will help to dry the meringues, making them crisp and crunchy.

Tiramisu

PREPARATION TIME:
20 MINUTES
COOKING TIME:
NONE
SERVES 6–8

3 cups strong black coffee, cooled
1/4 cup dark rum
2 eggs, separated
1/4 cup superfine sugar
1 cup mascarpone cheese
1 cup whipping cream, whipped
20 large sponge ladyfingers
2 teaspoons Dutch cocoa

1 Combine the coffee and rum in a glass bowl.
2 Using an electric mixer, beat the egg yolks and sugar in a small bowl for 3 minutes until the mixture is thick and pale. Add the mascarpone and beat until the ingredients are just combined. Fold in the whipped cream.
3 Using clean beaters, beat the egg whites until soft peaks form; then fold quickly and lightly into the cream mixture.
4 Dip half the ladyfingers, one at a time, into the coffee mixture. Drain off any excess and arrange in the base of a serving dish about 8 x 10 in and 2 1/2 in deep. Spread half the cream mixture over the ladyfingers.
5 Dip the remaining ladyfingers into the coffee mixture and repeat layering with the ladyfingers and cream mixture. Smooth the surface and dust with cocoa. Refrigerate for 2 hours, to allow the flavors to develop, or until firm. Serve with fresh fruit.

Summer Berry Tart

PREPARATION TIME:
35 MINUTES +
20 MINUTES
REFRIGERATION
COOKING TIME:
35 MINUTES
SERVES 4–6

1 cup all-purpose flour
2 tablespoons confectioner's sugar
1/3 cup butter, chopped

FILLING
3 egg yolks
2 tablespoons superfine sugar
2 tablespoons cornstarch
1 cup milk
1 teaspoon vanilla extract
8 oz strawberries, halved
3/4 cup blueberries
1 cup raspberries
1–2 tablespoons apricot jam

1 Sift flour and sugar into a bowl and add the butter. Rub in the butter with your fingertips until it resembles fine bread crumbs. Make a well in the center, add 1–2 tablespoons water and mix with a flat-bladed knife, using a cutting action, until the mixture comes together in beads. Add more water if necessary. Gently gather dough together; lift onto a lightly floured surface. Press together until smooth.

2 Roll out the pastry to fit an 8 in round fluted tart pan. Line the pan with the pastry, trim edges, and refrigerate for 20 minutes. Preheat oven to 350°F. Cut a sheet of waxed paper to cover the pastry-lined pan. Spread a layer of dried beans or rice evenly over the paper and bake for 15 minutes. Remove from oven, and discard the paper and rice. Return to the oven for 15 minutes, or until lightly golden.

3 To make the filling: Place the egg yolks, sugar and cornstarch in a bowl, and whisk until pale. Heat the milk in a small pan until almost boiling, then remove from the heat. Add the milk gradually to the egg mixture, beating constantly. Strain into the pan, and stir constantly over low heat for 3 minutes, or until it boils and thickens. Remove from heat, and add the vanilla. Transfer to a bowl, cover with plastic wrap, and allow to cool.

4 Spread the filling in the cooled pastry shell and top with the berries. Gently warm the apricot jam until it liquefies, then sieve. Brush the warmed jam over the fruit with a pastry brush before serving.

Storage time: The pastry can be cooked up to a day ahead. Store in an airtight container and fill up to 4 hours before serving.

Banana Caramel Tart

PREPARATION TIME: 35 MINUTES + 50 MINUTES REFRIGERATION
COOKING TIME: 40 MINUTES
SERVES 8

1 1/4 cups all-purpose flour
2 tablespoons confectioner's sugar
3/4 cup ground walnuts
1/3 cup butter, chopped
1/4 cup iced water

FILLING
14 oz can sweetened condensed milk
2 tablespoons butter
1 tablespoon light treacle or honey
4 medium bananas, sliced
1 cup whipping cream, whipped
1/2 cup heavy whipping cream
1/4 cup semisweet chocolate chips, melted

1 Sift the flour and sugar into a large mixing bowl; add walnuts and butter. Rub the butter into the flour until fine and crumbly. Add almost all of the iced water, and mix with a flat-bladed knife to a firm dough. Add more water if needed. Turn out onto a lightly floured surface, and press together until smooth. Roll out and ease into a 9 in round fluted tart pan; trim edges. Cover with plastic wrap. Refrigerate for 20 minutes.
2 Preheat oven to 350°F. Cover the pastry-lined pan with a sheet of waxed paper, and spread dried beans or rice over the paper. Bake for 15 minutes, then remove paper and beans. Return pastry to oven for 20 minutes, until golden. Set aside to cool completely.
3 To make the filling: Place the condensed milk, butter and treacle in a small, heavy-based pan. Stir constantly over medium heat for 5 minutes, until the mixture boils, thickens and turns a light caramel color. Cool slightly. Arrange sliced bananas over the pastry, then pour on the caramel, and smooth with the back of a spoon. Refrigerate for 30 minutes.
4 Lightly fold the creams together. Drop dollops of cream over the caramel, and arrange slices of banana on top. Drizzle

New York Cheesecake

PREPARATION TIME: 1 HOUR + CHILLING
COOKING TIME: 1 HOUR 50 MINUTES
SERVES 10–12

1 1/2 cups all-purpose flour
1/2 teaspoon baking powder
1/4 cup superfine sugar
1 teaspoon grated lemon rind
1/3 cup butter, chopped
1 egg

FILLING
1 lb 8 oz cream cheese, softened
1 cup superfine sugar
1/4 cup all-purpose flour
2 teaspoons grated orange rind
2 teaspoons grated lemon rind
4 eggs
2/3 cup whipping cream

CANDIED PEEL
1 cup superfine sugar
peel of 3 limes, 3 lemons and 3 oranges, shredded
1 1/2 cups whipping cream

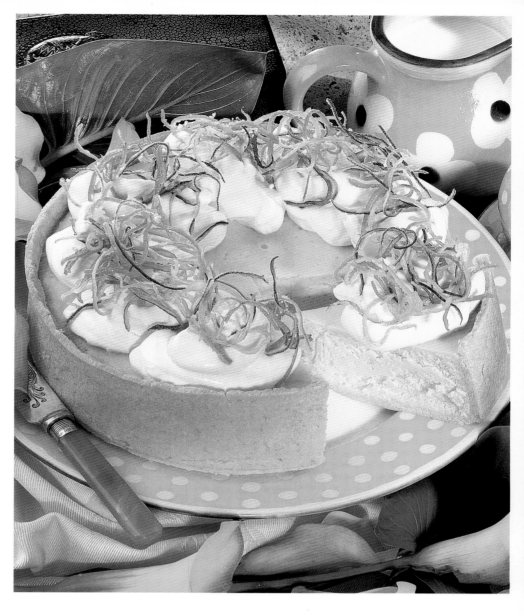

1 Sift the flour and baking powder into a large bowl, and add sugar, lemon rind and butter. Rub in the butter with your fingertips until mixture resembles fine bread crumbs. Make a well in the center and add the egg. Mix with a flat-bladed knife, using a cutting action, until the mixture comes together in beads. Gently gather dough together; lift onto a lightly floured surface. Press together, wrap in plastic wrap. Refrigerate for 20 minutes, or until firm.
2 Preheat the oven to 425°F. Roll the pastry between 2 sheets of baking (silicone) paper until large enough to fit the base and side of a greased 9 in round springform pan. Ease pastry into the pan and trim the edges. Line with a piece of crumpled baking paper and pour in some beans or rice. Bake for 10 minutes, remove the paper and beans, flatten the pastry lightly with the back of a spoon and bake for another 5 minutes. Allow to cool.
3 To make the filling: Reduce the oven to 300°F. Beat the cream cheese, sugar, flour and rinds until smooth. Add eggs, one at a time, beating after each addition. Beat in the cream, pour the filling into the pastry shell and bake for 1 hour 25–35 minutes, or until almost set. Cool, then refrigerate.
4 To make the Candied Peel: Put the sugar in a pan with 1/4 cup water and stir over low heat until dissolved. Add the peel, bring to a boil, reduce heat and simmer for 5–6 minutes. Allow to cool and drain the peel (you can also save the syrup to serve with the cheesecake). Whip the cream, spoon over the cold cheesecake and top with Candied Peel.

Chinese Fortune Cookies

PREPARATION TIME:
15 MINUTES
COOKING TIME:
ABOUT 5 MINUTES FOR EACH TRAY.
MAKES ABOUT 30

3 egg whites
1/2 cup confectioner's sugar, sifted
3 tablespoons unsalted butter
1/2 cup all-purpose flour

1 Preheat the oven to 350°F and line a baking sheet with baking (silicone) paper. Draw three 3 in circles on the paper.
2 Place the egg whites in a medium bowl and whisk until they are just frothy. Add the confectioner's sugar and butter and stir until the mixture is smooth. Add the flour, mix until smooth then set the mixture aside for 15 minutes. Using a flexible metal spatula, spread 1 1/2 level teaspoons of the mixture over each circle. Bake the cookies for 5 minutes, or until they are slightly brown around the edges.
2 Working quickly, remove the cookies from the trays by sliding the spatula under each round.
3 Place a written or typed fortune message in the center of each cookie. Fold the cookie in half, then in half again over a blunt-edged object. Set aside to cool on a wire rack. Cook the remaining mixture the same way.

Storage time: Fortune Cookies may be stored for up to 2 days in an airtight container.
Hint: Make only two or three cookies at a time, or they will harden before you have time to fold them and will break during folding.
Note: Fortune Cookies make a great after-dinner talking point and guests will be impressed if you make your own. It also allows you to have some fun personalizing the messages.

Amaretti

PREPARATION TIME:
25 MINUTES +
1 HOUR
STANDING
COOKING TIME:
15 MINUTES
MAKES 40

1 tablespoon all-purpose flour
1 tablespoon cornstarch
1 teaspoon ground cinnamon
3/4 cup superfine sugar
1 teaspoon grated lemon rind
1 cup ground almonds
2 egg whites
1/4 cup confectioner's sugar

1 Line two large baking sheets with baking (silicone) paper and preheat the oven to 350°F.
2 Sift the flour, cornstarch, cinnamon and half the superfine sugar into a large bowl. Stir in the lemon rind and ground almonds.
3 Place the egg whites in a small, dry mixing bowl. Using an electric mixer, beat until firm peaks form. Add the remaining superfine sugar gradually, beating constantly until the mixture is thick and glossy and all sugar has dissolved. Fold the egg white mixture into the dry ingredients until just combined and mixture forms a soft dough.
4 With wet or oiled hands, roll 2 level teaspoons of the mixture at a time into a ball, and arrange on the prepared baking sheets, allowing room for spreading. Sift confectioner's sugar liberally over the cookies, and bake for 15 minutes, or until the cookies are lightly browned. Transfer to wire rack to cool.

Sugar and Spice Palmiers

PREPARATION TIME:
20 MINUTES
COOKING TIME:
20 MINUTES
MAKES 32

1 sheet frozen butter puff pastry
2 tablespoons raw (Barbados or Demerara) sugar
1 teaspoon mixed pie spice
1 teaspoon ground cinnamon
3 tablespoons butter, melted
confectioner's sugar, to dust

1 Preheat the oven to 425°F. Brush two baking sheets with melted butter or oil, and line with baking (silicone) paper.

2 Thaw the pastry sheet as directed on the package. Meanwhile, combine the raw sugar and spices in a small bowl. Cut the sheet of pastry in half and brush with some of the melted butter. Sprinkle generously with the sugar mixture, reserving 2 teaspoons.

3 Fold the long edges of pastry inwards, then fold again so that the edges almost meet in the center. Fold once more, then place the pastry on a tray and refrigerate for 15 minutes. Using a small, sharp knife, cut the pastry rolls into 16 slices each.

4 Arrange the palmiers cut-side up on the prepared baking sheets, brush with remaining butter and sprinkle lightly with reserved sugar mixture. Bake for 20 minutes, or until golden. Cool on a wire rack and dust lightly with confectioner's sugar before

Mixed Nut Biscotti

PREPARATION TIME:
30 MINUTES
COOKING TIME:
45 MINUTES
MAKES
ABOUT 50

2 tablespoons whole blanched almonds
2 tablespoons hazelnuts
1/2 cup shelled unsalted pistachios
3 egg whites
1/2 cup superfine sugar
3/4 cup all-purpose flour

1 Preheat oven to 350°F. Brush a 10 x 3 x 1 3/4 in loaf pan with oil or melted butter, and line the base and sides with baking (silicone) paper. Spread the almonds, hazelnuts and pistachios onto a baking sheet and place in the oven for 2–3 minutes, or until the nuts are just toasted. Allow to cool.

2 Place the egg whites in a small, clean, dry mixing bowl. Using an electric mixer, beat the egg whites until stiff peaks form. Add the sugar gradually, beating constantly until the mixture is thick and glossy and all the sugar has dissolved.

3 Transfer the mixture to a large mixing bowl. Add the sifted flour and nuts. Gently fold the ingredients together until well combined. Spread the mixture into the prepared pan and smooth the surface. Bake for 25 minutes, then remove from the oven and cool completely in the pan.

4 Preheat the oven to 325°F. Using a sharp, serrated knife, cut the baked loaf into 1/4 in slices. Spread the slices onto baking sheets and bake for about 15 minutes, turning once halfway through cooking, until the slices are light golden and crisp. Delicious dipped into coffee, or served with a sweet dessert wine.

index

USEFUL INFORMATION

The recipes in this book are written using convenient cup measurements. You can buy special measuring cups in the supermarket or use an ordinary household cup: first you need to check it holds 8 fl oz by filling it with water and measuring the water (pour it into a liquid measure or even an empty yogurt carton). This cup can then be used for both liquid and dry cup measurements.

OUR POT RATING: When we test recipes, we rate them for ease of preparation. The following cookery ratings are used in this book.
A single pot indicates a recipe that is simple and generally quick to make—perfect for beginners.
Two pots indicate the need for just a little more care, or perhaps a little more time.

Liquid cup measures

1/4 cup	2 fluid oz
1/3 cup	2 1/2 fluid oz
1/2 cup	4 fluid oz
3/4 cup	6 fluid oz
1 cup	8 fluid oz

Spoon measures

1/4 teaspoon	15 drops
1/2 teaspoon	30 drops
1 teaspoon	1/3 tablespoon
1 tablespoon	3 teaspoons or 1/2 fluid oz

Cup conversions

1 cup all-purpose/self-rising flour	4 oz
1 cup grated Parmesan cheese	3 1/2 oz
1 cup shredded Cheddar cheese	4 oz
1 cup bread crumbs (fresh)	2 3/4 oz
1 cup bread crumbs (dry)	3 1/2 oz
1 cup dried chickpeas	7 oz
1 cup chopped chocolate	4 oz
1 cup rice, uncooked	6 1/2 oz
1 cup rice, cooked	6 oz
1 cup superfine/granulated sugar	8 oz
1 cup confectioners' sugar	4 oz
1 cup fresh basil/cilantro/mint leaves, firmly packed	1 oz
1 cup chopped fresh basil/cilantro/mint leaves, firmly packed	2 oz

Weight

10 g	1/4 oz	220 g	7 oz	425 g	14 oz
30 g	1 oz	250 g	8 oz	475 g	15 oz
60 g	2 oz	275 g	9 oz	500 g	1 lb
90 g	3 oz	300 g	10 oz	600 g	1 1/4 lb
125 g	4 oz	330 g	11 oz	650 g	1 lb 5 oz
150 g	5 oz	375 g	12 oz	750 g	1 1/2 lb
185 g	6 oz	400 g	13 oz	1 kg	2 lb

Alternative names

bicarbonate of soda	—	baking soda
capsicum	—	red or green (bell) pepper
chickpeas	—	garbanzo beans
cornflour	—	cornstarch
fresh coriander	—	cilantro
cream	—	single cream
dark chocolate	—	plain/bittersweet chocolate
eggplant	—	aubergine
flat-leaf parsley	—	Italian parsley
golden syrup	—	light corn syrup
hazelnut	—	filbert
heat bead	—	barbecue briquette/ barbecue charcoal
icing sugar	—	confectioners' sugar
plain flour	—	all-purpose flour
prawns	—	shrimp
sambal oelek	—	chilli paste
snow pea	—	mange tout
spring onion	—	scallion
thick cream	—	double/heavy cream
tomato paste (US/Aus.)	—	tomato purée (UK)
Weber barbecue	—	Kettle grill/Covered barbecue
zucchini	—	courgette

Thunder Bay Press
An imprint of the Advantage Publishers Group
5880 Oberlin Drive, San Diego, CA 92121-4794
www.thunderbaybooks.com

Library of Congress Cataloging-in-Publication Data available upon request.

Printed by Toppan Printing Hong Kong Co. Ltd. PRINTED IN CHINA
ISBN 1-59223-083-0. First printed in 1997. Reprinted 2003.
1 2 3 4 5   07 06 05 04 03

Editor: Sally Feldman **Designer:** Michelle Withers **Chief Executive:** Juliet Rogers **Publisher:** Kay Scarlett